HATE YOU

REBEL INK BOOK ONE

Copyright © 2020 by Tracy Lorraine

All rights reserved.

No part of this book may be reproduced in any form or by any electronic or mechanical means, including information storage and retrieval systems, without written permission from the author, except for the use of brief quotations in a book review.

Editing by Pinpoint Editing

Proofreading by Paige Sawyer Proofreading

Cover designed by Sammi Bee Designs

Andy and Amelia x

A NOTE

Hate You is written in British English and contains British spelling and grammar. This may appear incorrect to some readers when compared to US English books.

Tracy xo

PROLOGUE

TABITHA

I STARE DOWN at my gran's pale skin. Her cheeks are sunken and her eyes tired. She's been fighting this for too long now, and as much as I hate to even think it, it's time she found some peace.

I take her cool hand in mine and lift her knuckles to my lips.

"It's Tabitha," I whisper. I've no idea if she's awake, but I don't want to startle her.

Her eyes flicker open. After a second they must adjust to the light and she looks right at me. My chest tightens as if someone's wrapping an elastic band around it. I hate seeing my once so full of life gran like this. She was always so happy and full of cheer. She didn't deserve this end. But cancer doesn't care what kind of person you are, it hits whoever it fancies and ruins lives.

Pulling a chair closer, I drop onto it, not taking my eyes from her.

"How are you doing today?" I hate asking the question, because there really is only one answer. She's waiting, waiting for her time to come to put her out of her misery.

"I'm good. Christopher upped my morphine. I'm on top of the world."

She might be living her last days, but it doesn't stop her eyes sparkling a little as she mentions her male nurse. If I've heard the words 'if I were forty years younger' once while she's been here, then I've heard them a million times. She's joking, of course. My gran spent her life with my incredible grandpa until he had a stroke a few years ago. Thankfully, I guess, his end was much quicker and less painful than Gran's. It was awful at the time to have him healthy one moment and then gone in a matter of hours, but this right now is pure torture, and I'm not the one lying on the hospital bed with meds constantly being pumped into my body.

"Turn the frown upside down, Tabby Cat. I'm fine. I want to remember you smiling, not like your world's about to come crashing down."

"I know, I'm sorry. I just—" a sob breaks from my throat. "I don't know how I'm going to live without you." Dramatic? Yeah. But Gran has been my go-to person my whole life. When my parents get on my last nerve, which is often, she's the one who talks me down, makes me see things differently. She's also the only one who's encouraged me to live the life I want, not the one I'm constantly being pushed into.

That's the reason I'm the only one visiting her right now.

When my parents discovered that she was the one encouraging my 'reckless behaviour', as they called it, they cut contact. I can see the pain in her eyes about that every time she looks at me, but she's too stubborn to do anything about it, even now.

"You're going to be fine. You're stronger than you give yourself credit for. How many times have I told you, you just need to follow your heart. Follow your heart and just breathe. Spread your wings and fly, Tabby Cat."

Those were the last words she said to me.

CHAPTER ONE

TABITHA

THE HEAVY BASS rattles my bones. The incredible music does help to lift my spirits, but I find it increasingly hard to see the positives in my life while I'm hanging out with my friends these days. They've all got something exciting going on—incredible job prospects, marriage, exotic holidays on the horizon—and here I am, drowning in my one-person pity party. It's been two months since Gran left me, and I'm still wondering what the hell I'm meant to be doing with my life.

"Oh my god, they are so fucking awesome," Danni squeals in my ear as one song comes to an end. I didn't really have her down as a rock fan, but she was almost as excited as James when he announced that this was what we were doing for his birthday this year. Although I do wonder if it's the music or the frontman who's really captured her attention. She'd never admit it, but she's got a thing for bad boys.

I glance over at him with his arm wrapped around Shannon's shoulders and a smile twitches my lips. They're so cute. They've got the kind of relationship everyone craves. It seems so easy yet full of love and affection. Ripping my eyes from the couple, I focus back on the stage and try to block out that I'm about as far away from having that kind of connection with anyone as physically possible.

I sing along with the songs I've heard on the radio a million times and jump around with my friends, but I just can't quite totally get on board with tonight. Maybe I just need more alcohol.

"Where to next?" Shannon asks once we've left the arena and the ringing in our ears has begun to fade.

"Your choice," James says, looking down at her with utter devotion shining in his eyes. It wasn't a great surprise when Shannon sent a photo of her giant engagement ring to our group chat a couple of months ago. We all knew it was coming—Danni especially, seeing as it turned out that she helped choose the ring.

Shannon directs us all to a cocktail bar a few streets over and I make quick work of manoeuvring my way through the crowd to get to the bar, my need for a drink beginning to get the better of me. The others disappear off somewhere in the hope of finding a table

"Can we have two jugs of..." I quickly glance at the menu. "Margaritas please."

"Coming right up, sweetheart." The barman winks at me before his eyes drop to my chest. Hooking up on a night out isn't really my thing, but hell if it doesn't make me feel a little better about myself. He's cute too, and just the kind of guy who would give both my parents a heart attack if I were to bring him home. Both his forearms are covered in tattoos, he's got gauges in both his ears, and a lip ring. A smile tugs at the corner of my mouth as I imagine the looks on their faces.

My gran's words suddenly hit me.

Just breathe.

My hand lifts and my fingers run over the healing skin just below my bra. My smile widens.

I watch the barman prepare our cocktails, my eyes focused on the ink on his arms. I've always been obsessed by art, any kind of art, and that most definitely includes on skin.

I'm lost in my own head, so when he places the jugs in front of me, I startle, feeling ridiculous.

"T-Thank you," I mutter, but when I lift my eyes, I find him staring intently at me.

"You're welcome. I'm Christian, by the way."

"Oh, hi." A sly smile creeps onto my lips. "I'm Biff."

"Biff?" His brows draw together in a way I'm all too used to when I say my name.

"It's short for Tabitha."

"That's pretty. So... uh... how do you feel about—"

"Christian, a little help?" one of the other barmen shouts, pulling Christian's attention from me.

"Sorry, I'll hopefully see you again later?"

I nod at him, not wanting to give him any false hope. Like I said, he's cute, but after my last string of bad dates and even worse short-term boyfriends, I'm happy flying solo right now. I've got a top of the range vibrating friend in my bedside table; I don't need a man.

Picking up the tray in front of me, I turn and go in search of my friends. It takes forever, but eventually I find them tucked around a tiny table in the back corner of the bar.

"What the hell took so long? We thought you'd pulled and abandoned us."

"Yes and no," I say, ensuring every head turns my way.

"Tell us more," Danni, my best friend, demands.

"It was nothing. The barman was about to ask me out, but it got busy."

"Why the hell did you come back? Get over there. We all know you could do with a little... loosening up," James says with a wink.

"I'm good. He wasn't my type."

"Oh, of course. You only date posh boys."

"That is not true."

"Is it not?" Danni asks, chipping in once she's filled all the glasses.

"No..." I think back over the previous few guys they met. "Wayne wasn't posh," I argue when I realise they're kind of right.

"No, he was just a wanker."

Blowing out a long breath, I try to come up with an argument, but quite honestly, it's true. My shoulders slump as I realise that I've been subconsciously dating guys my parents would approve of. It's like my need to follow their orders is so well ingrained by now that I don't even realise I'm doing it. Shame that their ideas about my life, what I should do, and whom I should date don't exactly line up with mine.

Glancing over my shoulder at the bar, I catch a glimpse of Christian's head. Maybe I should take him up on his almost offer. What's the worst that could happen?

Deciding some liquid courage is in order, I grab my margarita and swallow half down in one go.

I'm so fed up of attempting to live my parents' idea of a perfect life. I promised Gran I'd do things my way. I need to start living up to my promise.

BY THE TIME I'm tipsy enough to walk back to the bar and chat up Christian, he's nowhere to be seen. I'm kind of disappointed seeing as the others had convinced me to throw caution to the wind (something that I'm really bad at doing), but I think I'm mostly relieved to be able go home and lock myself inside my flat alone and not have to worry about anyone else.

With my arm linked through Danni's, we make our way out to the street, ready to make our journeys home, and Shannon jumps into an idling Uber while Danni waits for another to go in the opposite direction.

"You sure you don't want to be dropped off? I don't mind."

"No, I'm sure. I could do with the fresh air." It's not a lie—the alcohol from one too many cocktails is making my head a little fuzzy. I hate going to sleep with the room spinning. I'd much rather that feeling fade before lying down.

"Okay. Promise me you'll text me when you're home."

"I promise." I wrap my arms around my best friend and then wave her off in her own Uber.

Turning on my heels, I start the short walk home.

I've been a London girl all my life, and while some might be afraid to walk home after dark, I love it. I love seeing a different side to this city, the quiet side when most people are hiding in their flats, not flooding the streets on their daily commutes.

My mind is flicking back and forth between my promise to Gran and my missed opportunity tonight when a shop front that I walk past on almost a daily basis makes me stop.

It's a tattoo studio I've been inside of once in my life. I never really pay it much attention, but the new sign in the window catches my eye and I stop to look.

Admin help wanted. Enquire within.

Something stirs in my belly, and it's not just my need to do something to piss my parents off—although getting a job in a place like this is sure to do that. I'm pretty sure it's excitement.

Tattoos fascinate me, or more so, the artists.

I'm surprised to see the open sign still illuminated, so before I can change my mind, I push the door open. A little bell rings above it, and after a few seconds of standing in reception alone, a head pops out from around the door.

"Evening. What can I do you for?" The guy's smile is soft and kind despite his otherwise slightly harsh features and ink.

"Oh um..." I hesitate under his intense dark stare. I glance over my shoulder, the back of the piece of paper catching my eye and reminding me why I walked in here. "I just saw the job ad in the window. Is the position still open?"

His eyes drop from mine and take in what I'm wearing. Seeing as tonight's outing involved a rock concert, I'm dressed much like him in all black and looking a little edgy with my skinny black jeans, ripped AC/DC t-shirt and heavy black makeup. I must admit it's not a look I usually go for, but it was fitting for tonight.

He nods, apparently happy with what he sees.

"Experience?" he asks, making my stomach drop.

"Not really, but I'm studying for a Masters so I'm not an idiot. I know my way around a computer, Excel, and I'm super organised."

"Right..." he trails off, like he's thinking about the best way to get rid of me.

"I'm a really quick learner. I'm punctual, methodical and really easy to get along with."

"It's okay, you had me sold at organised. I'm Dawson, although everyone around here calls me D."

"Nice to meet you." I stick my hand out for him to shake, and an amused smile plays at his lips. Stretching out an inked arm, he takes my hand and gives it a very firm shake that my dad would be impressed by—if he could look past the tattoos, that is. "I'm Tabitha, but everyone calls me Biff."

"Biff, I like it. When can you start?"

"Don't you want to interview me?"

"You sound like you could be perfect. When can you start?"

"Err... tomorrow?" I ask, totally taken aback. He doesn't know me from Adam.

"Yes!" He practically snaps my hand off. "Can you be here for two o'clock? I can show you around before clients start turning up. I'll apologise now for dropping you in the deep end, we've not had anyone for a few weeks and things are starting to get a little crazy."

"I can cope with crazy."

"Good to know. This place can be nuts." I smile at him, more grateful than he could know to have a distraction and a focus.

My Masters should be enough to keep my mind busy, but since Gran went, I can't seem to lose myself in it like I could previously. Hopefully, sorting this place's admin out might be exactly what I need.

"Two o'clock tomorrow then," I say, turning to leave. "I'll bring ID. Do you need a reference? I've done some voluntary work recently, I'm sure they'll write something for me."

"Just turn up on time and do your job and you're golden."

I walk out with more of a spring in my step than I have in a long time. I'm determined to find something that's going to make me happy, not just my parents. I've lived in their shadow for long enough.

I LOOK myself over before leaving my flat for my first shift at the tattoo studio. I'm dressed a little more like myself today in a pair of dark skinny jeans, a white blouse and a black blazer. It's simple and smart. I'm not sure if there's a dress code—D never specified what I should wear. With my hair straightened and hanging down my back and my makeup light, I feel like I can take on whatever crazy he throws at me.

With a final spritz of perfume, I grab my bag from the unit in the hall and pull open my door. My home is a top floor flat in an old London warehouse. They were converted a few years ago by my father's company, and I managed to get myself first dibs. They might drive me insane on the best of days, but at least I get this place rent-free. It almost makes up for their controlling and stuck-up ways... almost.

Ignoring the lift like I always do, I head for the stairs. My heels click against the polished concrete until I'm at the bottom and out to the busy city. I love London. I love that no matter what the time, there's always something going on or someone who's awake.

The spring afternoon is still a little fresh, making me regret not grabbing my coat, or even a scarf, before I left. I pull my blazer tighter around myself and make the short journey to the shop.

The door's locked when I get there, and the bright neon sign that clearly showed it was open last night is currently saying closed.

Unsure of what to do, I lift my hand to knock. Only a second later, the shop front is illuminated, and the sound of movement inside filters down to me, but when the door opens it's not the guy from last night.

"Oh... uh... hi. Is... uh... D here?"

The guy folds his arms over his chest and looks me up and down. He chuckles, although I've no idea what he finds so amusing.

"D," he shouts over his shoulder, "there's some posh bird here to see you."

My teeth grind that he's stereotyped me quite so quickly, but I refuse to allow him to see that his assumptions about me affect me in any way.

"Ah, good. I was worried you might change your mind."

"Not at all," I say, stepping past the judgemental arsehole and into the studio reception-cum-waiting room.

"That's Spike. Feel free to ignore him. He's not got

laid in about a million years, it makes him a little cranky." I fight to contain a laugh, especially when I turn toward Spike to find his lips pursed and his eyes narrowed in frustration. All it does is confirm that D's words are correct.

"Is that fucking necessary? Posh doesn't need to know how inactive my cock is, especially not when she's only just walked through the fucking door. Unless..." He stalks towards me and I automatically back up. I can't deny that he's a good looking guy, but there's no way I'm going there.

"I don't think so."

"You sure? You look like you could do with a bit of rough." He winks, and I want the ground to swallow me up.

"Down, Spike. This is Tabitha, or Biff. She's our new admin, so I suggest you be nice to her if you want to stop organising your own appointments and shit. I don't need a sexual harassment case on my hands before she's even fucking started."

I can't help but laugh at the look on Spike's face. "Don't worry. I'm sure you'll find some desperate old spinster soon."

He looks me up and down again, something in his eyes changed. "Appearances aside, I think you're going to get on well here."

I smile at him. "Mine's a coffee. Milk, no sugar. I'm already sweet enough." His chin drops.

"I thought you were our new assistant. Why am I still making the coffee?"

"Know your place, Spike. Now do as the lady says. You know my order."

"Yeah, it comes with a side of fuck off!" He flips D off

before disappearing through a door that I can only assume goes to a kitchen.

"I probably should have warned you that you've agreed to work around a bunch of arseholes."

"I know how to handle myself around horny men, don't worry."

After finishing my A levels, before I grew any kind of backbone where my parents were concerned, I agreed to work for my dad. I was his little office bitch and spent an horrendous year of my life being bossed around by men who thought that just because they had a cock hanging between their legs it made them better than me. I might have fucking hated that year, but it taught me a few things, not just about business but also how to deal with men who think they're something fucking special just because they're a tiny bit successful and make more money than me. I've no doubt that my time at Anderson Development Group gave me all the skills I'm going to need to handle these artists.

"So I see. So, this is your desk. When you're on shift you'll be the first person people see when they're inside, so it's important that you look good. But from what I've seen, I don't think we'll have an issue. I've sorted you out logins for the computer and the software we use. Most of it is pretty self-explanatory. I'm pretty IT illiterate and I've figured most of it out, put it that way."

D's showing me how they book clients in when someone else joins us. This time it's someone I recognise from my previous visit, although it's immediately obvious that he doesn't remember me like I do him. But then I guess he was the one delivering the pain, not receiving it.

"Biff, this is Titch. Titch, this is Biff, our new admin. Be nice."

"Nice? I'm always nice. Nice to meet you, Biff. You have any issues with this one, you come and see me. He might look tough, but I know all his secrets." Titch winks, a smile curling at his lips that shows he's a little more interested than he's making out, and quickly disappears towards his room.

It's not long until the first clients of the afternoon arrive, and I'm left alone to try to get to grips with everything.

Between clients, D pops his head out of his room to check I'm okay, and every hour I make a round of coffee for everyone. That sure seems to get me in their good books.

"I think I could get used to having you around," Spike says when I deliver probably his fourth coffee of the day. "Only thing that would make it better is if it were whisky."

"Not sure the person at the end of your needle would agree." He chuckles and turns back to the design he was working on when I interrupted.

My first day flies by. D tells me to head home not long after nine o'clock. They've all got hours of tattooing to go yet, seeing as Saturday night is their busiest night of the week, but he insists I get a decent night's sleep.

CHAPTER TWO

TABITHA

WITH BOTH UNI and my new job, the next week is over before I've realised it's even begun. I'm only doing my Masters part time, so I don't need to go into uni all that often. I spend most of my time working at home. My new hours at the studio are exactly what I was missing. It gets me out and I get to meet new people. It might not be my forever job, but it's perfect for right now.

It's almost four o'clock the following Friday when I walk into the studio reception with a takeout tray of coffee in my hand for everyone. The guys are all in their rooms setting up for a busy night of inking and piercing Londoners. Music pumps through the speakers that fill the studio, and I wiggle my hips in time as I make my coffee deliveries.

"How did we survive without you?" D asks when I pass his black coffee over.

"Just doing my bit to keep you going all night."

"We appreciate it. Have you had a chance to look at tonight's bookings? Are we full?"

"Pretty much straight through to two AM. Only a few drop-in slots open."

He blows out a breath. "You'd better send a few more of these down my way then."

"Didn't sleep well?" I ask, now noticing the dark circles under his eyes.

"Something like that," he mutters.

"Well, if you need anything, just shout." Turning on my heels, I leave him to set up.

About thirty minutes before we turn the closed sign to open, all three of the guys appear. After checking out their bookings for the night, they fall down onto the black leather sofas that fill the waiting room.

I'm busy inputting clients' information so I don't pay much attention to what they're talking about, but when the bell rings above the door, my eyes automatically lift from my screen. I don't see who's entered because D stands, blocking my view.

"I'm sorry, we're not open until—" My warning is cut off when D opens his arms to the visitor.

"You're back!" he exclaims, pulling the guy into a one-armed hug. "Didn't think you were planning on turning up until next week."

"I wasn't, but they're set up and don't need me getting under their feet." His deep, rumbling voice does something to me. Goosebumps break out across my skin and I lean over in my seat in the hope of seeing the face that voice belongs to. Unfortunately, I lean just that little bit too far and the chair moves in the opposite direction, leaving me in a heap on the floor.

"What was that?" the deep voice asks.

"That? That was our new admin. You're going to love her, she's exactly what we've been looking for."

"Why didn't you tell me you'd hired?"

"Because your parting words to me were, and I quote, 'just get it fucking sorted'. So I did just that. You're gonna love her."

Smoothing my hair down, I find my feet, ready to get up and meet the mystery man with the deep voice. I stand, wiping any dust off my arse from the concrete floor, and look up into a pair of blue eyes that I've not seen in years.

My chin drops as I take him in.

Zach Abbot.

The school's bad boy, sex god, the guy everyone wanted to be friends with or have on their arm. He's arrogant, obnoxious, and from what I remember downright rude. And right now, he's staring at me like I'm less than a piece of shit on his shoe. *Nothing new there.* My heart pounds in my chest. What the hell is he doing here, and why was D talking to him like he owned the fucking place?

"Her? You hired *her* as our admin? You can't be serious."

My eyes open so wide I'm afraid they might just pop out.

"She's awesome, Zach. Just give her a chance."

"You're fucking serious. Have you looked at her? She looks like she should be working a shift at a golf club not a fucking tat studio." His eyes drop down my body, taking in my simple, black V-neck jumper and tan skinny jeans.

My skin prickles with his attention and red hot anger blooms in my belly. And now I remember why I hated him so much at school. Not only is he all those things I previously mentioned, but he's a massive fucking dickhead.

I step out from around my desk and stand before him. A few things have changed since I was at school and totally intimidated by the likes of Zach Abbot and his crew of self-righteous arseholes. I've learnt who I am. I've discovered that I'm not some weak girl who needs to cower away from bullies. I'm Tabitha fucking Anderson, and I'm not afraid to stand up for what's right. Maybe my dad did teach me something with his controlling ways all these years.

"Problem?" I ask, standing almost toe-to-toe with him. I try to ignore my thundering heart and the fact that my hands are trembling. His unique manly, woodsy scent hits my nose and makes my mouth water.

Damn him for being so fucking tempting.

There was a time when we were at school when I'd have given my right arm to be this close to him, every girl would have. But I sat and watched. Being practically invisible back then seriously helped with that little endeavour, and I discovered that he wasn't worthy of standing close to, let alone wanting anything else to do with him.

"Yeah. You don't fit in in my studio." He dismisses me with a nod of his chin.

"Your studio?" My eyes narrow in confusion. That can't be right.

He tilts his head to the side as if he's talking to an idiot. It does nothing but fire me up. "Yeah. *My* studio."

My brow creases. There's something else I should

probably mention about Zach Abbot. His little sister is now my best friend. I had no idea when I first met Danni at uni. I assumed the surname was a coincidence—after all, there must be hundreds of Abbots out there. She's a couple of years younger and I didn't remember her from school; equally she didn't know me, but that wasn't a shock to me as I lived my life in the shadows. Danni and her family seem to think Zach, the middle child, spends his days living the high life off of his trust fund. Yet, he's standing before me right now claiming to own a successful chain of tattoo studios. I had no idea when I first started, but this isn't the only Rebel Ink in the world. There are four others in England and no less than three in America. And apparently, they all belong to him.

I stare at him, holding his captivating blue eyes hostage, struggling to believe that this man before me is the same one the Abbot family spends its time moaning about and making excuses for.

"What's her name?" he asks over his shoulder.

"I'm standing right here." If it were possible, steam would be bellowing from my ears right this second.

"So you are."

"I'm Biff. I'm the one who's been sorting out your shocking filing system, inputting your clients' details that have been floating around on scraps of paper—have you even heard of GDPR?— and actually responding to some emails."

"She also makes great coffee," Spike adds.

His eyes hold mine, the blue getting colder by the second. He sucks his bottom lip into his mouth as his gaze drops. My skin prickles as he runs it over my breasts, down my waist and all the way to my boots. My nipples pebble and my blood turns to lava with his undivided attention on me. It only makes me angrier. Nothing this guy does should affect me. Okay, so he's hot. Even more so than I remember from school. He's filled out, his shoulders are wider, his arms more muscular, and the way his t-shirt hugs his body leads me to believe there's something delicious hiding underneath. Shame about the personality.

"You don't fit in here. A posh girl sitting behind that desk does not give off the right first impressions. Sort yourself out, or kindly fuck off."

A gasp sounds out behind me.

"What the fuck, man?"

D comes to stand next to me and I'm grateful for his support, but as I look over the four of them dressed head-to-toe in black, tattoos covering their skin and gauges in their ears, and lip and brow piercings catching the spotlights above, I realise that what Zach's saying is right. I don't fit in here. My Ralph Lauren jumper, my Versace jeans and my Louboutin boots most definitely don't belong in a dark tattoo studio.

Sucking in a deep breath, I reach behind the desk and pull my pink Kate Spade bag from the bottom drawer. Looking at its soft pastel colour is more proof that, although said extremely poorly, Zach is correct.

"You're right."

"Biff, no." D pleads. "Ignore this dickhead. You're exactly what we need here. What you look like shouldn't affect that."

"It's okay. Thank you for fighting for me." I touch his forearm lightly as I pass.

They might think I'm about to walk out for good, but I will not cower to the likes of Zach Abbot, even if he is right. He's just set out a challenge, and I never back down.

D, Spike and Titch's voices ring out behind me as I allow the door to shut. It's obvious none of them are happy about their boss' opinion, but I already know they're not going to change his mind.

Pulling my phone from my bag, I find my best friend's phone number and hit call.

"Hey, how's it going?"

"Good. Do you have plans tonight?"

"I don't, actually. What are you thinking?"

"I've got a challenge for you. Be at mine in an hour."

CHAPTER THREE

ZACH

I'M FUCKING EXHAUSTED. The jet lag from my long-haul flight is kicking my arse, but my need to stop in the studio to make sure things are okay gets the better of me. I know D and the guys are more than capable, but that place is like my baby so the temptation to poke my head in is too much to deny.

I regret it the second I step inside and find her.

What the fuck does D think he's playing at, employing a posh fucking princess to be the face of Rebel Ink? She's not rebel fucking anything, and she's everything I try to distance myself from on a daily basis. She looks just like the kids I was forced to spend time with as a child, the kind of woman my mother would probably say is the perfect match for me. She was dressed exactly like my sister does and talked like the posh kids I had no choice but to spend my days with at that pretentious private school my parents insisted on before I was old enough to get the hell away and live my own life.

She doesn't belong here, and I don't care how much stick I get from the guys or how good she is at her job. She's not staying.

Am I an arsehole for making her leave? Yes, I can't deny that, but it's just the way it's got to be.

"I can't believe you just did that."

"Believe it," I mutter, falling onto one of the sofas, propping my feet up on the coffee table and letting my head fall back as three pairs of eyes burn into me.

"She's not right for this place," I say without even opening my eyes.

"Who gives a fuck what she looks like? She whipped us right into shape."

"And gave us coffee," Titch says again.

"Who gives a fuck about the coffee? I'll buy you all machines for your rooms if I have to. I refuse to have clients walk in and think they've entered a fucking spa not a studio. This isn't up for discussion."

D blows out a frustrated breath. I've listened to him almost all of my career. He's had my back since the day I showed an interest in this life, but this is one thing we're just going to have to agree to disagree about.

"So how was it?" he asks, changing the subject.

"Really good. The location is spot on, and Corey was fitting in like he lived all his life there by the time I left." Corey is one of my best artists, not that I'm going to admit that to any of these guys. He'd previously been in charge of my Manchester studio, but when I mentioned to him that I wanted another US place he jumped at the chance to relocate. He helped out all the way with location and hiring staff. If it continues the way it has the past couple of weeks then I think it could be one of our most successful studios.

Having one tattoo studio where I could do my thing was a dream of mine since the day I drew my first design, but with everyone around me focused on the family antique business, I knew they wouldn't understand. The only person who got me was my best friend, Jonathan. He shared my desire to break away from what was expected of us, to be rebellious and do our own thing. He'd be proud of all this. I lift my hand to the dog tag that's hanging around my neck and run my fingertip over the cold metal.

"If anyone can make it happen then it's Corey," Spike adds.

"I've no doubts in him. So aside from your lapse in judgement on our new appointment, anything else I need to know about?"

"Err... We had new ink delivered. Our main supplier has changed name but the products are the same. We've pretty much been booked solid and been turning walk-ins away."

"You think it's time for a new artist?"

"Not if you're planning on sticking around."

"I'm here as long as the others are running smoothly."

"Anyone want a coffee? I guess it's down to us to make it again now," Titch says.

"Do you care about anything other than coffee?" Spike barks.

"Um... yeah. Pussy."

"Fucking hell," I say, getting up and heading towards

my room. "I'll be here for a few minutes, but I'm heading to bed in a bit. I'm fucking dead."

I walk into the room where I laid down my first ink aged fourteen and breathe in the familiar smell. This room is my home. I feel more at peace in here than I have anywhere in my life, and I crave it when I'm away too long.

Picking up my gun, I turn it on and let the buzz flow through my body. I've not inked anyone in what feels like forever, and I'm desperate to make my mark on someone. I love running my own business, but it takes me away from what I really love at times: creating art.

I turn it off before I'm tempted to drag one of the guys in here and demand they let me add to their growing collections. It's only once I've placed it back down that I realise how tidy the place is.

"What the hell happened in there? It's like my mum marched in and tidied my bedroom without permission." We all know that's not what happened because no one outside of my Rebel Ink family knows what I do on a daily basis. Do I feel guilty about keeping my growing empire from my family? Sometimes. I know they'd support me, they're good people, but that doesn't mean I need them in my business giving me their opinion and trying to help. I've been an outcast from the day I was born, I may as well keep it a tradition.

"*She* happened." D nods towards the door that his new recruit stormed through not so long ago. "I told you, she's good for the place. We didn't even ask her to tidy up, she just took it upon herself to remove all the growing coffee mugs you'd abandoned in your room." I think back to the state I know I left it in. I didn't think anyone would care, seeing as my room is private. These guys know I don't share. Not where my room is concerned, anyway.

"Try all you like, you're not going to make me feel guilty about this. I'll stand by my opinion that she's not right."

"Whatever. I've got work to do. Maybe you should do some admin before you hit the sack, seeing as we're back to no one else doing it," D suggests before disappearing into his room.

Frustration that he can't see where I'm coming from on this has anger licking at my insides. We're usually on the same page. He's been my sounding board for almost everything since I was a kid. We've never been so far apart as we apparently are on this particular subject.

Titch looks at me and opens his mouth. Knowing something I don't want to hear is about to fall from his lips, I cut him off. "Enough. I've made my decision. End of. I'm going to bed." Turning my back on the two of them, I walk through the small kitchen and out the back door that leads me to the flat above.

I could easily afford to move out of this place and have a decent sized flat, or house for that matter, but why would I when I basically live downstairs or at one of my other studios?

The small space smells musty as I push the front door open. Kicking my boots off, I open every window I walk past.

Pulling open the fridge, I find one can of beer, a tub of butter and some cheese.

Slamming it shut, I decide against food and go straight for the bedroom instead.

The sheets are still a mess and there's a used condom and its empty wrapper sitting on the bedside table. I have a vague recollection of the night before my flight to America. I'd gone out with Titch after finishing up here for the night and pulled some blonde girl. *Ava, Anna, Amy...* something like that. All I remember was that she kept me up the rest of the night, meaning that I was able to get some sleep on the plane and almost get myself on US time from the second I landed. Shame I didn't have the same for the journey home.

My muscles grow heavy as I start pulling my clothes from my body with my need to crash. The second I'm down to my boxers, I fall face-first into my bed. I can faintly smell that chick's perfume, but no sooner have I had the thought than I pass out.

IT'S GONE midday by the time I open my eyes, totally confused as to where I am and what day it is, or why it's so cold.

Reaching over for my phone, I find the bedside table where it usually sits empty. Groaning, I lean over the side of the bed until I find my jeans and dig in my pockets until I find it.

Saturday, right.

I spend a couple of hours cleaning the place up. I've been gone almost three weeks, but now I'm back it feels like I never left. I throw the contents of my suitcase into the washing machine and pull up an online shopping app to get myself some food delivered, or more importantly, some alcohol.

I'm randomly adding shit to my basket when a message comes through.

D: You come to your senses now you've had some sleep? Here's her phone number so you can call, apologise, and beg her to come back.

Rolling my eyes at him, I return to what I was doing, not understanding what his obsession with the posh girl is. He knows my background, understands the life I've distanced myself from. I'd have thought he'd have known that I wouldn't have been up for having a *Made in Chelsea* reject sitting behind the desk downstairs.

He's probably banging her, a little voice says in my head. I bet she's terrible in the sack. All the stuck-up ones are. They seem to think their looks and beauty are all they need.

An hour before we open for the day, I head down to get a sense for how things have really been while I've been away. I trust D with my life, but it's good to see what's been happening with my own eyes.

With a huge mug of coffee I fall down onto the chair in my room and power up my computer. I check my emails and respond to any urgent ones, leaving the rest for later, then I pull up our appointments and have to do a double-take when I find it looks completely different to when I left. Each of us has been colour coded, and it's so much easier to see what we're all up to on each day. *Why didn't I know this programme did that?* I also find that all the accounts are up to date. Every single purchase that's been made has been categorised and is ready to go to my accountant.

"What the hell?" I ask myself, liking but equally confused by this kind of organisation. A little bit of doubt starts to creep in. Did I do the wrong thing last night? I know I flew off the handle a little when I first saw her. I was jetlagged, I couldn't help it. But is D right? Despite appearances is she what we need?

I push the thought away. We can find someone who can effectively do this shit and look the part at the same time. We've had someone before, and we'll find them again.

I open up a new tab and type in the recruitment site I've used in the past when trying to find staff to see if the ad needs updating when the front door to the shop opens.

I look to the door, waiting for one of the guys to poke their head around the frame but no one does. The sound of someone shuffling around continues to sound out.

My curiosity gets the better of me and I head out to see what's going on. When I get to the reception entrance, I find a woman standing with her back to me. Her hair's pink on the tips, she's wearing a short leather jacket and a pair of skinny jeans so tight they should be fucking illegal, and a pair of biker boots on her feet. My eyes stay on her arse and the delicious curve of her hips a little too long before I find it in me to speak.

"I'm sorry, but we're not actually open yet."

She stiffens at the sound of my voice, and after a beat she speaks. "I'm aware."

My brows draw together in confusion. *Who the hell is this woman?*

Then she turns and my chin damn near hits the floor. "You?"

The smile that curls at her lips has something stirring beneath my skin, and I already know I'm in trouble.

CHAPTER FOUR

TABITHA

BANG ON AN HOUR later and the buzzer to my flat is ringing out. I rush to let Danni in, my excitement for what I've got planned beginning to get the better of me.

The second I stepped out of Rebel Ink I booked an Uber and went straight to the closest supermarket. I begged the driver to wait for me and had the quickest trip around that shop that I've ever had in my life, but when I emerged less than ten minutes later, I had everything I'd need to put my plan into place.

"What the hell's going on?" Danni asks as she follows me toward my kitchen and accepts the glass of sauvignon I hand her.

"I've got a new job," I announce.

"Oh? I didn't know you were looking."

"I wasn't, but I saw a poster and took it as a sign. I made that promise to Gran and quite honestly, I feel like I've been letting her down. I promised her I'd start living my own life, not the one my parents want for me, but I've just continued down on the same path."

"That's not true, you're doing your Masters."

One side of my mouth twists. "I was already doing that."

"Okay, fair point. So this job?" she asks again, curling her feet up underneath her and getting comfortable on my sofa.

"It's in a tattoo studio."

Danni almost spits her wine out in shock. "It's in a what?"

"A tattoo studio," I repeat, although I've no idea why. It's obvious she heard the first time.

"Why?"

I shrug. "Thought it might be fun."

"Working with a group of tatted up, biker thugs?"

"Stereotypical much? Not everyone who has a tattoo is a thug, Dan." I lift my cami to show her my ribs as a point.

"Obviously I know that, but tattoo artists are—"

"Are what? Please enlighten me, I'd love to hear your opinion seeing as you've probably never spoken to one." Of course, this is very much not true seeing as I've discovered her very own brother is one, and my new boss it seems. He might have been all kinds of arsehole tonight, but I'm not going to out him to his sister, not yet anyway. I want to fight this battle myself as his pissed-off employee, not his sister's best friend.

"Okay, fine. I've no idea. You tell me, what are they like?"

"Mostly pretty awesome." I talk about D, Titch and Spike and all their crazy quirks that I've discovered that make them so fun to work with.

"So it's all guys... and you?"

"Yep," I state proudly.

"I bet that's a sight to see."

"Yeah well, that's kind of why you're here. I want to... fit in more."

"Okaaay," she drawls hesitantly, leaning forward to put her glass on the coffee table.

I get up and grab the bag from the shop. "Yep, you're going to help me embrace my wild side." I pull out the box of hair dye and place it next to her wine.

"Pink?"

"Pink," I agree with a smile, excitement exploding in my belly for the first time in a long time.

"What else is in the bag?" I tip out the contents and watch as she inspects each one. "You bought supermarket makeup? That'll be beyond shit."

"I didn't have time for anything else. I'm sure it'll do the job just fine. So are you going to help me or what?"

"You mean am I going to watch as you turn yourself into someone who's going to give your dad a heart attack? Hell yes!"

Danni picks up both our glasses of wine and I collect up the bottles and tubes littering my coffee table. Together we head towards my bathroom.

"So the whole lot pink?"

"No, just my blonde tips. You're probably going to need to paint it on. I'll grab you a brush." I leave her in the bathroom in favour of one of my spare bedrooms that I've turned into my studio and rummage through my brushes until I find one suitable that I'm willing to ruin.

"This is London, you know. I'm s[ure we could have] found a salon," she shouts.

"Probably, I just thought this wou[ld be fun. If I don't] like it, I can go and get it done properly [later.]"

The next hour passes by with lots [of giggling] from my friend and another glass of wine each while we're surrounded by the stench of the ammonia in the dye. I refuse to look in the mirror until she's dried and straightened it.

My hair's been pretty boring most of my life. The girl who hid in the shadows at school had non-descript mousy brown, cut straight across hair. It was never in the latest fashion like the 'cool' kids and it had never been anywhere near any dye. I got a little braver as I got closer to my twenties and had some blonde highlights added, but, still under my parents' thumbs, I was afraid to do anything too wild that they would disapprove of.

Until a few minutes ago, it was brown and blonde ombre. I loved that it had the hint of following the fashion but still kept my parents happy. What we've just done, on the other hand, is going to go down like a lead balloon. If the dye's worked as I'm imagining then the bottom of my hair will no longer be honey blonde but a striking pink.

My hands tremble slightly with my excitement to see how it's turned out.

Danni takes her time. I'm not sure if she's torturing me on purpose for being so crazy or just doing a thorough job, but my impatience is getting the better of me.

"Are you done yet?"

"Just about."

She straightens the final layer before gently brushing it through.

"Go on then."

suck in a breath and stand. I count to three and lift my eyes to the mirror. "Oh my god," I gasp, my fingers coming up to touch the pink staring back at me. "I love it."

"Really?" I glance at Danni who's over my shoulder in the mirror, looking a little hesitant.

"Yeah, really. Why didn't I do this years ago?"

"Because—"

"Don't say it," I interrupt. I don't need her to tell me how weak I've been when it comes to my parents. Her mum and dad are so supportive of everything she does. She's no idea what it was like for me growing up with them breathing down my neck every second, ensuring I do what pleases them.

She shrugs at me but her eyes tell me exactly what she's thinking. I refill our once again empty glasses and Danni orders our favourite Chinese dishes to be delivered, and we continue on our impromptu girly night in. It's been too long since I had a night like this. We usually end up out in one of the many cocktail bars across the city, but this right now is perfect. A bit of one-on-one time with my bestie, even if I do feel guilty about keeping quite a big secret from her.

It would be so easy to open my mouth and explain how her youngest older brother is now my boss, but for one I doubt she'd believe me; they all think they know Zach, turns out they have no idea. But also because for some fucked-up reason I feel the need to keep his secret. I've no idea why, I owe him nothing, especially after the way he treated me tonight, but something stops the words falling from my lips.

"I'm so excited for this time next week. I've got an epic night planned," she says, putting her phone down on the arm of the chair, grabbing her wine and turning to me.

"Oh come on, tell me," I whine. Danni's oldest brother, Harrison, is getting married in two weeks. Technically they're already married, seeing as they had a spur of the moment Vegas wedding a few years ago. His already wife, Summer, has entrusted Danni as her maid of honour and chief organiser of the hen do. Personally, I think she's crazy. Summer is quite quiet and reserved, and I have a feeling that her hen do is going to be anything but, especially if the current twinkle in my best friend's eye is anything to go by.

Danni introduced me to Summer at uni when she first started. She's an art undergrad, so we're often in the department together, and our love of art meant we bonded pretty fast.

"Nope, you'll have to wait to find out just like everyone else."

I huff, trying to come up with a way to get the information I need. "Okay, well... what should I wear?"

"Your most awesome dress, obviously." She rolls her eyes like it was the most ridiculous question in the world.

"She's going to hate you if you embarrass her, you know that right?"

"She'll get over it. It's her last hurrah, it needs to be all kinds of awesome." I don't disagree with that, but I fear Summer's and Danni's ideas of awesome vary somewhat.

"Oh, dinner's here," Danni announces, dragging me from my thoughts and practically running for the door.

I WALK OUT of the flat with a newfound confidence the next day. I spent all morning in my studio working on a project for uni before jumping in the shower, washing all the paint off me and getting ready for my busy Saturday shift at work.

A shudder runs up my spine as I think about Zach's cold eyes as he stared at me last night. He really hated me on sight. I want to say he disliked me at school, but honestly, that would mean he'd have had to have noticed me. I was like a ghost in that place; the girl who loitered in the shadows, afraid of doing anything that would disrespect my parents. Dad had hopes of making more contacts with the parents of the private school kids I spent my days with. I think he hoped I would befriend the wealthiest and would be able to form a connection with their parents. Needless to say, I wasn't friends with any of the kids he would have liked me to have been.

I'm ready early and already antsy about turning up at the studio looking like a totally different version of myself, so instead of pacing my living room, I book an Uber and head off into the city for a little retail therapy before starting work. I've got a pretty vast wardrobe but it mostly consists of 'posh girl' (as I'm sure Zach would put it) blouses, jumpers and trousers. If I'm going to fully own this new look of mine then I need to make some additions.

I walk up to the heavy front doors of Selfridge's and smile to myself. You can take the girl out of the posh clothes, but you can't take the labels off them. Shaking my head at my thoughts and the fact that this shop was my first thought, I continue inside to see what I can find.

I head to my usual favourites and find the most perfect All Saints leather jacket to finish off my outfit before doubling back on myself when I walk past a pair of Jimmy Choo biker boots. I grab a few other bits, some vests along with a red leather skirt and tights to wear underneath.

I'm feeling pleased with myself when I walk back out with my yellow bags swinging from my fingertips. Where I might be a fan of designer labels, I'm not usually that much of a fan of shopping because I always find myself buying the same items, items that could equally be hanging in my mother's wardrobe as well as mine, but this morning as I walked around I felt the buzz of excitement that something new and big was happening. At least I was taking life by the balls and doing something for me. Something to show the world who Tabitha Anderson really is. One thing I know for sure is that she's not a meek and mild younger version of her mother.

I have the sudden urge to go home and burn all my old clothes, but as I slide into the back of an Uber, I look at the clock on my phone and realise that I don't have time. That shop totally took over my afternoon, and if the driver doesn't step on it I'm going to be late.

I laugh quietly to myself. Maybe I should be late just to piss him off further. I almost ask the driver to go the long way around, but as I sit forward to do so, I change my mind. He already dislikes me and is probably hoping that I'm not going to reappear today.

I quickly change my Converse for my new boots and pull my leather jacket up my arms before thanking the driver and stepping from his car.

The neon light still shows closed, and when I get to the door it's locked. I pull the key D gave me from the pocket of my bag and let myself in.

The place is in silence so I assume that I'm the first one in. I push my Selfridge's bags under my desk and go into the kitchen to power up the coffee machine ready for the others' arrival. I set my coffee going and then wander out to reception. I start up my computer and stand looking at the artwork on the walls while everything comes to life and the smell of freshly brewed coffee permeates the air.

The sound of his footsteps hits my ears and I freeze, my spine stiffening. *This is it, Tabitha. You need to bring your A game to stand a chance against this arsehole.*

I suck in a deep breath, hoping to drag in a little extra confidence with it. I'm just about to turn to face him when he speaks. The air I was holding in my lungs comes rushing out at the sound of his voice.

"I'm sorry, but we're not actually open yet." My skin pricks at the deep roughness. It makes my temperature spike and my irritation levels grow. I've not even looked at him yet.

"I'm aware," I snap, but I can't help a smile appearing on my lips. He has no idea it's me. Excitement explodes in my stomach. He clearly thinks I'm a client, which means he must think I belong here. Well, the back of me at least.

I don't bother preparing myself this time. His voice has already knocked me for six so I'm not sure I will ever be as prepared as I need to be to see him.

I spin on the balls of my feet, revealing myself to him.

My eyes run from his styled blonde hair, over his blue eyes, his straight nose and strong jaw. The moment his full lips part in shock, I know I've achieved what I intended to. Accomplishment blooms within me and I fight to keep the smug smile that's threatening under control.

"You?"

His eyes run the length of me, darkening as they go.

He takes a step forward, but the second he does, his face hardens like he doesn't actually want to come closer and his body's moving of its own accord.

"Well, you didn't actually fire me," I state, popping my hip out.

"That doesn't mean I think you'd come back, or change... for my benefit." His eyes sparkle as the realisation that he has some kind of power over me must hit him.

I take a step towards him, squaring my shoulders and preparing to tell him what I really think of him. "Let's get something straight here, Zachary. I did not, and will not ever change for a man, especially one as rude and arrogant as you. So you can get the idea that you had anything to do with this out of your massive egotistical head right now. I did this for me. I'll give you the credit that you helped give me the push I needed, but that's it."

A smirk widens on his lips, and my hand twitches to reach out and slap it away. "Riiight." He closes the space between us even more and something sparks the second I feel his heat seeping into my skin. I tell myself it's my loathing for his attitude, but I fear it might be something else. "And what will your boyfriend think of this little change? I can't imagine he'll be all that impressed, seeing as he probably keeps you around to look good on his arm and make his mother happy."

I bare my teeth in anger and he just laughs, making me want to hurt him.

"I'm no one's trophy. No one owns me or has any influence over what I choose to wear." A little voice in my head tells me that's not true, seeing as I've been listening to my parents for far too many years of my life, but I slam her back inside the trapdoor she belongs behind.

"So you're single then."

I open my mouth to respond, but really he can't be closer to the truth. A smile spreads across his face, making a dimple pop in his cheek, and damn him if it doesn't make him look even better.

"If you turn out to be a shit admin, I guess I could make use of you in other ways."

My eyes almost pop out of my head. "Did you just call me a hooker?"

He laughs, full on laughs in my face. "You think I'd need to pay you to get you into my bed?"

"There's nothing in this world you could do that would get me there."

He's so close that our noses are almost touching, our breaths mingling. All I can smell is him, and fuck if it's not making my knickers a little damp. His arrogance should not be affecting me right now. I should be turned off.

"I'll take that as a challenge then, Tabby Cat."

I suck in a huge breath through my nose, my eyes burning at hearing that nickname. Only Gran ever got away with calling me that. "Don't. Don't ever call me that. It's Biff, Tabitha if you must, but not ever that."

"Touch a nerve, did I, sweetheart?" He lifts his hand to tuck a lock of my pink hair behind my ear and I fight like hell not to lean into his soft touch. I refuse to allow him to affect me. I hate him.

"Fuck you."

"Oh, my little pussy cat, I fully intend to."

My teeth grind so hard I'm worried it'll crack one.

We're still staring daggers at each other when the bell above the door chimes, announcing someone else's arrival.

"Whoa girl, what happened to you?" Titch takes my hand and thankfully tugs me away from Zach. He lifts his arm and encourages me to spin. I'm halfway around when

HATE YOU

Zach's angry blue eyes catch mine. But this time, they're not staring at me. He's directing his death stare at Titch.

"Have you two just about fucking finished?" Zach seethes.

"Jesus, who pissed in your coffee this morning?"

"Go and do some work and stop eye-fucking our admin girl."

The girl comment grates on me, but I decide to let it slide seeing as Zach now really is pumped for a fight.

"Aw, come on, man. Even you've got to admit how banging she's looking. You might have been a wanker last night, but I'm tempted to say it was worth it seeing as this is the result."

Zach mumbles something under his breath and turns to walk away.

"What you so pissy about? You basically told her to do this."

He pauses in the doorway but obviously chooses not to respond, as a second later he continues again.

CHAPTER FIVE

ZACH

MY HEAD'S fucking spinning as I close my studio door behind me and lean back against it. Is Titch right? Is all that my fault?

I should have let her continue in her posh girl clothes. At least then all she did was piss me off. Now, she pisses me off while I picture doing wicked things to her in my head that are no good for anyone.

Don't fuck your staff no matter how hot they are, I say to myself as a reminder.

I need to stay away from her—not that that's going to be all that easy when she spends her time only feet away from me.

Fucking hell.

Trying to push the image of her from my head, I fall

on my chair and pull up today's schedule. I'm packed out all day, it doesn't even look like I'm getting a fucking lunch break. Well, I guess that's what happens when I disappear on regulars for almost three weeks.

It can't be ten minutes later when there's a knock at my door. Assuming it's my first client, I call out for whoever it is to enter but keep my eyes on my screen as I try to rack my brain for what we were working on before I went away.

Sadly, when the door's cracked open, I know who it is even before she speaks. Her perfume fills the room and my mouth waters.

"I... uh... brought you a coffee. Not that you deserve it." She mutters the last bit under her breath.

"I pay your wages, I'm pretty sure I deserve it." I spin on my chair and pin her with a look that stops her walking any farther into the room.

"No, that just means that I should do my job. At no point have I seen anywhere that it's required for me to be nice to you." The second she says it she slams her lips together, her eyes widening in shock.

Her panic that she's just spoken that way to her boss tells me a lot about her. Mostly that she probably is the posh girl I believe her to be who follows orders and doesn't ever speak out of turn—apart from with me, it seems.

Pushing my chair out behind me, I stand and stalk over to her, my eyes taking a slow perusal of her body as I move.

"You know... there's a tradition around here. I'm not sure if Titch told you." She bites down on her bottom lip and shakes her head slightly, her chest beginning to rise and fall rapidly with my approach. "Yeah, see, in order to work here, you need ink. And that ink can only be applied by me."

"Who says I haven't got any already?"

"You might have a tat or two hiding under these clothes, Tabby Cat. Although I very much doubt it." She bristles at my use of the nickname she apparently hates so much. I lean in to whisper and chuckle when she tries to move away. Sadly the only place she's going is up against the wall, which isn't a terrible idea. "But, if there is then I know for a fucking fact that I didn't do it. I assure you that if you were laid out on my table that I'd remember. I'm pretty sure you would too."

"Y-yeah, why's that?" she asks, but the way she tenses makes me wonder if she's already regretting the question.

"I always remember the virgins." I pull back and look at her. Her usually grey eyes flash with a little blue.

"Well, like I said, I'm not. So if you don't mind, I've got work to do." She presses her delicate hands to my chest and my heart pounds against them. I don't know whether to knock them off or to pull her closer. New looks aside, everything about this woman is everything I hate and everything I've tried to escape from.

"Prove it," I taunt.

She takes a step away but holds my eyes. "No." They narrow with contempt. My need to win the challenge she unknowingly set out in reception becomes even more possible to deny. The only question is, how long am I going to be able to hold off? Should I just fuck her now and send her on her merry way back to her privileged life, or should I have a little fun first?

The bell from the front door fills the silent space around us as our eye contact holds, the air crackling with hate and desire. She's trying to look unaffected by me, but she's doing a really shitty job of it.

"You should probably go and see who that is. You know, do that job I pay you for."

She sucks in a breath and shoves my coffee into my chest. The hot liquid splashes over the side, lightly scalding my skin before she turns to leave.

"Tabby Cat?" She stops but she doesn't turn back to me. "I will find that ink. If it so exists."

"No fucking chance." And then she's gone, leaving only her tempting scent behind her.

I don't get to dwell on it because no sooner has she gone than my first client of the day is standing in my doorway. The second I see him, I remember exactly what we were working on.

"It's good to see you, Mark. Grab a seat."

We chat for a few minutes to confirm what we're adding to his design before he drops his jeans to the chair on the other side on the room and climbs up into position.

The second my gun comes to life, I forget about everything with Tabitha and just focus on the task in hand. Just as it's always been since I did my first tattoo at fourteen, the world falls away and the only thing that matters is the marks I'm making, the permanent art that my client is allowing me to stain their skin with.

I stop a few times to drink what's left in my mug of coffee and to give Mark a short break as I work on the design we started a while ago on his leg.

By the time he's done, my hand aches but the muscles that were knotted in my shoulder have all relaxed and I feel more like myself than I have done in a while.

I expect my next client to appear seeing as we've now got a receptionist who's good at her job according to the others, but even long after Mark has left no one appears at my door.

With a sigh, I get up and walk her way. I come to a stop in the doorway to reception and take her in. She's sitting behind the desk, her full attention on the screen in front of her while her lips move in time with the music that's quietly playing.

She doesn't notice me approach, so when I do announce my arrival she almost jumps out of her seat.

"Where's my next client? I thought you said I was fully booked."

"Jesus, Zach. Are you trying to kill me?"

"Chance would be a fine thing. I can't even get rid of you," I mutter, but from the narrowing of her eyes I'm thinking she heard me.

"I don't know. I've tried ringing her but it keeps going to voicemail, so I'm assuming she's not coming."

I lean myself against the door frame as I look her over. "I guess I've got time then. Wanna play?"

"Not with you."

"Burn," Titch says, emerging from his room just as Tabitha tries to put me in my place. "He bothering you again?"

"Isn't he always?"

"I can kick his arse for you, if you like."

"Fuck off can you." I laugh, but it's not because it's true. His nickname might be Titch but don't make the mistake that it's because he's small—he's anything but. He's also spent time in the London underground fighting ring, so I most definitely wouldn't back myself should he turn on me.

"I'm not sure I could handle hearing you scream like a

little pussy when I put you down. But don't think I won't for this one."

My fists curl as he walks over to her desk and drops down in front of it so he can have a private conversation with her. I've no fucking clue what they're talking about, for all I know it's something as innocent as his next appointment, but fuck if seeing them together sharing some kind of secret doesn't make something stir uncomfortably in my stomach. I want to be the one to make her squirm, to make her scream.

Stop it, she's your employee.

"Something going on here I should know about?" I stalk towards the desk, looking between the two of them and hoping that I look pissed off rather than the other feeling that's racing wildly through my veins that I don't want to identify.

"We're good. Titch was just being nice. I'm not sure that's something you'd understand."

"Try me." She shakes her head, takes something from Titch's hand and stands from the desk.

"I'm just popping out. I won't be long, I'm sure you're more than capable of holding the fort."

"This is my fucking business," I fume.

"Exactly," she sneers at me.

I should walk away, but my eyes refuse to move as she grabs her jacket from the coat rack behind her and pulls it on. Her t-shirt lifts and reveals an inch of perfect milky skin. My mouth waters but not before I feel the burning stare of my best friend.

"I won't be long," she says to Titch, walking towards the door.

"Wait," I bark. "Pick me up some lunch while you're out."

"No," she says, a smirk playing on her lips when she turns back to look at me.

"No?"

"No. Not unless you ask nicely."

I roll my eyes. Is this woman for fucking real? "*Please, Tabby Cat, could you get me some lunch?*"

"I'll see what I can do." She's gone before I have the opportunity to tell her what I want.

"What?" I snap at Titch who's still staring at me like I've grown a second head.

"You like her, don't you?"

"No, she's fucking annoying and everything I hate. You should know that."

"So, hot as shit, witty as fuck, and totally your type is everything you hate?"

"She's just..." I trail off, trying to find the right words to describe my newest pain in the arse employee that I had nothing to do with hiring.

"Everything you want?"

"No, she's really fucking not."

"That's good, because I think she's awesome."

"Good for you."

"So you don't mind if I make a move?" I can't tell if he's being serious or just trying to piss me off enough to get a reaction out of me. Whatever it is, I refuse to show that his words affect me in any way.

"Nope. Eat your heart out."

A wicked smile turns up at the corner of his mouth. "Was thinking about a work night out. Welcome her to Rebel properly. What do you say?"

"Whatever. I've got work to do."

I walk away from him before the warning on the tip of

my tongue to stay away from her sneaks out, giving away everything I'm thinking right now.

There's no fucking way he's sinking his teeth into Tabitha. If anyone's going to get her then it's me. When I want, where I want, and exactly how I want.

I disappear back to my room, leaving Titch to plan his night out. If he really thinks that he's going to get a chance with Tabitha then he's got another think coming.

I click about on the computer for a bit but don't do anything of any importance. I can't get the hopeful look in Titch's eyes from my head, or the way they leaned into each other as they whispered about fuck knows what.

When her soft knock sounds out on my door, I'm just about ready to call it a day and get out of here and leave her and Titch to it, but I've got a ton of clients to get through yet.

"What?" I bark, pushing my chair out with such force it slams against the unit behind me.

"Did you want this now?"

CHAPTER SIX

TABITHA

I DROP Titch's lunch into his studio first, mainly because he's nice and asked me very politely if I'd run to the closest McDonalds for him seeing as he had clients all afternoon. He gave me money and his order and I had no issue.

The boss, on the other hand. Him I had an issue with.

I can still feel the tingles just beneath my skin from the way he was looking at the two of us as Titch leaned forward to whisper his order to me. His wink clued me in to the fact that he was merely doing it to piss Zach off, and the second I saw the murderous look on his face I couldn't help but think it was an awesome idea. It was instantly obvious that I'm not the only one feeling this weird vibe between us. Things aren't all that different from when we were kids in that he's still an arrogant arse, I hate him, and he's still the hottest man in probably any room he walks into. But—and this is a big but, one that's irritating the hell out of me—why can't I stop imagining what he might look like if he were to whip his shirt off and put his lips on my skin? My core clenches now even at the thought.

He's wrong. Everything I've never wanted. But man, I can't help but crave a taste right now. He's trying to piss me off because he clearly hates me for some reason as much as I do him, but with every insult that falls from his lips, my body just seems to want his more. *I really need to get laid.* It's been months since I ended my last disastrous attempt at a relationship, and things have been more than a little dry for me since then. I've been telling myself that my vibrating friend does the job perfectly well, but maybe I'm just kidding myself. Maybe what I need is a night with a man. A capable one who can blow my socks off, give me the release I need so I can focus on what I should be doing with my life. Not obsessing over my arsehole boss.

"You are a fucking legend, Biff." I can't help smiling at Titch's praise. He's a really good guy, despite his choice in friends.

"It's nothing. I got yours last so hopefully it'll still be hot."

"Appreciated," he says, unwrapping his burger and taking a giant bite. "What'd you get boss man?" he mumbles around the food.

I open the paper bag in my hand and show him the contents. He damn near spits out his half-chewed food as he barks a laugh.

"He's gonna love you for that."

"I don't know what you mean, I thought this was his kind of thing," I say innocently, shrugging my shoulder, but the smile that plays on my lips shows I'm anything but.

I turn to leave but a nondescript noise from Titch has me stopping at the door.

"Biff," he mumbles before swallowing. "Night out tonight. Celebrate our new member of staff. No excuses."

I nod, because it seems like that's the only choice I have. Although, to be honest a few drinks and a little dancing does sound like a fantastic idea. Maybe Zach will even remove the stick from his arse long enough to enjoy himself—if he even bothers coming. "Give me the details and I'm there."

I leave him to his lunch, having already seen way too much of his half-eaten burger in his mouth and hesitantly head towards Zach's closed door.

I knock but only to be polite. What I really want to do is storm inside his room and throw the lunch I so lovingly picked out at his head.

"Do you want this now?" I ask as I poke my head into the room.

"Yeah."

He doesn't move. He doesn't even turn to acknowledge I'm here, so I'm forced to take it over to him. I guess I could drop it to the floor, but then I won't see his reaction to my choice.

I lower the bag beside him and wait.

"A coffee wouldn't go amiss as well."

"I'll see what I can do."

I take a step back and butterflies erupt in my belly as he looks into the bag.

"What the fuck is this?" he asks, pulling out the vegan superfood salad I picked up for him followed by the disgusting green bottle of goodness that I thought would finish the meal nicely.

"You didn't specify, and I thought seeing as you obviously work out that maybe you're on a health kick."

"This isn't healthy, this is rabbit food." He stands and takes a step towards me, forcing me to take one back.

"I think it's the same thing," I counter.

"I can smell McDonald's."

"That's what Titch asked for."

"And you didn't think to get me something while you were there?"

My back hits the door I came through not so long ago as he continues to stalk towards me, his blue eyes sparkling with irritation and desire causing heat to zero in on my core.

"You didn't say what you wanted." I tilt my head to the side and try to look innocent. I'm not so sure it works.

His forearm lands on the door right beside my head, and he stares down at me. His scent surrounds me and I fight to keep control of my breathing with him so close, but I know it's not a battle that I'm winning.

"How about you go back and get me some real food? Something that involves meat, maybe."

"How about... go fuck yourself. You asked for food, I got you food. Maybe you should consider being more specific next time."

His jaw pops as his teeth grind. "I should have sacked you yesterday."

"Maybe, but you didn't." I probably shouldn't provoke him because he could still quite easily get rid of me, although my instincts tell me that he's enjoying me being around more than he'd ever admit.

His lips part with a comeback, but the second I look down at them he closes them again. The silence is heavy but nowhere near as suffocating as the tension that crackles between us.

He moves closer still and my eyelids are desperate to close, but I need to keep my wits about me. He might look like he's going to kiss me but I doubt that's what's actually going to happen.

"You need to get the fuck out of my room."

I don't move immediately other than to lift my eyes. When I find the dark blue staring back at me I'm frozen. My chest heaves as our breaths mingle and my breasts very lightly brush against his shirt. My nipples harden and my core floods with heat. I'm pretty sure that if he were to make any kind of move right now I wouldn't have it in me to stop him, no matter how much I dislike the wanker.

"Now." An amused smile curls at his lips as I scramble to get away from him and pull the door open.

I've almost made my escape when the arsehole calls me back. As if I need any more torture.

"What?" I bark, desperate for a few minutes alone to breathe.

"Once you've cooled off, go back and get me a fucking burger or two, hey?"

"Go your-fucking-self. I'm not your slave." His quick intake of breath is the last thing I hear before I slam his door shut and run to the kitchen.

Resting my back on the counter, I drop my head back and drag in a few deep breaths. This thing between us is going to go one of two ways: I'm either going to fall into bed with him and allow him to fuck my brains out, or I'm going to cause him some physical damage in an attempt to shut him the fuck up. I'm not sure which idea I prefer the most, if I'm being honest. Fucking him and hurting him both sound quite appealing.

Once I feel like I've somewhat composed myself. I grab my own lunch and sit myself at the little breakfast bar. Usually I'd sit out the front and eat, but seeing as I treated myself while I was getting Titch's lunch, not Zach's, I don't want to stink the reception out with my takeout grease smell.

I feel better once I've got a full belly, and, with a fresh coffee in hand, I make my way to my desk. I ignored both Zach's requests for a different lunch and a coffee. I've no idea what his last slave died of but I'm certainly not replacing her.

Turning my monitor on, I find a handful of new emails. One makes me roll my eyes. Does he really think he's being clever?

From: Zach Abbot
To: Tabitha Anderson
Subject: Why have a dog and bark myself?

Tabby Cat,
Don't worry. I welcomed my own client in.

I need:

A decent lunch. I'm starving
A cup of coffee
You, panting up against my wall once again
Z ;)

My curser hovers over the delete button. I don't want to give into his pettiness, but something stops me.

To: Zach Abbot
From: Tabitha Anderson
Subject: Read my job description

Get your own
Get your own
Get a dog

BIFF

I emphasize my name in the hope that one day soon he'll quit with the nickname that makes me want to cry every time I hear it. I've been called it many times over the years, but I fucking hate it. It was only my gran who kept it up, and coming from her mouth, it didn't annoy me quite so much. Unlike when I hear Zach say it and it makes me want to rip his tongue out.

I don't get a response so I can only assume that he's too busy working on the client I failed to let in. I'm only working here four days a week; he's going to have to get used to seeing his own clients in on the other days.

It must be almost an hour later when the bell above the door rings and a guy in a black and aqua jacket walks in carrying an insulated delivery bag.

"Delivery for Zach," the guy says, unzipping the bag and pulling out a brown paper bag that matches the one I put in the bin not so long ago. He goes to put it down on my desk, but like hell am I going to be the one who delivers it to Zach.

"Third door on the right." I point him down the

corridor and then turn back to my computer so he can't argue.

The rest of the night goes by fairly smoothly, but that's mostly because Zach stays hidden away and I refuse to step foot in his room. If he wants a drink then he must think better of it because I receive no more requests.

CHAPTER SEVEN

ZACH

MY IRRITATION DOESN'T LEAVE me all afternoon. Even the buzz of my gun does fuck all to get rid of it. The only thing I can see no matter what I'm inking is her dark, desire-filled eyes and her full red lips as she stared up at me earlier.

Titch has been in and out of my room like a fucking cuckoo, trying to convince me to come out with them tonight. I can't deny that a night out with the guys after being away doesn't sound good, but it's not just the guys, is it? *She's* going. And she's the reason it's happening at all. Because Titch wants to get into her pants. I shake my head as anger tightens my muscles just thinking about him trying it on with her.

HATE YOU

She's mine.

Whoa... no, no. She's messing with my fucking head. We've only been under this same roof together for a few hours. There's no way we're going to be able to put up with each other long term, and seeing as this is my business, I'm not going to be the one who's leaving. She is.

"All right, fine. I'll come. But," I add quickly, "I'm not spending all night watching you try to hit on Tabitha. I've got better shit to do with my life."

"You really need a drink and to get fucking laid, you know that right?"

I flip him off. Of course I fucking know it. My only issue is that I doubt anyone besides *her* is going to hit the spot.

AFTER MY LAST client of the night leaves, I sit on my stool hoping that the others will forget I'm here and go without me. I can hear them all chatting and laughing out in reception, but I know I'm on borrowed time. All four of them will have seen my client leave. They all know I'm done and can probably predict that I'm putting this off.

With a sigh, I start tidying up. My need for a pint outweighs my need to stay away from her by the time I've finished.

"Ah, here he is. We thought we were going to have to come and wrestle you out of your room."

I keep my eyes away from where she's sitting behind her desk. I don't want to give her the satisfaction that my hiding away might have had anything to do with her.

"We getting a fucking drink or sitting around here

having a fucking mothers' meeting?" I bark, kicking Titch's foot from the coffee table as I walk past him.

"We're going, just waiting for you and Biff to finish up." I feel her eyes burning into my back, but I still refuse to give her any attention.

"You guys go. I need to freshen up, then I'll meet you there in a bit."

"You sure? I can wait, it's no problem," Titch offers, pissing me the fuck off.

"She told us to go, now let's go." I push open the front door, expecting them to follow.

D and Spike step out seconds later, and Titch comes a minute after looking torn.

"I need a fucking pint. Come on."

Our local is only two streets over. The Pear Tree was an old fashioned London boozer until a couple of years ago when it was modernised into a bar that's always busy. Thankfully, by the time we usually finish on a Saturday most people have already hit the clubs and it's quietening down. And that's exactly as we find it when we walk through the door.

"Lads, long time no see," Leon, the manager, greets. "The usual?"

"Yes please." We find ourselves a booth and wait for him to bring our drinks over.

"So, what have you guys been up to?" I ask, needing to get my head out of the studio and away from Biff while I've got a reprieve.

"Same as, same as," D says, but he turns to Spike. "This one's got a new girl on the go." I raise an eyebrow, waiting for him to elaborate.

"It's nothing serious."

"That's not how it looked last weekend. She was clinging to you like a koala bear."

"Yeah, I'm pretty sure she thinks it's more than it is. She's a fucking good lay though, so I'll let her cling for a while longer. What about America? Those Cali girls are hot, right?"

I think back to the girls walking around on the beaches flaunting almost everything they had. "Ah man, I could have moved. They were something-fucking-else."

"Hook up much?"

"Every-fucking-night." Okay, so that's a lie, but I'm not telling them that. They think I live 'the life' and I'm not ruining it for them. "Came back for a rest."

"Lovely," a soft female voice says from behind me that sends shivers down my spine. "I'm sure the female population of California were gutted their personal sex god had to leave."

Her eyes hold mine, her disgust for my actions clear in her grey depths. I hate it, and my need to tell her that I'm exaggerating slightly is right on the end of my tongue.

"Whoa, you scrub up well, girl," Titch says. "Scoot up, D-man, let the girl in." Titch slaps D in the chest and he stands, allowing Tabitha to slide into that side of the booth.

Part of me wants to stop her sitting next to him—he could do anything beneath the shield of the table—but not wanting to show it affects me, I sit on my hands and keep my lips sealed. My eyes, however... they feast on her. She's still wearing the skin-tight jeans but she's now teamed it with a low cut, loose black top and a pair of black sky-high heels with little chrome studs on them. Her hair is as bright as it was earlier, but instead of straight, it's got a curl to it and her make-up is dark, making her look even more mysterious and appealing. The posh girl I first met is starting to disappear, and I need to keep hold of that image of her to stop me doing something I'm going to regret.

Titch's eyes are locked on the swell of her breasts, and it takes every bit of restraint I have not to lean over the table and slap him.

"What do you want to drink?" he asks.

"I doubt Leon stocks Crystal, Tabby Cat."

"Good thing that's not what I drink." She throws me a look that might make a weaker man crumble, but she needs to learn that I'm not going to be backing down from her attitude.

"Jack and Coke would be great."

"Double coming right up, baby."

My teeth grind that he's planning on getting her drunk so he can get what he wants. The fucker knows I'm on his wavelength too, because when he turns to go to the bar, he fucking winks at me.

The tension around the table crackles while D and Spike look between Tabitha and me like we're going to start a fist fight any moment.

"Don't let me stop your enlightening rundown of your American conquests," she says with a smirk.

"With pleasure." I want to look away from her, but because she's requested this, I look her straight in the eyes as I tell the story of one of my wilder nights in California. "They're fucking dirty over there. Corey and I went to this beach party. There were bikini clad girls everywhere, the music was banging, the alcohol was overflowing. It was like nothing I've ever seen before. Basically one big outside orgy. Girls and guy, girls and girl, guys and guys. No one was off limits." Tabitha's face scrunches in disgust. It's kind of cute. Unable to hold my stare, she looks to Spike when he starts talking.

"We're going on a work trip there, right?" Spike asks. He's basically salivating at the thought alone. Fucking dog. If Tabitha thinks I'm bad then she should hear some of Spike's tales. He's definitely one that no guy wants for his sister. I smile to myself, thinking that Danni would thankfully run in the opposite direction of any of my friends. I'll forever be grateful that her type seems to be suave bankers.

"I'll see what I can do," I say with a laugh. "Corey was loving it. It was clear he was right at home from the moment I arrived."

"Ah man, why didn't I offer to relocate?"

"Because the girl you were getting your cock wet in at the time was more important."

"Ugh, Krissy. Do you know that bitch gave me crabs?"

"Yeah, you might have mentioned it."

"You guys do realise we've got a woman present, right?" D asks, glancing at Tabitha.

"The second you employed her she sadly became one of us. She can deal, she knows where the door is."

I look back to her. Her back straightens and her shoulders square. "I've dealt with worse than you lot. I've probably even got a few stories of my own that would make you blush."

"That right, Biff baby?" Spike asks, his interest suddenly focused on her and her possible dirty story.

"Fuck off have you. You're so straight laced, you're probably a virgin."

"Have you about finished?" Titch asks, coming to a stop at the table with a tray full of drinks. "We're meant to be celebrating Biff starting with us, not scaring her off and dragging her darkest secrets from the closet."

"Just getting to know her better." Something crackles between us as our eyes hold. The guys seem to vanish around us as I try to dive into her head to find out if she's lying. I want to say she is, but that little saying 'beware of the quiet ones' rings out in my head.

CHAPTER EIGHT

TABITHA

MY HEART'S out of control in my chest as I hold Zach's stare, trying to appear like I'm telling the truth when in reality the wildest thing that's ever happened in my sex life is probably a really bad attempt at shower sex.

The last thing I wanted to do tonight was to have to sit and listen to Zach's American conquests while Titch tries to hit on me. I mean, he's cute, but that's all there is for me.

"Go on then, Tabby Cat. Enlighten us to your wild side," Zach taunts.

"Give it a rest." Titch places my drink in front of me. I'm desperate to reach out and down it in the hope it gives me a little confidence, but I don't want to break first. Zach already thinks he knows me; I refuse to appear weak. "Drink this and shut the fuck up or go home."

I pray that Zach takes that final suggestion and gets up, but he doesn't. He lifts his fresh pint and drinks it while watching me over the rim of the glass.

"So Biff, you're single, right?"

"Yep, exactly how I like it. I can have a little fun with no strings and no responsibilities."

"A-fucking-men, girl." He holds his glass out for me to tap mine to. "Welcome to the team. I think it's the start of something beautiful." I want to agree. I love the three of them, they're good fun. It's the boss who has my stomach in knots and my skin burning with awareness.

Choosing to ignore his piercing stare, I twist myself so I can focus on what the others have to say.

"YOU READY TO HIT THE dancefloor, Biff?"

"It's three in the morning, you can't be serious."

"Deadly. I want to see if you've got moves."

I was grateful for my little spur of the moment shopping trip this morning. It meant I had something to change into for this impromptu night out.

"Oh, I've got moves, don't you worry." I wink at Titch and down what's left of my drink. I've had enough in the past two hours that the thought of dancing the rest of the morning away doesn't sound totally insane. I've not pulled an all-nighter in years, so I guess it's about due.

"Well, what are we waiting for? Hoping Steve will be on the door and we'll get right in."

I don't get a chance to ask who Steve is because Titch takes my hand and pulls me from the booth. I assume the others follow, but I don't really care. My thoughts are focused on the impending pounding music as it flows through my body and allows me to forget the world as I move in time.

I'm introduced to Steve. He appears to be a client of one of the guys seeing as every inch of skin is covered in ink. We skip the line and in minutes we've got shots in our hands, courtesy of some barmaid who takes one look at Zach, bats her eyelashes and immediately pulls out a bottle of Jägermeister and lines up a row of shots. She gives me a warning look but I just smile sweetly. I've no intention of getting between her and my boss, if they're even a thing. I've got the impression from how he's acted and the way he spoke about his time in America that he's free and single.

"Cheers, Tam," Zach says as he necks his shot and looks at me expectantly. Does he really think I'm so stuck up that I don't know how to down a shot?

I make a show of picking mine up and licking my lips. Zach's eyes follow my tongue and the butterflies that have been gently fluttering away in my stomach take flight once again. He swallows, and the muscle in his neck ripples as he waits for me to drink.

Sucking in a deep breath, I rip my eyes from him and tip the glass to my lips.

It's fucking disgusting, reminding me why I never drink this shit, but I'm not being seen to refuse. He'll only assume that it's because I think I'm too good for it, which I don't at all. It's just not for me.

I manage not to show my distaste as I drop the glass to the bar.

"Right, are you ready for this, Biff? Some people say I could have been the next JT." He winks, and I laugh.

"Show me what you've got then."

In a flash we're heading towards the dancefloor and I'm pulled into Titch's body. His front presses into my back and his hands land on my hips as we move in time to the music.

Credit where credit's due, he does have rhythm. I'm not sure it's JT level, but then I've never danced with him to have anything to compare this to.

He leans into my ear, his breath tickling over my neck, but I don't react in the way I think he expects me to. There's no shudder of excitement, no rush of heat to any part of my body like I know would happen if someone else were dancing with me right now. I expect him to say something to try to pick me up, but what comes out of his mouth shocks the fuck out of me.

"Zach's going out of his mind right now. Do you have any idea how badly he wants you?"

I still at his words for a second before I remember I'm meant to be dancing.

"I very much doubt that. He hates me."

"That's what he wants us all to think, and he might. But that doesn't remove the fact that he wants to fuck you into next week." I suck in a breath. "Oh, don't act so surprised. The sexual tension between the two of you is so thick the rest of us can practically see it."

"It is not." I try to argue, but the rumble of a laugh I feel behind me tells me I'm failing miserably.

My body heats at Titch's words, but when I glance toward the bar, I find the real reason why I'm burning up. *His* eyes are focused on me. They're dark, his eyelids heavy while the muscle in his jaw ticks.

"So the question is... what are you going to do about it?"

"I... I..." I stutter, the desire flowing through my blood as I fight to drag my eyes from Zach, the alcohol in my veins making it really damn hard to concentrate. "Nothing. He can fuck off."

"Really?" A chuckle rumbles through Titch before his hands resting on my hips tighten and I'm turned to face him.

"He's my boss."

"Riiight," he says, a knowing smirk playing on his lips that I want to slap off.

"And I hate him."

He leans into my ear. To the people around us, Zach included, it probably looks intimate and nothing like the reality of the situation. I realise that all of this with Titch really has been a game. "Sometimes that makes for the best sex."

"Whatever you say." I continue moving with him, but my enthusiasm is waning. I might enjoy the little hate game I've got going on with Zach—it certainly fulfils a need I've had since I was an invisible little kid—but I've no intention of using Titch to get back at him. They're friends, there's no way I'm getting in the middle of them, and the way Titch's body is moving against mine right now and the burning stare I can still feel is proof that I'm doing just that.

"Excuse me, I need to use the bathroom."

I twist out of Titch's arms and walk away. When I glance back over my shoulder, he's pulled another woman into his body, but the stool Zach was sitting on is empty. My heart races at the thought that he's found his own woman to dance with and is about to put me through the same torture he just had to endure if Titch is right. *Of course Titch is right,* a little voice says as I follow the sign for the ladies. *You already know there's something between you. This isn't news.*

The queue for the toilets is insane. I didn't really need to go when I excused myself in there, I just needed to get away, but by the time I get to the front of the line, I'm glad I did.

I do what I need to do, wash my hands, top up my lipstick and run my fingers through my hair, separating the curls that have twisted together. With my head held high, I walk back out into the club. I intend on saying goodbye to Titch and the others and getting the hell out of here before Zach decides enough is enough and does something about his burning stare.

Pulling open the door, I take two steps when a hand wraps around my wrist and I'm harshly pulled back. I let out a squeal but not before his hand covers my mouth—not that anyone would hear with the volume of the music in here.

My heart's in my throat as I'm pulled back into a dark doorway at the back of the club. A shadow appears from behind me, but the second his light hair catches my eye, I relax, although not that much. The man might not be a stranger, but he's still dragged me down here against my will.

"What do you want?" I snap, ready to push from the wall and storm away from him.

"Are you doing it on purpose?" he asks. He stands right in front of me, crowding me and blocking off the rest of the club so it almost feels private. He lifts one arm so he's resting it on the wall beside my head. His scent fills my nose and damn if it doesn't make my mouth water.

"Doing what? Enjoying a night out? Yeah, I guess that's kind of intentional." I roll my eyes at his idiocy.

"Yeah, *enjoying* yourself. With *him.*"

"Oh, I see. You're jealous that Titch got to dance with me while you were forced to stay on the side-lines and watch. Well, I'm all yours now, aren't I? What are you going to do about it?"

He steps closer, the heat of his chest burning into mine, his usually light blue eyes almost navy with desire. They bounce between mine before dropping down to my lips. I desperately want to run my tongue along them, but I refuse to show him that I'm affected by this. Instead, I bite down on my cheek until a metallic taste fills my mouth.

"I don't know," he drawls. "So many options."

His hand lifts. Taking a lock of my hair between his fingers, he tucks it behind my ear. The second his skin brushes the shell of my ear, sparks shoot around my body.

My heart pounds impossibly hard against my ribs as heat blooms between my legs at his closeness.

His finger drops and skims down the smooth skin of my neck. Goosebumps follow his trail and I shudder. His lips twitch, telling me that he didn't miss it.

I gasp when his finger hits the swell of my breasts and runs along the hem of my vest.

He leans in to whisper in my ear. "You're everything I hate in a woman. Everything I've tried to leave behind. Yet you're here. Tempting me. Driving me crazy."

I swallow, shocked that he's admitting this.

"I need you out of my system."

He stops, his next words dying on his tongue as he continues to stare at me. I should use his moment of silence to push him away and run, but I don't. I'm frozen to the spot, desperate to discover what he's going to do next.

He reaches out, his fingers popping the button at my waist open in a flash.

"Oh god." This is wrong. He's my boss, a guy I can't stand, my best friend's brother—although he's not aware of that—and we're in a very public place right now. Yet, I still can't find it in me to wrap my fingers around his arm and stop him.

Flattening his hand, he pushes inside. He groans when he finds the lace of my knickers, but he doesn't stop there. He doesn't stop until he's parted me and his fingers are gliding through my wetness.

"Fucking knew you wanted me, Tabby Cat. Now I'm going to ruin you."

CHAPTER NINE

ZACH

I KNOW I've made a mistake the second her desire coats my fingers. The scent of her need fills my nose, and my mouth waters for more than I'm able to take right here because I'd be kidding myself if I said I didn't want everything from her. I might hate her, but that doesn't stop me wanting to take. I want to see her writhing beneath me, calling out my name as she understands the power I have over her. She might think she's something special with her designer clothes and posh girl demeanour, but she's nothing more than a plaything for me. And she's about to discover the real game here.

"Oh god," she whimpers, and my cock swells beneath my trousers.

I drop my head to her neck and breathe her in, but I

refuse to put my lips on her. Instead I lick up the smooth skin, feeling her racing pulse.

I circle her clit once more before dropping my fingers lower and dipping them just slightly inside her. Her muscles contract and try to suck me in deeper to get what she needs, but she's not the one in control right now.

"Zach, please." Fuck, if the sound of my name as a plea on her lips doesn't do something to me.

"You want more?"

"Yes," she begs. "I need... need more."

I thrust higher into her heat, wishing like fuck that it was my cock, not my fingers as she clamps down on me.

"Shatter, Tabby Cat. Fucking shatter for me." Lifting my head from the crook of her neck, I watch as pleasure hits her. Her eyes roll back and her teeth sink into her bottom lip.

"Ohhhh," she cries as she falls, her pussy clamping my fingers impossibly tight.

The second she's come down from her high, I rip my hand from her trousers and take a step back. It's not enough for anyone to see her, but it's enough that I've got no contact. She's already too tempting as it is.

Her chest heaves as she tries to catch her breath. She drags her heavy, lust-filled eyelids open and stares at me with glassy eyes. Her brows draw together as she tries to figure out what the hell just happened. I wish I had a fucking clue. All I know is that I couldn't watch her dancing with Titch a second longer without touching her myself. She's mine. Mine to taunt, mine to pleasure.

Unable to resist, I lift my hand and suck the two fingers that were just deep inside her pussy into my mouth.

Her chin drops and her eyes darken further as she watches the movement.

She's so fucking sweet.

"What now?" she taunts, her eyes narrowing in contempt.

"Now nothing."

Turning on my heels, I walk away from her. It's the hardest thing I've done in quite some fucking time. Every muscle in my body screams for me to go and take what I need, but I refuse to show her that she holds that kind of power. She doesn't need to know how crazy one look at her dancing with Titch made me.

I lose myself in the hundreds of people who are still filling this club despite the fact it's nearly dawn, and order myself another drink. I need the taste of her off my tongue. It makes me want to do crazy shit like find her and drag her back to my bed.

DECIDING TO LEAVE, I slam my glass down on the bar and turn for the exit. Sadly two others have a similar idea, because when I lift my eyes Titch and Tabitha are before me.

Titch's dark eyes are ablaze, telling me that he's drunk off his arse, while Tabitha refuses to look me in the eye, but I don't miss the blush that's still colouring her cheeks and down her neck.

Good.

"We're heading out."

I nod, not trusting myself to say anything.

"See you tomorrow then?" Titch asks hesitantly. He knows exactly what's up—well, maybe not exactly, but we've been friends for long enough for me to know when he's trying to play me.

"Great. Can't wait." They both turn to leave and my mouth runs away with me. "Titch?"

"Yeah?"

"Don't fuck my staff." He looks at Tabitha, who stands stock still beside him, her spine ramrod straight as if she's trying to appear unaffected by me. Big fat fail on that, love.

Titch salutes me, a small smirk appearing on his smug as fuck face, before placing his hand on the small of her back and guiding her towards the exit.

Deciding against following them out in case I'm wrong and he does actually want her, or more likely she's so fucking horny after our little moment that she's begging him to finish the job I started, I order another drink and try to think about anything other than her pussy.

Tammi, the barmaid I've fucked on many occasions, walks over when I gesture for her.

"The usual?" she asks.

"Make it a double."

"That good a day?"

"Something like that," I mumble. Not that she can hear me.

"Here you go." She slides the glass over and then leans forward on the bar, forcing her breasts together in a move that usually works wonders on me. Tonight, not so much. "You needing a friend to end the night with?"

"Nah, not tonight. Just a few of these." I lift my glass and down the contents in one. One of her brows lifts. She doesn't believe me and spends the rest of time I'm at the bar trying to convince me that spending the night with her will be exactly what I need. She might be right in that it's pussy I'm desperate for, but she's very much mistaken if she thinks it's hers I'm craving right now.

BY THE TIME I leave the club, I can barely feel my legs. The cold hits me, but with the alcohol flowing through my system I barely even shiver. The sun is rising and London is beginning to wake up, making me glad I don't have a boring nine to five like everyone else.

That was what was expected of me. To join the family antique business and continue the Abbot legacy. The problem with that is that from as early as I can remember, I've felt like anything but a member of that family. Yes, they're my parents, they've brought me up and given me every opportunity, but I've never been able to shake the feeling that I don't belong. Harrison, my brother, jokes about me being the milkman's, and to be honest, I wouldn't be surprised to find out I was. I'm the opposite to the rest of my family in every single way.

I come to a stop outside Rebel Ink with my keys in my hand. I look up at my dark flat and let out a sigh. I could have gone home with Tabitha tonight. I'd put money on it. With my fingers deep inside her I'm pretty sure she'd have done anything I asked of her. I wonder how she'd take to me turning up at her front door right now. Would she still be awake and willing for a little more of what we started? Or—and the thought makes my stomach turn over—did Titch not just walk her home? Is he there right now, taking what should be mine?

I look over my shoulder in the direction I know she lives in. It's not that far from the studio, and it would only take me minutes to be at her building. My cock swells at the thought and desire courses through me before it quickly turns to anger.

I shouldn't want her. She's the epitome of everything I dislike about my life. She's the posh little girl, living the posh little life. Okay, so she's clearly trying to make a statement by working for me here, but I'm under no illusion she's here because she wants to be. She's probably just trying to prove a point to her stuck-up parents. She's given me no sign that she even likes tattoos. She's just using me, and that makes me feel a hell of a lot better about using her back. I'll let her continue working, because despite my first impressions she's actually pretty damn good at her job, and eventually I'll get her in my bed, break her, and send her back to her privileged little life. Then I'll be able to continue with mine.

CHAPTER TEN

TABITHA

TITCH IS THE PERFECT GENTLEMAN. He ignores my obviously flushed state when I reappear from my little rendezvous with Zach, and when he suggests that he take me home, he does exactly that. He has an Uber waiting out the front of the club and he opens the door so my drunk, unsteady legs can climb in.

It's the alcohol's fault. If I weren't so intoxicated I'd have been able to tell Zach where to go the second he dragged me back into that little alcove. That's what I tell myself anyway. It's easy to pretend that what happened had nothing to do with the electricity I feel every time we're close. It had nothing to do with the sparks that shot around my body when he touched me, or the one whiff of his scent that had my mouth watering and my core heating faster than I could control.

"You okay from here, or would you like me to walk you right up?" Titch says, helping me from the car.

I look up to the front door. "I'm fine. Thank you so much. Tonight was... fun?" It's not meant to come out like a question, and my face scrunches in confusion when I realise it has.

"Tell me to shut up if you like but..." Titch hesitates, but after blowing out a breath, he continues. I'm pretty confident I know what's coming, but I'm powerless to stop him, too intrigued to find out how he's going to play this. "Zach's a really good guy. I know things are... weird between you, but just give him time."

"He's an arsehole. Why would I want to do that?"

He studies my face for a second. "Firstly, because you're good at your job and I like having you about." A smile curls at my lips at his honesty. "I love the guys, but there's something so awesome about having you there. You bring a different dynamic to the place and don't put up with our bullshit."

"And second?"

"He likes you." I bark out a laugh. "He's just—" He pauses, presumably trying to decide how much to give away, but in the end he sticks to vague. "He has no idea what he needs. Just give him time," he repeats.

"Yeah, you said that already."

"Well, that's because it's what you need to do. I'll see you tomorrow. Try to get some sleep." Titch winks at me and takes a step back toward the car.

"See you tomorrow." Turning on my heel, I make my way to the front door.

"Water and painkillers before sleep," Titch calls. I

laugh and wonder just how good a job I'm doing right now to appear sober.

After kicking off my heels, I follow orders and go through to my kitchen to down a pint of water. I pull my phone from my bag and look down at the screen. Five thirty in the morning. It's been a lot of years since I was up this late. Or early. But that's not the worst of it. I've got a missed call from my mother from early yesterday evening.

Ignoring the voicemail, knowing that I'm most definitely too drunk to hear whatever it is she's got to say, I close everything down and go in search of my bed. I don't start work until two, so I should get a good few hours in.

I strip out of my skinny jeans and vest. Leaving my underwear where it is, I crawl between the sheets and I swear I'm out before my head even hits the pillow.

AN INCESSANT RINGING eventually drags me from my peaceful sleep. I don't need to open my eyes to know that one: I didn't shut the curtains before I passed out last night, and two: I drank way too much.

I lie still for a few moments, hoping that the loud shrill of my phone will stop and I'll be able to fall back to sleep. But no sooner has it stopped than it starts again.

Groaning, I roll over and grab it.

'Mum' lights up my phone.

Brilliant.

Knowing she's already tried to get a hold of me a handful of times, I know I can't ignore her. Swiping the screen, I move the phone towards my ear and wince as I wait for her high-pitched voice.

"Darling, are you ignoring me?" she asks in the exact judgemental voice I was expecting.

"No, Mum. I was sleeping."

"It is ten o'clock in the morning, Tabitha. You should have been up hours ago."

"Well, I wasn't. I went out last night and—"

"Typical. Just typical. You know full well that today is our big meal. You should have been here thirty minutes ago and yet you're still between the sheets. You need to get yourself sorted, young lady. And if you turn up here smelling of last night's drink, so help me god."

"Right," I all but growl into the phone. How could I have possibly forgotten such a fun event that I'm forced to attend in the hope that one of dad's 'friends' will be able to convince me to begin a respectable career instead of *fannying around with pointless hobbies,* as my parents describe my love of art.

"Get out of bed, put on a nice dress, and get your backside over here pronto. We've got guests arriving and they're expecting to see you."

If I thought my head was spinning when I first woke up then it's nothing compared to right now. I've not had nearly enough sleep to deal with my parents today, let alone a whole bunch of their friends.

Knowing there's no way out of it if I want to keep this roof over my head, I roll my arse out of bed and head for the bathroom.

It's not until I'm standing with a towel wrapped around my body and a brush in my hand that I remember my hair.

Fuck. Mum's going to lose her shit. My stomach twists with nerves but I can't help a smile playing on my lips at the thought of her face.

In an attempt to make her happy, I quickly dry and curl it with my straighteners before pulling a dress and pair of shoes she'd approve of from my wardrobe. It's a simple floral summer dress that shows off a hint of cleavage. The light chiffon fabric skims over my thighs and comes to a stop at my knees. It's not something I'd choose; it's one of those dresses Mum bought for me over the years specifically for her events.

A large sigh falls from my lips as I grab my bag and head out the door. I don't intend on spending too long at my parents'. I'll show my face, eat a little, assuming the hangover starts to wear off, and then I'll make my excuses so I can get back here and changed before work this afternoon.

"TABITHA, what on earth have you done to your hair?" Mum snaps the second I walk into her kitchen. I might be late, but I'm still one of the first here.

"I coloured it, Mum. Wanted something different."

"Something different would have been walnut, or some copper hues. That... That's just... tasteless." Her top lip curls up in disgust, and I somehow manage to stop my eyes from rolling.

"Well, I like it. I was feeling a little wild and needed a change."

"It looks ridiculous. None of Dad's friends will even consider hiring you looking like that."

"I don't want them to hire me, Mum. I don't want to work for any of them."

"Tabitha, how many times do we need to go over this?

You need a respectable job, or you need a man who's willing to keep you."

A bitter laugh falls from my lips. "No, Mum. That's what you think I need. I, however, am perfectly happy with my life right now. I don't need a job just to impress you and Dad, and I most definitely do not want to be a kept woman."

She tuts but my dad joins us, thankfully cutting off any of her words.

"Tabi— whoa, what's going on with your hair?"

"I dyed it pink. Jesus, it's not like I became a crack whore or anything."

Mum gasps at my choice of words whereas Dad's chin just drops in horror.

"Well, I should hope not. Something like that would really tarnish the Anderson name."

Of course it would.

"Right, where do you need me? I'm not staying long."

Mum flaps around with the tea towel in her hand, looking like she's about to cry. Fuck knows why, she's not cooked a single dish in this kitchen. Everything's been delivered in perfect condition. "Just... just go and be nice. And try to be respectable, despite the hair."

"I'll try." I give them both the most insincere smile I can muster and walk from the room to the sound of Mum complaining to Dad.

Dying my hair might be me pushing back against the life they've dragged me into, but I know it's barely the tip of the iceberg. What I really need to do is tell them where to go and walk out, but there's a part of me that isn't ready. Walking away from them means walking away from the money and the flat. I might hate everything they stand for, and I know it makes me a huge hypocrite, but I can't help it. Going it alone is scary, especially when I don't have a proper job or any clue what I want to do. I could do as they suggest and get myself a job with one of the people spending the afternoon here, but it'll keep me tied to them. I want my own life, I just need to figure out what it looks like.

I end up sitting next to one of Dad's 'friends' while my mother gives me evils from across the table. Charles is one of Dad's associates, although I've not really got a clue what he does aside from drink too much and sleep with younger women behind his wife's back. She's sitting beside him, utterly clueless as he leers at me and spends more time looking at my cleavage than he does my face.

Every time I feel his gaze on me, my skin prickles and my stomach turns over.

"It's been lovely chatting to you, Charles, but I really must go."

"Oh, Tabitha. Stay a little longer." He lifts his wine to his lips at the same time he places his hand on my thigh. A little squeal of shock falls from my lips and I stand, forcing my chair to clatter to the floor. My mother's eyes narrow in frustration, and my father also glances my way, looking very unimpressed with my little outburst.

"I'm sorry. I have somewhere to be."

I march off before he has a chance to try to stop me again.

"Tabitha, what the hell was that?"

"He was trying to touch me up under the table."

"Charles? Really? His wife was sitting right the other side of him."

"Believe what you want. I'm leaving."

"You can't go. Your mother's not even served dessert yet."

"I'm not hungry, and I need to get to work."

"To work? You didn't tell us you'd got a job." No, and there's a very good reason for that.

"I haven't had a chance, but I've got to go or I'll be late."

"What sort of place has you starting work on a Sunday afternoon?"

"Does it matter?"

"Yes it does. We need to know where our daughter is spending her time."

"I'm twenty-seven years old. Is that really necessary?"

"Yes," they say in unison. Dropping my head back, I suck in a long breath as I try to keep my calm. The last thing any of us needs is me acting like a spoilt child.

"I'm working part time doing admin in a tattoo studio by me."

Mum's eyes go so wide I almost expect them to pop out and start rolling around on the floor. Dad, on the other hand, just starts laughing. Frown lines form between my brows as I try to figure out what's funny.

"That's a good one, Tabby. Next you'll be telling us you're a stripper."

The frustration that's been simmering just under the surface all day begins to erupt. "I'm not joking, Dad. I'm really working at a studio, and I'm actually really enjoying it."

"But... but the men who go to those places are—"

"Are a hell of a lot more respectful than the one you sat me beside this afternoon. Now if you'll excuse me, I'm already late."

I pull the front door open and march down my parents' driveway towards the Uber that's waiting for me.

"Change of plan," I tell him once I've climbed in, and

I rattle off the studio address. I'm late, and I really don't have time to change. Zach can screw it if he doesn't like it.

The neon sign has been turned to open and is shining bright. There are a couple of clients already sitting in the waiting room when I push the door open and step inside. Every single set of eyes turns to me and runs down my body. I get it, the floral dress really doesn't fit. My skin prickles with awareness, but it's not from their scrutiny. *He's* here somewhere. He's looking right at me.

I quickly glance around the room, but finding no one, I take a step towards my desk and drop my bag.

It's then that he makes himself known. He appears in the doorway to the kitchen. His eyes are narrowed, but not enough to miss the storm brewing beneath. His face is set and his jaw is ticking with frustration. His arms are crossed over his chest, the muscles in them bulging and straining against the dark fabric of his t-shirt.

"You're late," he snarls. His eyes drop from mine in favour of my body and his eyes widen before an evil, humourless laugh falls from his lips.

Stepping towards me, his fingers wrap around my wrist, his touch burning all the way to my core as he drags me towards his room and away from prying eyes.

"What the hell are you playing at?" he demands the second he slams the door shut behind me. He doesn't move, leaving me the choice of pressing my back against the cold door or my front to his warm chest. I decide that staying as far away from him as possible is the right thing to do.

"I'm sorry, I got stuck at this thing."

"What? The Queen's fucking tea party?"

"Well, no. It was just a meal at my parents' but—"

"But nothing, you look... you look... fuck." His hands

find his hair and he pulls it painfully hard as he takes a huge step back from me and turns around, cutting himself off from me.

"I've got clothes under my desk from yesterday. I'll quickly change and we're all good."

I push from the door and turn to reach for the handle, only when I wrap my hand around it I don't find cool metal but a hot hand instead.

"Stay here," he barks before pushing past me and storming back towards reception.

"O... okay," I mutter to myself as my heart thunders so hard in my chest I can feel it in my ears.

It's only seconds before the sound of his pounding feet heads back this way. I move away from the door, afraid he'll push it open so hard that it'll knock me off my feet and take a seat on the edge of his chair.

Anticipation fills me, making my hands tremble for what kind of Zach I'm going to find when he comes back.

The door shuts, but I refuse to look over. This arrogant arsehole isn't going to have me at his beck and call.

"Change," he demands, throwing the bags onto my lap.

"Only because you asked so nicely," I seethe, taking the bags in my hand and standing.

He turns, his eyes find mine, and my breath catches. They're so dark, but right now I've no idea if it's with anger or desire, and that thought has my thighs clenching with need. I might have been drunk last night, but that doesn't mean I don't remember exactly how it felt to have his hands on me. And although I know it was a mistake of epic proportions to allow it to happen, it doesn't mean I'm not standing here craving a repeat.

HATE YOU

"Don't," he warns, his thumb and finger gripping my chin, ensuring our connection holds.

"You're going to need to let go if you want me out of this dress." His eyes flash with heat. "Is that what this is all about? You don't really care about the dress, you just want me to strip out of it."

"Trust me, Tabby Cat. If I wanted you naked, I could think of easier ways than this."

My chest heaves as he continues to stare into my eyes. My breaths fan across his face where he's so close. His jaw clicks, but other than that he gives nothing away, whereas I feel like I'm about to melt into a puddle.

"Get moving, Kitten. You've got a fucking job to do."

"Well, if you'd let go I might have a chance."

His eyes drop to my lips when I bite down and wait. His fingers grip that little bit harder and I half expect him to give in and lean towards me, but when he does release me, he does the opposite. He lets go and pushes me enough that I fall back onto the chair.

I watch as he moves to the other side of the room. His shoulders are pulled tight with tension, the muscles in his back rippling as he lifts his hands to his hair once again.

"Get a move on, you've already wasted enough of my time."

Scrambling to my feet, I pull clothes from the bag that I purchased yesterday and left under the desk when we went out. Thankfully there's enough to make a full outfit, albeit a small one.

CHAPTER ELEVEN

ZACH

WHY I DIDN'T WALK out the door and leave her to it fuck only knows. I'm now standing staring at the collage of tattoo images I've done that are pinned to my wall as the sound of her rustling through her bags behind me fills my ears.

I was pissed off when I fell into my bed last night wondering if she'd fallen straight into hers with Titch, I really didn't need her to be late and then to turn up like she'd just had afternoon tea with fucking royalty. The dress is hot, don't get me wrong. It's the perfect tease with its slightly too low neckline revealing the swell of her tits, and the way it skims across her arse. I bite down on the inside of my cheek in an attempt to stop me turning around to find out just how sweet that arse really is.

I only last a few seconds. Resting my palms on the counter in front of me, my need to watch her becomes unbearable and I turn my head so I can see over my shoulder. She's too focused on what she's doing—pulling something on under her dress—for her to notice my attention, so I make the most of it.

She drops the fabric back down, covering whatever it was she put on before, blowing out a breath and reaching for the zip at the back of her dress.

She pulls it down painfully slowly. If she knew I was watching, I'd say she was doing it on purpose, but she's yet to look up at me.

The thin straps slip from her shoulders before the fabric pools at the floor around her feet. The sight of her standing in just a white lace bra has my breath catching and my cock even harder than before. My fingers curl into the wood beneath them as I fight to stay where I am and not go over and put my hands on her where they belong.

My teeth grind as I remember just how her curves felt last night beneath my hands. How her body moved with my every touch, begging for more.

A growl climbs up my throat, but I manage to catch it before it erupts.

Tabitha pulls a shirt from her bag and lifts her arms to pull it over her head.

"Wait," I say, turning, my long legs eating up the space between us as I move towards her.

She quickly tugs the fabric down her body, but it's too late. I've already seen it.

Sucking in a breath when I'm in touching distance, she drags her bottom lip into her mouth and waits.

My eyes search hers, expecting her to say something,

but instead she holds mine, her head tilted a little to the side in defiance.

Reaching out, I tuck my finger under the hem of her shirt and lift. My fingertip grazes the soft skin of her belly as I do so, eliciting a gasp from her.

I keep my eyes on hers, waiting for her to back away, to tell me to stop, but she doesn't.

Once I know the fabric is high enough, I lower my gaze to the ink that covers her right rib.

"Well, well, well... The princess has been marked." I run my finger over the delicate feather, delighting in the feeling of her body trembling under my touch. I'm halfway along before I pay enough attention for it to become recognisable. Hardly anyone else would notice, I'm sure. But I know my artists, and I sure as shit know my best friend.

"Motherfucker."

Standing to full height, I push past her and rip the door open.

Titch's door slams back against the wall, causing both him and his client to look up, their eyes wide in shock and their mouths hanging agape. I use their surprise to my advantage. Marching over, I take his still buzzing gun from his hand and pull him from his stool. His back slams against the wall with a thud and I pin him in place with his shirt. The fury raging through me is the one thing I can focus on, the image in my mind of his hands on what's mine too much to bear.

"Zach, what the fuck?"

"You put your motherfucking hands on her?"

"On... who?" He glances over my shoulder, his brows drawing together in confusion as, I assume, he stares at Tabitha. "What the fuck is going on?"

"Zach, leave it." Her soft voice just about manages to filter through my haze seconds before her warm hand lands on my forearm. The shock of her touch is enough to have me backing away from Titch.

"Fuck," I bark, risking a glance up at her. What the fuck did I just do?

"Talk. Now," Titch demands while I stand there with my chest heaving and my fingers curled into tight fists. He might be my best friend, but that doesn't mean I won't hit him.

"Ugh, he's freaking out because you did this." Tabitha lifts her shirt, revealing Titch's handiwork.

"Huh," he says, leaning closer and squinting slightly. "Sure looks like mine."

"That's because it is, arsehole."

"I do a lot of tats. See a lot of people. I don't remember everyone," he says, his arms flailing from his sides. "I don't need to tell you all this, Zach. Now, if I may..." He gestures to the woman who's still laid on her front on his bed, patiently waiting for him to return.

Anger swirls within me as I stare him dead in the eyes, but I can't deny that he's right. I don't remember even half of whom the skin I've inked belongs to. Just because Tabitha is one of us now, it doesn't mean he should have recognised her from that small tattoo.

"Fuck this." Turning, I storm from his room and out through the kitchen so I can have a few moments to breathe.

I PACE back and forth in my living room for a while, waiting for my heart to stop racing. What the fuck was that? I never lose my head over a woman. So what if Titch has inked her? It doesn't mean anything. He's a professional, it's unlikely he'll have offered any extra services, plus if he had I'm sure she'd have had something to say about it. She's not exactly backwards in coming forwards.

I desperately want to reach for my liquor cupboard, but with an evening full of clients, I can't very well do that.

I'm staring at the clock, knowing that I need to head back down before I piss my clients off, when a knock sounds out from the front door.

"Yeah," I bark. My heart's in my throat as I wait to see if it's Tabitha's head that's going to pop around the dark wood to rip me a new one.

I'm relieved when the first thing I see is the shaggy dark hair of my best friend. Although, one look at his pissed-off eyes and I soon realise he might not go easy on me, either.

"Here, I sent Biff for decent coffee. Thought you might need it."

"Need fucking more than this," I mutter, but I accept his offer.

"It's got a double shot."

I sip at the coffee and regret it the second the liquid burns the top layer off my tongue.

"Karma's a bitch, huh?" Titch asks as he watches me.

"Do we have to?"

"I really fucking think we need to, motherfucker." He drops down onto the other end of the sofa, wisely putting his coffee on the table to allow it to cool. "Start talking."

"Got nothing to say." I shrug, but I know he's not going to allow me to get away with that.

"Okay, let's try this a different way. You fucked her yet?"

I blanch at his blunt question, but it soon pisses me off because I wouldn't bat an eyelid if he were to ask me this about any other woman. "No," I mutter, looking to the window to stop him reading whatever might be in my eyes. He's a perceptive motherfucker, and I don't need him seeing more than I'm ready to admit to myself.

"So how'd you see the tat?"

"She was changing in my room. I wasn't a gentleman."

"No surprise there."

"Says Mother fucking Teresa."

"Hey, I'm not saying I'd act any differently. So... what's next?"

"Next, I've got a night full of clients. One of which is probably already downstairs waiting for me." He nods, proving that that is the case.

"And what about Biff."

"What about her?"

He sighs. "Zach, man. You need to start being honest with yourself, even if you can't be with me."

"I'm not—"

"You want her. We can all see it, and none of us can blame you. She's hot." My temperature begins to boil at his observation alone, telling me that I've got a serious issue here. "She also doesn't put up with your shit and gives as good as she gets. At first I thought it was going to be the fun of the chase, of winning, of proving you can have her no matter what, but now, the last few days, I see it's more than that. You want her, and not just because you can't have her."

By the time he's finished his little speech, I'm on my feet and ready to run away from having to deal with it.

I swipe my coffee up and march towards the door. "I don't want her. She's everything I don't want. I just want to play with her a bit, prove that women like her don't belong in this world."

He's laughing as I pull the door open and step out into the enclosed hallway.

My lips twist in frustration while every part of my body screams that every word I just said is bullshit. That may well be the case, but like fuck am I going to accept it.

This is a game. A game I'm in charge of and one that I'm going to win. I'll get her on her knees, I'll take what I want, and then I'll throw her back into the stuck-up, pretentious world she fell from. Her parents probably already have someone in their sights to marry their beloved daughter, and I can fucking guarantee that he doesn't have any tattoos.

Leaving Titch behind in my flat, I make my way back down to the studio. I have every intention of walking through reception and to my room without so much as looking her way, but the second I step foot into the waiting room my eyes seem to have a mind of their own.

I glance over our clients, nodding at the one who's patiently waiting for me before risking a look at her. The second my eyes land on her, my body freezes. She's sitting behind the desk, one hand on the mouse, but instead of looking at the computer she's staring right at me. Confusion and intrigue fill her eyes while she chews on her bottom lip.

Something sizzles between us before I drag my barriers back up and turn towards my next client. "You ready?"

"Sure am."

Without a word to Tabitha, I walk towards my room to get on with my job.

It's not until the door's shut and Isaac is on the bed ready that he speaks. "You're sure to get a few more clients through the door now you've got that hot bit of arse on the desk."

My fingers tighten around the gun in my hand that's about to make contact with the back of his thigh, and my teeth grind.

I suck in a few deep breaths. I can't afford for that bitch to ruin my reputation.

"She sure helps to keep our waiting clients distracted."

"She sure as shit does that, mate. Especially in that little skirt she's wearing. Damn, when she bent over I almost got a shot at the—ow."

I make a start without warning, pressing a little harder than necessary in an attempt to cut off his words. I don't need to hear that she's out there showing off anything. Especially not when I'm yet to see much beyond a tat on her ribs.

Trying to put her to the back of my mind, I focus on the task in hand and the amount of ink I need to lay down before I get to lock myself upstairs with just the image of his handiwork on her skin.

Motherfucker.

CHAPTER TWELVE

TABITHA

ANY BIT OF NOISE, any footsteps or closing of a door, has me looking up, nerves erupting in my stomach, just waiting for his eyes to land on mine once again.

Why I trusted him not to look earlier, I've no fucking clue. I should have demanded he left the room, but his close proximity does something to my brain, hence why I ended up with his hand in my knickers last night. My cheeks burn and my core clenches at the memory.

Looking back to the guys' waiting clients, I expect to find them staring at me, wondering what the hell is wrong with me, but they're all distracted with their phones or the magazines on the coffee table in the centre of the sofas.

Unable to concentrate on what I should be doing, I

pull a piece of paper from the printer and start doodling. I draw the same thing I always do. It relaxes me and helps me to block out the rest of the world as I focus on the ink marking the page. I'm transported back to a time when things were a little easier, lighter, even though seeing her words staring back at me still fill me with an all-consuming grief. I wonder if that will ever fade. If I'll ever be able to think about my gran without the pain of losing her filling every inch of my body.

Clients come and go, the guys—minus Zach—come out to get their next ones, to grab a drink and to check up on me I'm sure, especially Titch who looks at me with concerned eyes every time he appears. I smile at him and shake my head. I'm fine. What happened earlier was just a moment of madness on Zach's part. I'm not going to dwell on it and think it means anything other than the threats he's given me about wanting to break me, whatever that means. I roll my eyes at myself. I'm not sure what Zach's real intentions are, but I know for a fact that I'll never give him the power to ruin me like he says he wants to.

As the last hour of the night rolls around, I head out to the kitchen to make coffees for the guys. I deliver them to Titch, Spike and D, who are all grateful but barely drag their heads up from the bit of skin they're working on. Something in my chest aches when I pass Zach's door. The buzz from his gun sounds out loud and clear. He probably needs a final drink as much as the others to get him through the night, but nothing could get me to cross the threshold into his room right now. All I can hope is that I can escape soon after the clients leave and he'll stay in hiding. I'm not due back here until Thursday night—hopefully it'll be enough time for him to sort his head out.

You could leave, a little voice says in my head as I drop down onto my chair with a sigh. I could, yeah. But that's not what I'm going to do. I'm better, stronger, than the arsehole down the hall. I bent over backwards for him and his pathetic group of friends at school. I refuse to be that girl again.

Tabitha the teenager was weak. She didn't know her place or her worth. Tabitha the woman is a very different creature and has learnt that to get what she wants, the life she craves, then she needs to take what she deserves and not let others walk all over her... parents aside, of course. That's still something she needs to deal with.

Pulling my coffee into my hands, I allow the warmth to seep into my palms. It's the first time tonight I've been alone and the silence is unnerving. I fidget my toes in my boots, needing to move, but nothing short of getting out of here is going to work. Less than an hour then I can be at home. I can lock myself in my studio and paint until sunrise if need be.

I look down at the wooden desk for the sketch I was working on earlier, but I don't find it. Rolling the chair back, I glance around the floor, thinking it's blown off somewhere, but again I come up empty.

The phone ringing distracts me from my search, and after booking in some sessions for a client, I forget all about it.

I CAN'T CONTAIN my yawn as the last client walks out and I get up to turn the sign on the door to closed.

"We boring you, Biff?" Titch asks with a laugh as he walks through with a handful of dirty mugs.

"No, just a late night and a too early morning."

"Why don't you get going? We can all finish up."

"I've just got a few things to complete and then I'm heading home." He turns toward the kitchen, but I quickly call him back. "Titch?"

"Yeah?"

"I'm sorry about... about earlier. I should have mentioned that you..." I hesitate but point to my ribs.

"Girl, you've got nothing to apologise for. I'm just sorry I don't remember doing it." A little colour hits his cheeks. "All that was on Zach. Can I..." He trails off before taking another step.

"Can you what?" I ask, not liking the hesitation in his tone.

"Um..." He looks away from me. "Can I see it? I want to remember what I did." His voice is softer than usual, allowing me to see a different side to the brooding bad boy.

"Of course." Walking over, I lift my top enough to expose my ribs.

He drops down a little so he can see, his finger coming out to run over it, although he never makes contact.

"Huh... That's pretty good."

"I have good taste, you know. I didn't come here on the off chance, I'd heard about your reputation."

"It could be better," a deep, rumbling voice says. The atmosphere changes and becomes almost suffocating as his burning stare heats my body.

Titch stands, his eyes rolling in frustration that he's poked the bear again.

"I'm out. I'll see you in a couple of days, yeah?"

I nod, unable to speak as he places the mugs into the kitchen and makes his escape out of the front door. No other words are spoken, but the sound of Zach's heaving breaths are loud around me.

I suck in one calming breath after another in the hope that I'll be able to look at him and appear unaffected, like last night and this afternoon never happened.

Turning, I keep my eyes on the floor. "What do you want, Zach?"

He doesn't respond, but knowing I'm still the focus on his attention, I find myself lifting my eyes to him. He's wearing a slim pair of black jeans with rips in the knees and a plain white t-shirt. How he's standing with his fingers gripped onto the doorframe above his head, it makes his shirt rise, giving me an inch of his sculpted waist. My mouth waters and my fingers tighten on my hips with my need to go over and lift it a little more. Abs are my weakness, and I'm pretty confident there's a seriously impressive set hiding under that fabric.

I take my time making my way up, but when I find his blue eyes my breath catches in my throat.

"See something you like?" His head tilts to the side, a knowing smirk appearing on his full lips that I want to slap off.

"Can't say I do."

A laugh falls from his lips, but there's no amusement in it.

He takes a step towards me and I take one back, feeling like I'm about to be this lion's prey.

"Zach," I breathe. I was going for exasperated, but as he steps closer and his scent filters into my senses it sounds anything but. My cheeks flush, knowing he heard it exactly as I didn't intend for it to sound.

"Funny that, because last night you seemed like you

very much liked what I had to offer." His eyes bounced between mine before dropping to my lips.

"Moment of madness fuelled by alcohol."

"Right." A lopsided smile appears on his lips, and a bloody dimple pops up that I've not seen before. I want to lean forward and lick it, and the thought irritates the hell out of me.

"Fuelled by lust, you mean."

"Hate."

"Even better."

When he takes another step, my retreat attempts are ruined by my arse bumping up against my desk. My fingers drop to wrap around the edge of the wood. I expect him to close the space between us but he stops a little short and drops his eyes to my body as if he's not seen what I pulled on earlier in favour of the summer dress he took offence to.

My red leather skirt is short—too short without thick black tights under it. It exposes way more thigh than I'd usually deem appropriate. My black t-shirt is plain and simple, and the biker boots on my feet give the whole outfit an edge that I must admit that I'm loving. I'm not the only one, if Zach's perusal is anything to go by. I can't see his eyes, but the muscle in his neck pulses and his jaw ticks as he grinds his teeth.

He steps forward, the heat of his body burning into mine. His rough cheek brushes against mine as his hot breath tickles the shell of my ear. Goosebumps break out across my skin, and I fight to drag in the air I need with him so close. My nails dig into the underside of the desk in my attempt to keep them there and not reach out to find just how toned his torso really is. It would be so easy to lift my hands and slip them under the loose fabric of his t-shirt right now to explore in the way I've imagined.

"Get in my room," he breathes, his demand making my skin prickle, but I'm afraid to admit that it's not with irritation but desire.

"Za—"

"Don't argue." With that he steps away, turns his back on me and marches towards his room. "I don't have all night," he adds just before he disappears from my sight. I'm too distracted watching the muscles in his back pull and flex as he walks to pay much attention.

I should grab my bag and walk straight out the front door without so much as a glance back in his direction.

It's what I should do.

But in seconds I'm standing in the doorway of his room, my heart in my throat as I wait to find out what he wants from me.

He's sitting on the little wheelie stool he uses to work on with his back turned to me as he stares down at his desk.

"Shut the door."

"I think it's safer if I leave it open."

"Fine. Your call."

Taking a step inside, I glance over his shoulder and find something very familiar.

"My drawing. You stole it."

"I prefer to say borrowed. I have every intention of giving it back."

"What the fuck?" I mutter, more to myself than him. He stills and then spins, bringing my drawing with him.

"You can draw," he states, his eyes narrowed, assessing me as if I'm suddenly someone else.

"Yeah, and?"

"What else can you do?"

"Plenty."

"You got any more tattoo designs?"

"Aside from the one on my body, no."

"Hmmm..." he mumbles, deep in thought.

"What?" I bark, getting fed up with his randomness and lack of explanation.

"Where do you want it?"

"What?" I feel like a fucking parrot.

"This." He holds up my sketch and glances down at my body. "Where. Do. You. Want. It?"

"Back on my desk where you found it."

"Don't try to be clever. I told you everyone here has to have my ink on them."

I blow out a frustrated breath. "I'm leaving." I turn back to the door but pause when he speaks again.

"Don't pretend you didn't draw this for any other reason."

"The reason I drew this is none of your business," I snap.

He steps up behind me. His fingers wrap around my wrist and keep me in place.

"Maybe not, but we both know you're lying. Where do you want it?" he repeats, his breath in my ear sending sparks shooting around my body. He releases me and his fingertips trail up my exposed arm and across my shoulder. He continues down the ridges of my spine as heat blooms in my core and my stomach clenches with desire. "I think around here." He runs his fingers around my waist, the opposite side to my feather.

"I... uh..."

"The biggest butterfly here." He presses his finger into my skin and then continues to point out where the others could wrap around to my back and slightly up my spine. I can't deny that his vision doesn't sound perfect. "It would look incredible. Don't you think?"

My response is nothing more than a moan.

"So do you want my hands on you, Tabby Cat? Do you want to feel the vibrations of my gun against your skin, knowing that a part of me will live with you for the rest of your life?"

My clit aches as he continues talking, my skin getting clammy with my soaring temperature.

He spins me and pulls me into him. My breasts brush against his chest and I gasp at the sensation to my already peaked nipples.

The reason for our closeness soon becomes apparent when the door slams shut behind me. "You might be okay with everyone watching, but I'm fucking not. You're mine, Tabby Cat."

"I'm... I'm not..." He takes a step back and runs his eyes over me once again. The heat in them steals my words.

"Top off, Kitten, and hop up on the bed."

This is a really bad idea. *A really fucking bad idea.* So why is it I find myself gripping on to the hem of my t-shirt and doing exactly as he says.

His focus locks on my lace-covered breasts. Thankfully, the bra I chose this morning is padded enough to successfully hide just how hard my nipples are beneath.

"This is going to be so much fun."

"If you say so."

He bites down on his bottom lip, his eyes never leaving my body. "This is your one and only chance to change your mind. Once you're on that bed, you're mine."

Excitement and lust hit me so hard I almost stumble back. Am I okay with willingly handing myself over to him? One-hundred per cent not. But am I about to get dressed and walk out? No fucking chance.

I take a small step to my left and hop up onto the soft leather of Zach's tattoo bed.

"You did this in black pen. That how you want it? Or were you thinking something a little more elaborate?"

"What do you think?"

"It's not my body."

"You're the expert," I throw back.

"You giving me permission to do my worst?"

"Don't make me regret it."

"When it comes to me, Tabby Cat, I'm sure you're going to have plenty of regrets. And they'll start from the moment you walked in here looking for a job."

CHAPTER THIRTEEN

ZACH

THE SOUND of her heavy breathing as she lies waiting for me is the only thing I can think about. Much like the second I saw her drawing sitting on her desk, inking it onto her was the only thing I could imagine the second I picked it up. The artwork is stunning, there's no denying that. The detail she's put into her small butterflies is incredible and only goes to prove that I don't really know the woman I live to torment right now.

I debate with myself how I want to do this. I could do it black. It would still look incredible, and I'm sure she'd be more than happy with it. Or I could be a little more creative.

Making a decision, I get everything I need before turning around to face her.

Every muscle in my body locks tight as I take her in. Her white lace bra makes her look like the innocent woman she's trying so hard to hide with the black clothes and biker boots so she fits in. I run my eyes over the curve of her cleavage, my fingers wrapping around the kit in my hands with my need to reach out and run my fingers over her. I already know her skin is like silk to touch; I can only imagine how incredible they'd feel.

My cock swells, desire sitting heavy in my stomach as I take in her slim waist, leather-clad hips and long, slender legs. The mix of princess meets badass is a combination I'm finding harder and harder to resist.

Dragging my eyes from her, I place everything I need on my table and wheel myself closer to her.

Clearing my throat, I prepare to reach out and touch her, hesitant as to what's going to happen when we connect.

"So first one here, and then trailing around," I nudge her so she turns onto her side slightly. "Then come to a stop about here?"

Her breathing gets more laboured with my touch, if that's even possible, and her skin breaks out in goosebumps.

"Y-yeah, that sounds great. How... um... how long do you think it'll—"

"Two hours ish. That okay, or did you have plans?" I've no idea why I'm asking, I have no intention of allowing her out of this room to spend time with anyone else.

"Oh um... sure. I was only going home to—" she gasps as I move her into position and prepare to start. "Bed." She blows out a long, slow breath when I turn my gun on and her eyes flutter closed.

"Scared?"

"Of you? Yeah."

A smile curls my lips that she's willing to admit that. She scares the shit out of me too, but there's no fucking way those words are falling from my lips.

"I'll try not to hurt you... too much."

"Those words fill me with very little confidence."

I laugh, I can't help it. I move the gun towards her skin. She flinches with the first scratch, but she soon relaxes. Shame I can't say the same thing about myself, because I'm like a coiled fucking spring, and it only gets worse the longer I sit here with her so temptingly close.

Eventually, I get so lost in what I'm doing that I almost manage to forget whose body is laid out before me. Almost.

When I sit back and take in my masterpiece with a slight smile playing on my lips, it feels like no time has passed at all despite the crick in my neck and the beginnings of cramp in my hand after a whole day at it.

"Are you finished?" Her voice is soft, almost dream like, but I'm fully aware that this is real life. I really did just ink her design on her smooth, flawless skin. I'm also sitting here sporting the evidence of having my hands on her body for the past couple of hours.

I shift on the stool to try to loosen the fabric around my solid length. She looks over at just the wrong time and witnesses me doing it.

"You... uh... want to see?" Her eyebrows rise, but she doesn't respond to my dumb arse question. Of course she wants to fucking see what I've done to her.

Wheeling over to the side, I grab a handheld mirror and hold it up so she can look at the reflection over her shoulder.

"Oh my god, Zach. That's... that's unbelievable." She stares at my artwork, disbelief written all over her face.

"I thought those butterflies deserved some colour."

"I never could have imagined…" she trails off as she continues to stare. My chest swells with pride that she likes it. Going for a watercolour effect was a risk, but I knew it would be incredible. "I can't believe you just did that, from my sketch. You might be a wanker, Zach, but you're a bloody talented one."

"I'll take that as a compliment."

"Take it however you like. We done here?"

"Yeah. Just let me wrap it, hang on." I'm forced to get up to collect everything I need.

I make quick work of covering her new ink, but I can't help but let my fingers trail over her skin a little more than necessary. Her little gasps of surprise along with the shudder that runs through her convinces me to continue.

Once I'm happy it's all covered, I place my palm on her waist and turn her onto her back. Her eyes are tightly closed, but her pink lips are parted to allow her increased breaths to pass. Her chest heaves, her breasts swollen behind the fabric, only more evidence of how she's feeling right now.

My fingers grip her waist tighter, and it's the reminder she needs that I'm still here because her eyes fly open. Her usually grey eyes are dark, her pupils dilated with lust, and she sinks her teeth into her full bottom lip and sucks it into her mouth. My cock aches to feel just how hot that might be.

"Zach?" Her voice is no more than a breathy whisper that drags my eyes back to hers.

"Fuck," I grunt, my need for this woman all-consuming. She's the only thing I can focus on. How soft her body is under my hands, how sweet she might taste against my tongue.

Without giving myself enough time to be able to talk myself out of it, I lean over her. My hand skims her cheek and comes to rest across her jaw with my fingers threaded in her hair.

Her eyes bounce between mine, but at no point does she do anything to stop me.

"Zach?" My name is a plea on her lips, and it's my undoing.

Closing the space between us, I slam my mouth to hers. She hesitates for a second before her lips part when I run my tongue along the bottom one and allow it to pass. Hers sneaks out to join in. Her taste explodes on my tongue, turning the fire already raging inside me up a notch.

The kiss isn't my finest. Instead it's hot and dirty. It's teeth clashing, tongues duelling as we try to devour each other, putting everything we hate about each other into it.

She pulls my tongue into her mouth and sucks. I damn near lose my mind and come in my pants like a teenager. Needing more, I skim my hand up the smooth skin of her stomach and take her breast in my hand. I squeeze and she arches off the bed with her need for more.

With one goal in mind, I pull back from her lips, but only as far as her jaw.

"Zach, fuck," she moans, the vibration of her voice tingling against my lips as I kiss down her neck.

I graze my teeth over her collarbone, dropping kisses around the swell of her breasts before I'm met with the fabric of her bra.

I continue my descent, over her ribs and down to her bellybutton. I dip my tongue inside, her hands fisting in my hair, pushing me lower to my final prize.

"Oh god, oh god," she chants above. I know she's watching my journey, I can feel her stare burning into me. It's not until I hit the waistband of her skirt that I look up.

Her eyes are dark and pleading with me to continue, and her cheeks are flushed.

"I shouldn't want to taste you so badly," I admit, my hands running up her thighs and pushing the leather up around her waist, revealing a tiny white pair of knickers that are so sheer they may as well not be there. My gaze drops to her breasts, wishing the fabric there was just as see-through.

"The feeling's mutual. I shouldn't want you this badly either," she whispers, dragging my attention back up to her. Her eyes widen in shock as if she didn't mean to say those words out loud.

Running my finger down her centre, I growl like a wild fucking beast when I find the fabric dripping wet. Every muscle in my body aches with my need to sink inside of her, but I fear that if I allow that to happen then I'm only going to crave a repeat. There's something different about this woman to all those who have gone before, and I'm afraid it's not a good thing.

Unable to wait any longer, I hook my fingers through the fabric at her waist and pull her underwear down her thighs. I untangle them from her boots until they drop to the floor.

Taking each of her ankles in my hands, I place her feet on the bed as wide as possible and stare down at her bare pussy.

"Fuck, Pussy Cat." I repeat my earlier action, but this time there's no lace barrier between us. Her heat damn near burns my finger as I dip it between her folds, finding her clit and circling it exactly as she liked last night.

She purrs above me, her back arching with pleasure, begging for more.

I drop my finger lower, dipping it inside her just slightly.

"Zach. Come on. Not fair."

"Everything's fair in love and war, Kitten." Pressing my palms against the inside of her thighs, I spread her as wide as she'll allow, drop to my knees and press my tongue to her clit. Her taste explodes on my tongue and I immediately know that I've just made a massive mistake.

Her moans of pleasure fill the room as her fingers tighten to an almost painful grip on my hair, but at no point do I let up. I'm fucking addicted, and I'm not stopping until I feel her coming against my mouth.

With my tongue teasing her clit, I push two fingers deep inside her. I hope to fuck that Spike and D have already left, because there's no doubt they'd be hearing what's going on inside this room. This prim and proper princess is able to let go it seems, and I can't deny that hearing her chant my name as she nears release isn't a huge fucking turn on.

I bend my fingers, finding that perfect spot inside her. Her hips leave the bed, but I pin her down with my arm over her stomach. My fingers thrust fast as my tongue picks up speed, my need to feel her, to taste her as she comes getting too much to bear. My cock weeps to be released and to bury itself inside her tight, velvety core, but first things first: I need her screaming.

"Come for me, Kitten," I growl against her, and the extra vibrations must be what she needs because her muscles lock for a beat before she cries out my name and her body convulses beneath me.

"Fuck, fuck, fuck," she chants as she rides out her orgasm. I don't pull back until I'm confident she's finished, and when I do, I can't help the wide smile that spreads across my lips. I can't imagine any guy wouldn't feel at least an ounce of pride having made a woman cry out like that.

Movement in front of me drags me back to reality, but I still can't wipe the grin from my face as I glance at her looking down her body at me. Panic fills my eyes and my stomach twists, knowing what's about to happen. She's shut down. Her eyes might still be glassy and dark from her release, but I already know nothing else will be happening between us. Not tonight, anyway.

"Fuck," she murmurs, averting her gaze from me and staring at the wall. "I need to leave."

My pleas for her to stay die on my tongue. I refuse to allow her to see that I need more from her. I refuse to allow anyone to see that I need them. That's dangerous territory right there.

I stand and take a few steps back as she scrambles from the bed, pulling her skirt down to cover up and searching out her shirt that's lying in a pile on the floor.

"This was... this was a mistake," she whispers so quietly I almost miss it before she yanks the door open and all but runs through it.

My body urges me to chase her, to make her see sense and to take what I need, but the rational side of my brain knows that allowing her to run is the right thing to do.

Only minutes after she races out of my room do I hear the front door to the studio slam and lock behind her.

Falling down onto my chair, I rest my head back and close my eyes.

What have I just done?

CHAPTER FOURTEEN

TABITHA

MY HEART POUNDS against my ribs by the time I slam my front door and fall back against it. Anyone would think I was being chased by a mad man, but then maybe I am. What the fuck was I thinking allowing him to put his hands—mouth—on me again?

My head bangs back against the door as I chastise myself for falling under his spell like I'm sure every other female does. One look into those mesmerising blue eyes and I'm sure they bend over on demand.

"Fuck," I scream into my empty flat, dropping my head in my hands.

Why did it have to feel so fucking good? Why couldn't he have been a fumbling idiot who had no clue what he was doing? That would have made this so much easier. If he had no skills, I could have easily avoided a repeat, but as it is, my body is already crying out to experience that all over again.

I tell myself it was just the heat of the moment that made it so good. The fact that he'd just spent hours working on my body made us both do crazy things that in normal circumstances wouldn't happen. *But it happened last night too*, a little voice cries in my head, not helping with my attempt to rationalise what happened.

Knowing whatever I tell myself is pointless, I push off the door and head for my room, dropping my bags to the bed as I pass before proceeding to strip out of my clothes. What I really want is a shower to remove any lingering scent of him and sex from my body, but the ache down my side reminds me that that can't happen right now. The ink is barely dry.

Dropping my skirt, I'm reminded once again of what an epic mistake I made this evening when my bare bottom is revealed in the mirror I'm standing in front of.

I left my sodding knickers on his studio floor like a hussy. I roll my eyes at myself. I really need to get a grip.

Twisting, I get a look at my new ink. I can't deny that it's not incredible. Zach really is talented. And he wasn't wrong, I have been drawing it as a way of building my courage for getting it. I never could have imagined it would have happened quite like it did.

I sigh as I stare at the bright colours and sore skin. Every time I look at it I'm going to be reminded of him. Or more accurately, his mouth on me.

My core clenches with desire. It would have been so easy to stay and to enjoy whatever was to follow, and it was obvious there was going to be more, if the tenting of his trousers was anything to go by.

Getting frustrated, I drag myself away from the mirror and the lifetime reminder I have of it on my skin and pull a loose t-shirt from my draw and a fresh pair of knickers. After taking my make-up off—not that much is left after this long arse day—and brushing my hair, I crawl between the sheets and toss and turn as memories of his touch from both yesterday and tonight fill my mind, making me wonder what it might be like for him to give me his all. My core aches, overcome with emptiness.

For a fleeting moment I consider getting back up and going to his flat to finish the job so I can get some rest, but I tell myself that's a really stupid idea and force my body to lie there until sleep finally claims me.

It's long past morning when I finally open my eyes the next day. The fitful sleep I did eventually manage was full of dirty dreams about my boss and best friend's brother. Rolling over, I groan when my side hurts and I'm reminded that my night-time fantasies are partly reality.

I don't bother changing. Instead I get myself a coffee and head for my studio. I've spent all weekend either working or drinking; I'm so behind on my studies that I have every intention of locking myself in my flat and making some serious progress on my project until I'm forced to leave again Thursday night to face my boss. My cheeks flame at the thought alone. How the hell am I meant to show my face there again without wanting the floor to swallow me up?

Cutting myself off from the world, I turn my phone onto aeroplane mode, put my music on loud and set to work.

I PAINT, I drink coffee, I eat and get a little sleep. I'm totally in the zone and covered in paint after two whole days inside my studio. I've not bothered looking at my phone or stepping back into the real world. I desperately needed some time alone with a canvas, even if my back aches from leaning over and my hair's slick with grease after foregoing a shower the past few days. I tell myself that I'm letting my tattoo heal, but really, I'm just being lazy.

It's not until my buzzer starts ringing that I look at the clock and realise it's Wednesday evening already.

Glancing at myself in the mirror in the hall, I wince knowing that if it's my parents at the other side of the door they're going to have fit once again. *Proper ladies don't spend their days locked in a room with only paint for company.* I can hear my mother's voice loud and clear, as if she's already standing in front of me.

Pressing down the button, I hold my breath as I wait to hear who's at the other end.

"Biff? You in there or do I have to send out a search party?" my best friend's voice sounds out, and I sign with relief.

"I'm here, I'm alive. Come in."

I press the button to unlock the door and wait until I hear her do so. I've got no time to change, so I settle for retying my hair and tugging down the huge t-shirt I'm wearing, hoping it's enough to stop me flashing her. Not that it's an issue, she's probably seen my arse more times than I could count over the years.

I open the door and leave it on the latch as I go in search of wine. I really fucking hope I've got some in the fridge. I already know there's not much in the way of food.

Danni's heels click against my wooden floor, telling me that when I turn around I'm going to find her looking much more put together than I am right now.

"I brought dinner. I assumed you'd probably not eaten if you've been working." Turning, I find her placing two bags on my island. "And I picked you up some basics." She pulls some milk and bread from the bag and, more importantly, two bottles of wine. "And these are pre-chilled."

"Lifesaver."

"So how's it going?"

"It's... going." I think about the progress I've made on the set of impressionist paintings I've started. "I've still got a lot to do before I'm happy."

"Ugh, such a perfectionist. I'm sure they're stunning already."

I shrug before reaching to grab us two glasses.

Danni twists the top off the bottle and pours us each one.

"Don't take this the wrong way, but you really need to shower. The food will wait if you want to..." she gestures towards my bedroom.

"You saying I smell, Dan?"

"Something like that," she says into her glass.

"Fine. I can take a hint, but I'm taking this with me."

"Be my guest. I'll put the food in the oven for when you get back." She kicks her shoes off as I leave the room, making herself at home as she usually does.

I pull off my few clothes and drop them into the laundry basket as I pass before turning the shower on a little hotter than I usually like and step under once it's to temperature.

It burns my head a little, but at least it'll help wash the grease out.

Knowing I've got hot food waiting for me, I don't take half as long as I could. I gently wipe over my tattoo before getting out and wrapping both my body and hair in a towel.

I wash and moisturise my face before grabbing a pair of leggings and a vest.

With my half empty glass in hand I walk into the kitchen. "Right, where's this food? I'm bloody starving."

Danni drags herself from the sofa where she was watching TV and comes to help me. I bend over to retrieve the boxes she placed in the oven before my shower, but I don't get very far.

"Whoa, hold up a second. What the hell is that?"

My brows draw together for a beat, wondering what she's talking about until all the pieces fall into place.

"Oh, this? I had it done at work the other night." I lift my top to show her the whole design.

"Whoa, that's incredible. Is it based on your sketch?"

"It is, with a bit of creative licence."

"It's stunning. That artist has some mad skills."

I almost snort in response.

"Uh... yeah, he's uh... pretty good."

She eyes me curiously but doesn't ask any more when I go back to the job I started.

"So what's going on with you?" I ask once we're both sitting at my dining table with plates full of incredible smelling chicken and steamed vegetables. It's slightly more healthy than I'd have probably chosen for myself tonight, but I can't complain.

"Ugh." She rolls her eyes, lowering her knife and fork. "My mum is driving me crazy with all the wedding stuff.

And Zach's not helping. He didn't even show up to Harrison's stag do this weekend. Can you believe that? His own brother's stag do. No one knows where he is, if he's even in the country. Mum's beside herself thinking he won't show to up the wedding. Makes me never want to get married."

I bite my tongue from attempting to defend Zach. It's not my place to explain his whereabouts when he clearly doesn't want anyone knowing.

"Oh, and can I find a man who might be remotely interested in being my plus one? Can I fuck," she fumes, stabbing a piece of chicken and shoving it in her mouth.

"I'm sure Zach will be there. Has she tried calling him?" I know it's a stupid question, but I can't really think of anything else to say that won't drop either of us in it.

"Of course she has. He hardly ever answers, and when he does he makes some excuse that he's busy and has to go. What the fuck is he busy doing? Banging some chick and pissing his money up the wall."

I open my mouth to argue. The words are right there on the tip of my tongue, but the second Danni looks up at me expectantly, they die.

"Have... have you tried getting back on the dating apps?" I ask, referring to her other issue. "Or just go alone? It's twenty-twenty, you don't need a date for your brother's wedding."

"But who will I dance with?"

"Any single guys that attend. Me. I sure won't have a date." *Not that I have any intention of going.* I accepted the invitation months ago, but knowing what I do now, I need to figure a way to get out of it. I might have to come down with some incredibly contagious disease the day before or something.

"I just want it to be perfect."

"Stop putting so much pressure on yourself. You'll find him when you least expect it."

"I know. It'll just be such a romantic day, and I want someone to go back to my hotel room with after."

"Who says you won't?" I wink and she laughs.

"We can only hope."

BEFORE I KNOW IT, it's Thursday afternoon and it's time to head to work. A huge ball of dread sits heavy in my stomach. At least I've got Saturday night off for Summer's hen do, whatever that might entail, seeing as Danni still refuses to tell me what she's planned.

I turn up to the studio to find Titch, Spike and D hanging out on the sofas with coffees.

"Biff, here's one for you," Spike says when he looks up and finds me pushing the door closed. I take the coffee handed to me and take a sip.

"Thank you. I need this." I was up early again this morning working and I've barely stopped. "Just the three of you tonight?"

"It seems that way. Zach cancelled all his appointments this week and fucked off up to Manchester to check on the studio there at the last minute."

"Oh. Does he do that often?" Titch eyes me curiously. Clearly I'm not the only one wondering if I have something to do with his disappearance.

Despite not knowing if I had anything to do with it, I breathe a sigh of relief that I'm not going to have to deal with him tonight. It's not going to last forever though, so I need to make the most of the peace.

I enjoy the relief for about two hours. By that time, all the guys' clients are in with them and I'm sitting alone with my work and struggling to focus. I hate to admit it but crazy thoughts of being the reason he's disappeared consume me.

I pick up my phone multiple times to call him with some bullshit question just so I can talk to him and put my mind to rest that this isn't all my fault.

It's just gone eight o'clock when the bell above the front door rings, forcing my eyes up from the computer screen.

"Hi, how can I help you?" I ask politely as the woman walks towards me. She's so tall, slim and beautiful that I could easily believe she's a model. Her long, dark hair hangs around her shoulders like silk and her cheekbones and jawline are the things girls dream about.

"Oh, hi." Her eyes flick over my face as if she's sizing me up just as much as I am her. I'm not sure what it is, but something about her has me on edge. "Is Zach here? It's just I left something in his apartment when I visited the other night."

My mouth drops open as realisation slams into me. He's not left because of me. Why was I even stupid enough to even think it for a second? It's a total coincidence that something in Manchester has called him away.

"I'm sorry, but he's not actually in today. He's been called to another of his studios."

"Oh... um..." She chews on one of her perfectly manicured nails with her sparkling white teeth. Jesus, could she be any more perfect? "Is there any way of getting upstairs? It's my best friend's birthday and I left her gift up there."

"Let me see what I can do." Pushing my chair out behind me, I walk through to where the guys' rooms are. I hesitate for a second as to which one to go for but in the end, I stop at the first one and knock.

"Come in," a deep voice calls.

Pushing the door open, I poke my head around and find D working on his client.

"I'm so sorry," I say, looking at the client. "There's a woman here saying she's left something up in Zach's flat and wants to know if she can get up there to collect it."

"What is it? Her virginity?" D and his client laugh while my stomach turns like I'm about to puke on his floor.

"Probably," I mutter. But having looked at her, I would say that she wasn't that innocent. There's something in her dark eyes that tells me she knows exactly how to get a man to do what she wants. "It's her friend's birthday present or something." I roll my eyes, wondering what it was that could have possibly distracted her enough to forget it in the first place.

"The spare keys are in the top drawer in his room. Take her up there, make sure she only gets what she left and escort her out."

"Sure thing."

Stepping inside Zach's room, the first thing I look at is his tattoo bed, which is currently up in a sitting position. Memories from Sunday night slam into me. Urges that I hoped I'd be able to banish by now take me by surprise. My temperature spikes and my stomach clenches.

Damn him and his talented tongue.

Putting it all to the back of my mind, I move toward the drawer D said and pull it open. The first thing that catches my attention is my sketch. It's sitting on top of everything else.

He kept it. Why?

My hand twitches at my side as I debate what to do. In the end, I snatch it up and shove it into the back pocket of my skirt. I drew it, therefore it belongs to me. Rummaging through the random contents of what seems to be a junk drawer, I eventually find a keyring with a couple of keys on it.

Wrapping my fingers around the cold metal, I find the woman exactly where I left her.

"Follow me."

She falls into step behind me, her heels clicking on the tiled floor. I've not yet opened the door that leads to the flat upstairs, and to be honest, I never thought I would. Being alone with Zach down here is dangerous enough, let alone venturing up here. I guess it's safe with him miles away.

Typically, the key that opens the front door is the last one I try. The second I open it to reveal the open plan living space beyond, my movements falter. A smell that is purely Zach hits me. I almost stumble back, thinking that I'm about to come face to face with the man himself.

"Do you know where it might be?" I bark.

"I left it by the sofa, I think." She pushes past me and goes to look but comes up empty.

Grumbling, she heads off down the hallway. I don't want to, but knowing that I can't leave her alone unsupervised in his private space, I follow her. From the second she walked in, I believed her little story, but now we're up here I realise that it could all be a master plan to do something she shouldn't be.

She turns into a room and I come to a stop in the

doorway of what appears to be Zach's bedroom. The walls are white, just like the rest of the flat, but everything else in here is black. Pretty much what I was expecting from the tattooed bad boy himself.

"Ah, there it is." She picks up a Selfridge's carrier bag from the side and hooks it over her wrist. "Ha, would you look at that. It seems we didn't use the whole box," she says with a shrug, putting something back down on the side that I didn't see her pick up.

My eyes lock on the box of condoms beside her.

My lips purse at the thought of him bringing her up here and doing what I didn't allow him to get from me.

"Are you done?"

She takes a step towards me, her eyes dropping down my body. "Jealousy doesn't look good on you, sweetheart. I suggest you get over yourself. He'd never want you." With that said, she marches past me, ensuring our shoulders collide as she leaves the flat. Her footsteps down the stairs sound out, but I'm frozen to the spot.

I had no idea how I was feeling was written over my face, but it seems that I really need to do something about my feelings for my boss. Absolutely nothing good can come of them for many, many reasons.

After a final look around the mostly tidy room, I make my way back to the front door to lock up.

Numb, I head back to my desk and fall down on the chair, staring at my now black computer screen. The woman is nowhere to be seen, so I can only assume she left.

"Is everything okay?" D asks when he comes out of his room sometime later. His deep voice startles me and I turn, my eyes wide.

"Yeah, yeah. Sorry, I just zoned out there for a

minute." In reality I was back on Zach's bed with his head between my legs, something I keep telling myself I need to stop thinking about, but it seems it's impossible. That fucker's got himself in my head, and I can't push him out no matter what I try.

He nods, accepting my answer before leaving me to it while he waits for his next client to arrive.

The whole evening is busy as it usually is, but the time doesn't fly by like I'm becoming used to. I hate that it's his fault. I'm usually sitting here on edge, waiting to discover what he's going to do or say when he appears, but with that not being a worry tonight the time drags.

It's ten minutes before closing when the phone on my desk rings.

"Good evening, Rebel Ink. How may I help you?"

There's silence on the other end, but I don't miss the mistakable sound of increased breathing. My skin prickles with awareness and I chastise myself for being affected when he's not even spoken.

"Is D in? He's not answering his phone." I release a breath I had no idea I was holding when he finally speaks. The timbre of his rumbling voice vibrates through me as if he says the words against my skin.

"Oh," I breathe. It sounds needy even to my own ears, and I straighten my spine before I allow myself to say anything else. "He is and his last client just left. Would you like me to take the phone to him?"

"No, how about you..." he pauses, whatever sarcastic comment he was going to say dying on his lips. "Yeah, that would be great."

Pushing the chair out behind me, I make the short journey to D's room with Zach breathing in my ear.

Goosebumps race across my skin as if I can actually feel it.

I hand the phone over and get out of the room as soon as possible to start closing up for the night. I need to get out of here. He might not be in the building, but his presence is here no matter what, and it's driving me to insanity.

CHAPTER FIFTEEN

ZACH

I DIDN'T REALLY NEED to go to Manchester, but the thought of watching Tabitha walk back through the door and sit behind her desk when the only thing I could think about was how hot and tight she'd be as I slid my cock into her didn't really appeal.

So I took the easy way out and I ran. It was a pussy move, I'm fully aware of that. And to be honest, it did fuck all. If anything, I think it was worse being so far away and not knowing what was going on. Was Titch making a play again just because I wasn't there to stop him? Did any of our clients take a liking to her and ask her out after their appointment?

The whole thing was a massive head fuck and only pointed to one thing: I need to fuck her to get her out of my system so I can move the fuck on with my life without being tempted by the princess in my waiting room.

Knowing she's got the weekend off, I head back to London late on Friday night. I avoid the studio when I get there and instead head straight up to my flat for some sleep.

Finding the box of condoms I'd bought and abandoned on the dresser doesn't help with my blue ball situation. I've jacked off countless times since Sunday night but much like the taste of her, nothing seems to get rid of it.

WAKING up the next morning to my ringing phone should be a sign for how my day's going to go. Rolling over, I grab it from the bedside table and groan. It's my mother again.

I know I'm on her shit list after bailing on my brother's stag do last week, but fuck if I wanted to spend my Saturday night with a bunch of stuck-up tossers and then an entire Sunday playing golf. Fucking golf, I've not got time for that bullshit.

Knowing that I can only ignore her for so long, I reluctantly swipe the screen and put the phone to my ear.

"Hello."

"Ah, you're alive. Good to know." She tries to make her words sound like a joke, but I don't miss the anger that sneaks in.

"Yeah, I'm sorry I've missed your calls, I've been busy."

"Is that right? Too busy to attend—"

"Look, I'm sorry, okay? But that sort of thing just isn't

me. Harrison and his friends wouldn't have wanted me there anyway."

"He's your brother, Zachary. Of course he wanted you there."

"Well, what's done is done," I say in the hope she'll drop it and move on to something else.

"Yes, well I guess so. I was just ringing to make sure you still planned on attending the actual wedding."

"Of course, I wouldn't miss it for the world." I attempt to make it sound as convincing as possible, but I'm not sure Mum falls for it and that's only confirmed when she speaks again.

"Really?" Really? No, attending a wedding, whether it be my brother's or anyone else's isn't exactly my idea of a fun day, but until I want to be outcast more than I already am then I know it's in my best interest to go. My family are good people, they just don't understand me. *They might if you give them a chance,* a little voice inside my head says, but I shake it away. "Anyway, Summer is finalising the table plan and she needs to know if you intend on bringing a plus one."

"Uh—" I start but soon get interrupted.

"I was only talking to Vince and Paula the other day— you remember them, don't you? The Bastilles? Their daughter Jessica is single. We wondered if—"

"No, Mum." I shudder at the thought. Jessica, or JJ as I knew her back in school, was the bane of my fucking life. Okay, so I gave her my virginity, but I was young and stupid back then and only thought with my teenage hormones and my dick. She's a fucking nightmare, and as far as I can tell, she's only got worse as she's got older, clinging to every man who might be able to give her the easy life she desires. "I'll find my own plus one."

Thoughts of asking Tabitha filter through my mind, but I push them back out as fast as they come. I'm sure my parents would love her, but no fucking way am I allowing her to think there could be something between us. Yes, I want to get between her legs again, but that's it. There will be no family meetings or any of that shit. She's from this part of my life, and my family is a whole other ballgame. I need to keep my worlds separate.

"Okay, so I'll tell Summer you'll need two seats?"

"Please." Although I've no fucking clue who I'll bring. I rack my brain for someone who'll fit in but will be loyal enough to keep my secrets to themselves. Or I could take a randomer, a fake girlfriend maybe. I'm sure there are plenty of girls out there who'd happily spend their Saturday at a luxury wedding with incredible food and an open bar.

Mum chats away about the plans as if I give a fuck and I humour her with some well-timed ohhs and ahhs. My patience with this shit only lasts so long though, because eventually I find myself making my excuses and bringing the call to a close. This whole wedding is a bit of a joke if you ask me, seeing as they're already married. But what do I know?

"Are you in the country right now?" I consider lying because I know what's coming next, but, feeling guilty for shooting her hopes down already, I tell the truth.

"I am. In London, actually."

"Any chance you fancy coming to dinner? I miss you." She tugs on my heart strings with her soft voice, and I immediately feel bad for not visiting as often as I should.

"I'll see what I can do."

She accepts that as a solid maybe and allows me to hang up.

HATE YOU

THANKFULLY, my Saturday afternoon and evening are booked solid with clients so I don't get all that much time to focus on the empty reception desk out the front. The four of us keep our doors open and listen out for customers coming in, but thankfully we only get a couple of walk-ins that we have to turn away.

I'm standing in the kitchen doorway, sipping on a coffee, when my next client walks through the front door.

"Long time no see. How's it going, man?" I say, walking over and slapping him on the back.

"It's good, man. Sorry it's been so long."

"Working hard?"

"Always, always."

"Come on through, you can tell me all about the women you have hanging off you every weekend while I cause you some pain." He laughs but walks through to my room when I gesture for him to do so.

Christian was one of my very first clients when I took over this place and turned it into my own. He didn't bat an eyelid at having me ink him up despite my lack of experience. He reckoned back then he could tell I was talented just by looking at me. I say he's an idiot, but whatever.

"Remind me where we're at." He hops up on my chair and lifts his leg for me, revealing his half completed artwork. "Jesus, it's taken you too long to get back for this."

"Tell me about it, things have been mental. I took on a bar job because things got a bit quiet. Huge mistake because the calls keep coming. I'm working two jobs most weekends. I shouldn't complain though, the money is pretty killer right now."

"That's awesome. I'm assuming you've not got a job tonight?" I ask, thinking that no one wants their stripper to have red raw skin and a wrapped tattoo hindering their view.

"Ha well, that was the plan but I got a call earlier. One of the other guys' missus has gone into labour and they're a guy short for a hen do. It's a hard life, but someone's got to do it."

I laugh. "Yeah, rather you then me."

"Nah, what are you chatting about, man? The girls would love you."

"My body maybe, but I've got the rhythm of a plank of fucking wood."

He barks out a laugh. "I'm not sure most of them really give a fuck, to be honest. They're usually drunk off their arses and just up for a good time."

"It's still a hard pass from me."

"You should come. Apparently, there's like four other hen dos at the club tonight aside from the one I'm booked for. They'll be hot, horny women everywhere. Plus, it's ladies night so..."

"Yeah?" I ask, sounding more enthusiastic than I actually feel about it.

"I'm not booked until ten-thirty, so come after you finish here and we'll get a drink. I'll put you on the VIP list. I need a good wing man, things have been a little dry recently."

"You're a male stripper with women hanging off you on a daily basis. How can you possibly be having a dry spell?"

"Five days, mate. I've not had a shag for five days."

"That's your dry spell?" I laugh at him and focus back on his leg. "The women not going to mind this?" I nod to his skin that's already starting to glow.

"You really think they're going to be looking at the back of my leg?"

Okay, so he has a point there.

I work on his design for another hour while we shoot the shit, and before he leaves, he tells me that tonight is non-negotiable and that he's expecting me at the bar no later than eleven-thirty. I agree but mostly so it'll get him to leave so I can start my next client.

The reception is cold and empty as I follow him out and greet my next victim. I hate the way my stomach twists with disappointment that Tabitha's not sitting there doing her best to ignore my presence.

Once again pushing her from my mind, I get back to work. Maybe Christian's right. All I need is a few drinks and a woman to sort my head out.

THE STRIP CLUB IS PACKED, the queue of women to get in wrapping around the building. The things that fall from their mouths as I walk past them would make a sailor blush. I turn towards where a couple of the more descriptive comments come from and run my eyes over the women. Some of them are hot. Some are totally my type, but I still don't get quite the same excitement racing through my veins as I usually would.

Walking up to the bouncer, I give him my name and he opens the rope for me. "Be careful in there," he warns. "This lot might eat you alive."

"I can handle horny women." He laughs and lets me

enter before turning back to attempt to calm down the women at the front of his queue who are offering him sexual favours in order to be allowed inside. Why do I get the idea that his job isn't as fun tonight as it would seem on paper?

The pounding, sexy beat of the music vibrates through the floor and up my legs. Women walk past laughing with their friends. A few have to be held upright after already having had one too many, but I ignore them all in favour of the bar.

As I make my way over, I see that Christian was right. There are multiple women wearing different versions of 'I'm the maid of honour' t-shirts, veils, and learner plates.

A little guilt hits me for missing my brother's stag. Maybe if he had it in a strip club then I might have made a bit more of an effort. I've no idea what his soon to be bride is doing for hers, but I can only assume it's something equally as dull. She's a painter, so probably some crappy life drawing class followed by afternoon tea. Yawn.

The barman who comes over looks run ragged. "Having a fun night?" I ask when he leans forward in an attempt to hear my order.

"Like you wouldn't believe." His eyes roll so far back in his head, I'm almost worried they might stay there.

"Pint of lager... and a shot of whisky," I add, thinking that I'm going to need more than a pint is going to be able to give me.

I'm earlier than I expected seeing as my last client of the night was a no-show. I down the whisky the second it's handed over then turn so my back is resting against the bar with my pint in hand.

I glance around at all the overly excited women as a

couple of men gyrate on the stage. I doubt they can see everything that's happening down here with the intensity of the lights shining on them. It's probably a good thing. Some of these women are wild.

Running my eyes from the main stage to a smaller one beside me, I find Christian doing his thing. I almost look away, not wanting to watch a friend get his kit off in front of me while wiggling his hips quite like that, but the second he reaches into the crowd to grab a willing woman, I can't help but see how lucky he's about to be. He's told me plenty of tales about the women he's had to dance for in the past, so I can't help being intrigued.

That all goes to shit when a flash of bright pink hair fills my eyes before a body I recognise very well steps up on to the stage.

My body tenses, my grip around my glass so tight I swear it's going to smash any second.

What the actual fuck?

CHAPTER SIXTEEN

TABITHA

"YOU PLANNED Summer's hen do at a strip club? Do you even know her?" I ask Danni in utter disbelief when the limo that picked us all up earlier pulls up out the front of a club.

I look over to the bride to be who's animatedly chatting with some friends and Danni's Mum while sipping on her second glass of champagne. She's yet to notice we've stopped, but I can only imagine that she's going to be horrified. This sort of thing isn't really her scene. In the whole time I've known her, I think she's been in a club about three times, and those were only because it was others' birthday's, including mine, and she felt like she had to be there. She's much more suited to a day of pampering and afternoon tea than this.

"What? It's ladies' night, she's going to love it." My brows rise at her enthusiasm and positivity. "We're here," she calls, halting all other conversations that are happening around us.

A few of the ladies scream in delight when they see our secret location. Summer and Diane both look out of the window at the same time, and I watch as the colour drains from their faces.

"Danni, are you sure—" Diane starts but is soon interrupted.

"Oh come on. It's Summer's last night as a single woman, kind of. We need to send her off in style. Now pull up those granny pants and lets go." Diane looks about ready to pop a vein as her daughter's words settle into her.

Everyone else seems excited, so reluctantly they both follow along when we start climbing out and entering the club.

The place is already heaving, the music almost unbearably loud, but it's not until we walk into the main room that almost all our mouths drop. There are half naked men everywhere and women staring at them, eyes practically popping out of their heads like they're cartoon characters.

"I think this was a mistake," I mumble. I know Danni won't hear, but I feel better for saying it.

It turns out that Danni has booked us a section right in front of one of the smaller stages. I can only hope that will make it easier for Summer and Diane.

A female member of staff, dressed in only a tiny pair of hot pants and a barely there tank, comes over and talks to Danni as if they're long lost friends. She lifts the hot pink rope for us to enter the sectioned off space and gestures for a waiter to bring over two trays of shots.

Hopefully they'll help wipe the shock off Summer's face and get her into the spirit of things. I think it's too late for Diane. She just looks terrified by the whole experience.

Everyone takes a shot when they're offered around. I keep my eyes on Summer and don't miss the tremble of her hand as she lifts it to her mouth.

Everyone starts to take a seat to watch the guy who's just walked out from backstage, but Summer doesn't move.

"Well, this wasn't what I was expecting," she shouts at me when I get close to her.

"Me either. But it should be fun. It'll be good to let your hair down."

"They'd better not try to get me up on that stage, I can't think of anything worse." A shudder runs through me at the thought. I'm all for being here, watching the show and enjoying everything these guys have to offer, but I'm fully with Summer. I don't want them wiggling their junk in my face.

My traitorous mind chooses that moment to conjure up an image of a guy I wouldn't mind getting up close and personal to. A guy who I've still not seen since our little rendezvous in his studio last weekend, or spoken to since our very awkward conversation on the phone the other night. I also still have no idea why he left so suddenly. All the unknowns are driving me slightly crazy, but I tell myself that it's just Zach. It's what he does. It's the reason why none of his family knows what he does.

"It'll be fine. Danni knows you better than that," I say, hoping like hell I'm right.

Summer laughs, but it's nervous at best. I glance down at her cute floral dress that screams afternoon tea and wonder what she's really thinking right now. The second Danni sent me a photo of her dress for tonight, I knew it wasn't going to be a quiet one. I never would have put money on male strippers though. After rummaging through my wardrobe to find something to wear, I eventually decided on another shopping trip for something that better fit my new look. I found a little black dress in Selfridge's that I just fell in love with. It's short, very short, and covered in heavy lace. The long arms make me feel a little less exposed, seeing as the back is totally open. It's perfect to show off the new artwork that curls around my side. Seeing as I had some time this morning, I'd booked myself a hair appointment to get the pink done properly and to have it put up for tonight. The pink is much more vibrant and looks incredible with the up-do my stylist spent hours creating.

I feel like a million dollars. It's just a shame I can't get *him* out of my head because a night of meaningless, hot and sweaty sex does sound appealing right about now.

Thankfully, as the evening progresses Summer has a few more drinks and she really starts to get into the swing of it, and much to my surprise Diane does too as she starts pointing out things that guys are doing up on stage.

"Well, I've got to admit that maybe this wasn't a horrendous idea. She looks like she's enjoying it," I say to Danni when she comes over with a fresh drink for me.

"There's something to be said for living outside your comfort zone every now and then." I agree, but when my mind sends me back to Zach's tattoo chair, I start to wonder if there's actually a lot to be said for living in your comfort zone, safely and without any risks.

"Just tell me you haven't done anything crazy like book her a lap dance."

Danni winks and I groan. "In for a penny in for a pound, Biff."

"She's going to fucking hate you."

"It's a risk I'm willing to take. She's about to become family, so it's not like she can avoid me."

Shaking my head at my best friend, I glance up as the lighting changes around us. Spotlights shine brightly on the stage and everyone around me stops and looks.

A new guy steps up. He's vaguely familiar for some reason, but I can't pinpoint from where. When I take in the inches upon inches of ink that covers the skin already on show, I wonder if he's a client at the studio.

He dances around for a bit, building some excitement before he comes to a stop at the edge of the stage by where we're congregating.

I look at Danni who's wearing a shit-eating grin, and then to Summer who looks like she could puke at any moment.

"Right, where's my lucky lady?"

He looks around, but seeing as Summer's wearing a veil and bride to be sash it's not exactly hard to find her in our crowd.

My heart races and my skin starts to prickle. I'm not even the one he's looking for and I'm panicking.

My eyes are locked on Summer as realisation as to what's about to happen settles into her. She shakes her head, her eyes going impossibly wide as she starts to back away.

"Come on, Sum. Say goodbye to single life in style," Danni encourages, alongside some of her more adventurous friends.

"No, no way am I getting up on this stage."

I've got no fucking clue what comes over me, but my

need to get this guy and Danni off her case has me stepping forward. "I'll do it on her behalf."

"No, no you don't—" Summer tries to argue, but I see the relief that fills her eyes.

"This is Summer's night," Danni argues.

"She's terrified, Dan, and she quite obviously doesn't want to do it."

Danni looks between the two of us and huffs. "Whatever." She waves me off and disappears in search of another drink. I'm surprised. I thought she might willingly put herself up on stage in Summer's—or my—place but she just leaves us to it.

"Right, who's it going to be then, ladies?"

Dragging in a huge breath that I hope might bring some confidence with it, I raise my hand to the guy and allow him to pull me up on stage. When I look at Summer, she mouths a thanks to me. *She damn well owes me one for this.* The rest of the ladies in our group cheer as I'm guided to a seat in the middle of the stage.

The guy—who is even more familiar now he's close up—puts his hand on the back of the chair over my shoulders and grinds himself into me.

"At least look like you're enjoying it, sweetheart. What's your name?"

"B-Biff," I stutter, not really wanting to have a full on conversation with this guy moments before he gets naked.

"Biff? I knew I recognised you."

I tilt my head to the side as I focus on him trying to rack my brain for where I've met him before when it hits me. He's the barman I almost went back for.

"Christian?"

"The one and only. Now, are you ready for the best night of your life?" He winks before standing back and turning so I've no choice but to stare at his arse as he bends over in front of me.

I might have been interested in him when he was the hot, tattooed barman but now... not so much.

He tugs at his trousers and they leave his body in one fell swoop, enticing a cheer from the exuberant crowd below that vanished to nothing the second he pulled me onto this stage. The only things I can see are him and the blinding lights. There could be a million people or absolutely no one in front of me. Sadly the noise they all make tells me that this mortifying moment of mine is being witnessed by hundreds of other women, most of which are probably dying to be sitting where I am right now.

My eyes drop from Christian's thong-clad arse and down his inked legs. I notice the clear wrap on the back of his calf and wonder how recently he had that done. I picture him at work sitting on one of the chairs with the gun pressed to his leg.

Thoughts of Zach don't exactly make this experience any more comfortable. Just thinking about how capable his hands are, both for creating everlasting artwork and with how he teased my body into a frenzy, has my temperature rising. I tell myself it's the spotlights.

I wonder if he can dance like that? I'm sure I'd be much more interested if it were him about to expose himself. I'm desperate to discover what he's hiding, seeing as he's taken his fill of most of my naked body.

I'm totally lost in my musings when Christian comes back to me. "That's better. You look a little more into it now." I refrain from telling him that it's thoughts of my boss that has this current look on my face and allow him to continue with his routine, following his lead when he wants me to run my hands down his back. Danni was right, in for a penny…

By the time I'm hopping down off the stage, sweat clings to my body and I'm desperate for a drink. Thankfully someone thrusts one into my hand after demanding to know exactly how that was.

Mortifying. Embarrassing. Long.

Christian is still up on stage driving the crowd wild, but I keep my back turned, needing to forget everything about what just happened. Before he let me down he asked if I wanted to have a drink with him after his set. He's probably never received such a quick refusal in his life. Even his offer of a more private show didn't spark any excitement inside me.

I felt like I'd shut down on that stage. Nothing he did aroused me in anyway, I was too desperate to hide back into the crowd, or even better, under my duvet.

Thankfully, the rest of the evening passes with little drama. Summer, Diane and I stay as far away from the stage as possible and Danni forgets her mission of embarrassing the hell out of the bride to be and settles for getting her nice and drunk instead, which Summer complies with. Danni matches her drink for drink, and by the time we're getting ready to leave she can barely stand up.

With my arm wrapped around her waist for support, we follow the other ladies out to the limo when we all decide it's time to call it a night. The drinks I've had buzz through my system making the room spin a little, but I'm nowhere near as drunk as some of the others and I'm pretty confident I'll still remember every mortifying detail about tonight when I wake up in the morning.

We're almost at the exit when my name is called.

Looking over my shoulder, I find Christian, thankfully now fully dressed in a white t-shirt and a pair of slim fit jeans. He looks good with his hair still wet from a shower and the muscles we all got an eyeful of earlier straining the fabric covering him.

"Oh hey," I don't mean for my voice to sound flat, but really, I just want to go home now. My feet are aching and I really could just do with a couple of painkillers and a pint of water in the hope of keeping tomorrow morning's hangover at bay.

"I was wondering if you'd like to go and get a drink sometime." He lifts his arm, his hand rubbing at the back of his neck. It's weird to see him a little unsure of himself after he was flashing his naked body for anyone who cared to look only moments ago.

Danni seems to perk up all of a sudden and pinches my side when I don't say anything.

"I... um..."

"She'd love to," Danni slurs.

I turn my death stare on her, but she doesn't even bat an eyelid. "Danni," I seethe through gritted teeth.

"What? He's hot. You've already seen the goods, so why not?" Her voice is nowhere near as quiet as it should be, and when I glance over at Christian he's got an amused smirk on his lips.

"She's got a point," he says. "Can I get your number?" He holds his phone out for me, and not wanting to be rude, I take it from his hands and tap it in. For a brief moment I almost consider giving him a fake one, but the nice, honest girl inside me doesn't allow it. Christian seems like a good enough guy. I should probably at least give him a chance, even if everyone standing behind me has already seen his cock.

"I'll call you." His smile is wide as he takes his phone back, ensuring our fingers touch in the process. I instantly notice the absence of any tingles, like the ones I get the second another inked-up guy touches me.

Chastising myself for thinking of *him* once again. I smile at Christian. "I'm sorry, but I really need to get this one home."

"No worries. It's been a long night. I'll talk to you tomorrow?"

"Sure." My stomach twists, but it's not with excitement as Danni and I turn back the way we were going and leave Christian behind.

The journey back in the limo is very different to the one here. Everyone is looking a little worse for wear, and some are actually asleep as the huge vehicle makes its way through London.

Thankfully, seeing as Danni was the one who booked it, it stops at my flat first. Danni hauls her giant bag from the floor that she left in here earlier and clambers out after me once she's said her goodbyes to everyone. It's tradition that she stays here after a night out. If we're still awake, we often watch reruns of *Friends* or *Sex and the City* with junk food to soak up any remaining alcohol before crashing and ordering the most unhealthy breakfast we can come up with the next morning, so I wasn't surprised when I found her overnight bag in the limo when they picked me up earlier.

"I need sleep," she complains when I force her to walk up the stairs. "What's wrong with the lift?"

"You know I hate using it."

"Yeah, but..." she whines like a petulant little child.

"Suck it up, sweetheart. We're nearly there."

"Ugh." She stops halfway up, plonks her arse down on the steps and pulls her shoes off.

Taking her bag off her in the hope it'll speed her up, I continue the climb.

The second we're in my flat, she immediately heads for my guest room, also known as her room, and begins stripping out of her dress.

Dropping her bag on the kitchen counter, I get us both a glass of water and take everything through to her. By the time I get there, she's already in bed.

"You should at least take your make-up off. You know what they say about sleeping in it."

"I don't care." She pulls the duvet up around her neck and snuggles down.

"Drink this. I don't want to deal with you puking all morning."

There's no response other than her breathing getting heavier.

Leaving her to it, I take my own glass of water and shut her door behind me.

I'm just at my bedroom when I swear I hear a knock on my front door. Stopping for a second, I wait to see if I'm going crazy. I'm just about to move, putting it down to the alcohol when it happens again. If someone wanted me, they'd use the buzzer. Unless it's a neighbour.

My curiosity getting the better of me, I head back to the door and pull it open. The person I find standing on the other side takes my breath away.

CHAPTER SEVENTEEN

TABITHA

I STARE into his darkened eyes, trying to figure out what the hell is going on. Glancing behind him, I find he's alone.

"Zach?" My voice is no more than a breathy whisper and I wish it were stronger. "Wha—what are you doing here? Is everything okay?"

My heart races as I stare at him, desperately trying to figure this out.

"That all depends."

My brows draw together. "On what?"

"On what you do next."

I gasp as he slams his hand down on the front door, forcing it so wide that it crashes back against the wall. I wince at the noise this late, but I'm soon distracted when he steps up to me. His body heat hits my front, and every muscle in my body aches for me to reach out for him, to touch him and take what I've been desperate for.

I open my mouth to respond, to try to get the answers I crave, but he uses that as his opportunity. His hand glides across my jaw line and his fingers thread into my hair as his lips crash down on mine. He doesn't wait to find out if I'm going to respond, he just takes charge. His tongue delves into my mouth, searching out mine as our bodies press together.

It takes me a second to register what's happening, but the moment I do, I join in. My tongue duels with his as our teeth clash and low moans of desire escape from both of us.

He walks us into the flat and I just about register the sound of the door closing behind us before I'm spun and pushed up against it.

"Fuck, this dress," he mutters, pulling back from me and running his eyes down the length of my body. "Been dying to get you out of it all night."

His words confuse me, but I don't have time to focus on them because his lips find mine once again and the only thing I can think about is him. He consumes every part of my body with his kiss alone. It's a heady feeling and one I could become very used to very easily. It's a terrifying thought.

His hands run down my sides, his thumbs teasing the underside of my breasts which are desperate for more attention before he skims them over my waist and to my exposed thighs. In one quick move, he has me off the floor and my legs wrapped around his waist. His hard length presses against my core and a throaty groan of approval rumbles up my throat.

"Can't. Get. E-fucking-nough. Of. You." His admission has desire pooling in my lower stomach and lava filling my veins. My heart hammers so hard against my chest as I fight to drag in the air I need with his lips still connected to mine. "All I can think about," he says, peppering kisses along my jaw until he finds the sensitive spot under my ear that makes me shudder with need, "is you."

"Oh god, Zach." My chest heaves, my nipples press painfully against the confines of my dress, and my knickers are soaked with my need for him to touch me. To feel his skin against mine.

My fingers have a mind of their own as I reach out to release the fabric of his black t-shirt. I pull it up from his waist, desperate to see more of him at last. I drag it up his torso, revealing his sculpted abs and a deep V that makes my mouth water.

"Off," I demand. He lifts his arms up for me and together we somehow manage to free him from the fabric and it falls to the floor somewhere around us.

"Fuuuuck." The word is quiet and drawn out as I stare at his inked body. It only fuels the fire that's out of control within me. The chain hanging around his neck intrigues me, but I'm not able to focus on it.

"Your turn." He finds the little button that's holding my dress together at the base of my neck and has it open in record time. He peels the lace from my shoulders until he reveals my bare breasts beneath.

"Fuck, Pussy Cat. These are fucking perfect." He doesn't allow me to remove my arms, so they stay pinned at my sides by the fabric as he lifts me a little higher and begins feasting on my nipples.

I cry out in pleasure as he bites down on one, sending a bolt of lust straight to my core.

"More, Zach. More, please," I beg.

Suddenly we're moving.

"Tell me which room is yours, unless you want me to fuck you on the sofa." His words are like gasoline on my raging desire.

"Sec-second on the left," I stutter, struggling to form words.

Using my back, he pushes the door open before kicking it shut. The slam hits my ears and allows a little reality to slip back in.

Fuck. His sister is passed out in my guest room.

Panic hits me, the butterflies in my stomach suddenly reacting to more than just my desire. But it only lasts a few minutes because Zach allows my body to slide down his until my feet hit the floor. His hands cup my face and he brings his lips to mine.

His tongue gently sweeps past my lips. It's much softer than it was out in the hallway, and I fear he's lost interest. But after a few seconds he seems to come back to himself. His hands sweep down over my shoulders before he finds my breasts once again. He pinches both my nipples and I gasp, pulling back from his kiss in surprise. My arms are still trapped at my sides. I'm desperate to touch him, to feel his muscles bunch and the softness of his skin when we connect.

Our eyes lock. His blue ones are dark, giving away the fire that's burning within, his lips are swollen from my kiss and parted slightly as he tries to catch his breath. Knowing that I was the one to put that look on his face makes my chest swell with pride.

"I can't get enough of you," he repeats before making

quick work of removing my dress from my hips and freeing my hands. I lift my arms immediately and reach out for him, only for his fingers to encircle my wrists and stop any chance of it happening.

He presses me against the wall. The coldness bites into the skin of my back and makes me shiver, but with his eyes on my almost naked body, I'm anything but cold.

He lifts my arms above my head and holds both wrists with one hand. His free hand lands gently on my cheek, and as his eyes stare deep into mine, I'm rendered motionless as something intense washes through me.

"Zach?" I question, needing him to do something and stop looking at me as if he's seeing deeper than I want him to.

Shit, does he remember me? It's not something I've worried about since our first meeting, because it was very obvious that he didn't have a clue who I was.

Another thought hits me. "When did you see me in this dress?"

His eyes narrow as if he didn't hear me, but after another second his lips part. "I was at Pulse tonight." He steps forward, the length of his body pressing against mine, his arousal obvious against my stomach. Heat floods my core, knowing he's as desperate for this as me right now.

"On ladies' night? Something you need to tell me, boss?"

A small smirk twitches at the corner of his lips. "Not at all. I was there for the ladies."

"Oh." Something unpleasant twists my stomach.

"I've got a friend who works there, but I wasn't expecting to find you looking like fucking sin." My cheeks flush. "I watched you up on stage. I wanted to kill that motherfucker for getting so close to you."

"Jealous?" I ask, curious as to how he's going to play this.

"Like you wouldn't fucking believe."

"But I thought you wanted to *ruin* me?" I ask, using his own words against him.

"Oh, Tabby Cat. I'm going to do that and then some."

One moment I'm pressed up against the wall and the next I'm bouncing on my bed as Zach sheds his trousers and boxer briefs. My eyes drop to his cock that's hard and ready. My mouth waters as I wonder just how he'll taste. Sadly, I don't get a chance to find out because he reaches forward and drags my knickers down my legs. He tugs them over my shoes before throwing them over his shoulder.

"That's better." Before I have time to think, he's pushing my thighs wide and his finger is running down my centre. "So fucking wet."

"Zach," I plead, my legs quivering with my need for more.

"Zach what? You're going to need to be more specific, Kitten."

"Your mouth. On me. Now."

With his eyes holding mine, he lowers towards my throbbing clit. I look down my body as the heat of his breath hits me.

"Have you been thinking about this since the last time?" His eyebrow quirks, telling me that he knows exactly how good he is. His arrogance should be a turn off, but at this very moment, with his face between my legs, it's anything but.

"Yes," I breathe, lifting my hips from the bed, offering myself to him, desperate for his touch.

"Patience, Kitten," he murmurs, his finger making contact once again and circling my entrance.

"Fuck, please, please." My hands fist the sheets beneath me as I fight to stay in control.

"Fucking love it when you beg."

"Why doesn't that surprise meeee." His tongue presses against my little nub and I snap. My hands release the sheets in favour of his hair so I can pull him closer. He chuckles against me, but it feels too fucking good to care. Pleasure ripples around my body as he licks, sucks and even bites down on my clit. Unintelligible words and pleas for more fall from my lips, but I don't register them as Zach goes to town on my body. His hands reach up and palm my breasts before pinching my nipples and sending me careering towards a release so strong I already know it's going to knock me for six.

Why does it have to be courtesy of a man I can't stand?

His tongue lowers and spears inside me. My fingers grip onto his hair so hard I can only imagine it must seriously hurt, but I don't give a shit, and nor does he because at no point does he let up.

"Oh god, Zach. Zach," I cry as he builds me higher and higher.

One hand releases my breast and he slips two fingers deep inside me, finding my g-spot almost instantly as he puts pressure on my clit with his tongue.

"Come," he rumbles against me, and the vibrations of his deep voice are the final straw. My body locks up tight before I crash over the edge. He continues licking and gently fucking me as my body convulses and twitches as I ride out the most intense pleasure I've ever experienced.

It borders on being too much, too intense, but before it's even subsided, I know that I want to experience it all over again.

I'm too focused on the aftershocks of my orgasm to notice that Zach pulls back. It's not until the bed dips as he crawls onto it that I manage to drag my eyes open.

His hair flops over his forehead as he crawls over my body, the cool metal of his dog tag landing on the heated skin of my stomach and making me shudder. His eyes flick over my face, taking in the effects of my pleasure as my chest heaves for the air I so desperately need.

"Fuck, Tabby Cat. What are you doing to me?" His question confuses me, but I don't get a chance to ask before his lips find mine and his tongue delves in. The taste of myself only makes me more desperate for him. I eagerly open up for him, my hands landing on his taut back. He settles between my legs, his cock teasing my entrance. I'm so fucking desperate to feel him pushing inside me that I lift up, trying to make it happen.

"Fuck," he groans, almost as if he's in pain.

My hands slide all the way down his back, his muscles bunching as I descend, until I find his arse. I squeeze, trying to pull him closer.

"And here I thought you were a good little posh girl," he whispers in my ear, proving just how wrong he's got me.

"Fuck me, Zach. I need you. Need you buried deep in —ahhhh." He listens to my demand, finds my entrance and in one quick thrust he's deep inside me. "Oh god, yes. Fuck." He stills for a second to allow me to adjust. I'm surprised by his consideration but equally as grateful as it's been quite a while since my body has experienced a real cock and not one made of plastic.

HATE YOU

"Jesus, Kitten. So fucking tight." He drops his head into the crook of my neck, his lips kissing the sensitive skin as he starts to move. I meet him thrust for thrust, but it's not long before we both need more.

He sits up, revealing his incredibly sculpted chest and abs covered in ink that I'm desperate to know the story behind. I reach out to his dog tag, but he sees where I'm heading and instead pulls it over his head and reaches over to drop it to my bedside table.

"Now, where were we?"

Taking both of my hands in his, he lifts them above my head as his hips pick up speed.

Sweat clings to my skin as he moves above me, hitting an incredibly deep place inside me with every thrust.

With both of my hands in one of his, he drops his free hand and slips it between the sheets and my arse, managing to change the angle of my hips. My back arches as the pleasure takes over and he catches one of my nipples in his mouth.

Our bodies move together, my hands raking up and down his back in an attempt to get more of what I need to push me to the edge once again. One orgasm from him wasn't enough, and I'm pretty sure two won't be either.

Fuck, I'm becoming addicted to this arrogant motherfucker.

"Look at me, Kitten."

I drag my eyes open and find him staring down at me, his eyes almost black, his jaw tense and the muscles in his neck and across his shoulders straining. He's never looked so fucking hot.

"Now, come for me. Let me feel you coming around my cock."

He lifts me a little higher, causing him to rub against

my clit as well as stroking me on the inside, and I detonate like a fucking rocket.

"Jesus, Kitten, fuck," Zach grunts as I clamp down on him, riding out my pleasure. It's only seconds later that I feel his cock twitch deep inside me before his face pulls tight as he releases everything he has. It's in that moment that something happens in my chest. It tightens almost painfully, and I know that I'm not going to be able to walk away from this easily and that it's going to hurt like fuck when he turns his back on me now he's got what he wanted.

His weight falls on top of me, pressing me into my memory foam mattress, and I love the feeling of his body on mine, knowing that I caused his current sated state.

A bang from the room next to mine has his head lifting.

"What was that?"

My heart pounds as I think about the woman sleeping just the other side of the wall. I really shouldn't be doing this with her so close. Both of them will hate me when they find out I've been lying to them.

"Oh... uh... it's just my friend. She got drunk off her arse and passed out the second she hit the bed."

"As long as she doesn't interrupt, I don't give a fuck." Something tells me that statement wouldn't be true if he knew who my friend was, but when he starts kissing down my neck and across my collarbone I forget all about it.

"What are you doing?" I ask, embarrassment immediately hitting my cheeks at my stupid question.

He pauses right above my breast. My nipples beg for attention, and I have to fight to stop myself lifting them towards his face.

Amusement fills his eyes as they hold mine. "*Ruining* you."

My lips form an O but no words come out. I kinda thought we were done, but I'm delighted that it seems we've only just started.

"Why are you looking at me like that?"

"It's nothing. I just thought—"

"I'd got what I came for?"

I nod, feeling vulnerable for allowing him to know my thoughts.

"Well, I hope you're not tired, Tabby Cat, because I've only just started."

A small shriek rips from my lips as he flips me over, his palm landing on the fullness of my arse, shocking the hell out of me. I've never been spanked before, but I think I like it. Heat floods my core as realisation hits that we're not done.

"Tabitha?" he asks, his voice sounding serious all of a sudden. I look over my shoulder to find him sitting across the back of my legs. He looks fucking incredible with his hair all mussed up, his swollen lips and his cock standing proud once again. My mouth waters. He really is a piece of art.

"Y-yeah?"

"Are you on birth control?"

I tense as I realise that he just took me bare and I didn't even blink. *Shit.* But that's what this arsehole does to me—he steals all my senses and totally consumes my entire body.

"I-I'm on the pill."

"Good. I'm clean. I've never..." He trails off, averting his eyes. I'm desperate to reach out to pull his eyes back to me so I can read his thoughts.

"Never what?" I ask innocently.

"I've never gone bare before." He looks back to me, and I understand why he turned his head. He feels it too. This connection. This pull between us that neither of us can deny. "I've never forgotten before. Fuck, Kitten." He drops his gaze and shakes his head as if he can't believe it. "I'm meant to be ruining you, not the other way around."

My breath catches at his honesty. "Zach," I breathe, but he makes it clear we're done talking about this when his palm collides with my arse once again.

"Fucking love this arse. Now get on your hands and knees."

I scramble to do as I'm told and in seconds he's filling me. I didn't think it would be possible, but this position means he gets even deeper.

He ploughs into me with such force, the bed bangs against the wall and my body's forced up the mattress even with his hands gripping my hips almost painfully tight.

When we're both on the brink of release, he pulls me up so my back is against his chest. One of his hands drops and his fingers begin to strum my clit while the other lifts and wraps around my throat.

"Mine," he grates in my ear as his cock swells inside me and I crash into oblivion, quickly followed by him.

CHAPTER EIGHTEEN

ZACH

I WAKE UP HOT. No, burning up. I throw the covers off, but it's not until I crack my eye open and find the naked body beside me that memories from last night come back to me. I glance around her bedroom. It's pretty much as I expected it to be. It's not a penthouse like I assumed but a nice flat in an edgy converted warehouse. Knowing Tabitha as I do now, it kind of suits her. It's got the whole posh girl with an edge vibe that she seems to like.

She moans in her sleep and my cock jumps to attention. Looking over and seeing the bare smooth skin of her back beside me and the swell of her arse, my fingers twitch for more.

She blew me away last night. Remembering the things that fell from her mouth, her demands for more, her descriptive way of telling me exactly what she needed... Fuck, my cock weeps to slide deep inside her tight little pussy again.

Unable to stop myself, my hand slips under the sheet and palms her arse. Even in her sleep she reacts to me, pushing herself into my hand.

She whimpers when I place my lips to her bare shoulder and pepper kisses across her soft skin.

I should leave. I should walk out right now and forget last night ever happened. I try reminding myself that I hate this woman. A woman who stands for everything I've spent my life getting away from. The pretence, the fakeness, the thinking that because there's money sitting in a bank, they're better than others. I fucking hate it, and she's part of that world. I don't know who her parents are, but I sure as shit know the type of people they are.

But there's more to her than just the posh girl you first saw, a little voice in my head says. I push it down and focus on the task at hand.

Dropping my hand lower when Tabitha once again pushes her arse into me, I find her slit. She's already wet for me, even in her sleep.

My heart pounds as I try not to focus on that not meaning anything more than her being as desperate for sex as I was last night. I mean, she'd spent the night watching strippers dancing around Pulse, of course she was up for it.

"Zach." The plea for more fires me up. I circle her entrance and dip a finger inside. She hums in pleasure and I add another digit. "Oh god," she whimpers. "I thought I was dreaming."

"Were you dreaming about me fucking you, Tabby Cat?"

"Uh huh." She gasps as I hit her magic spot. I wish I could see her face right now, her flushed cheeks both from what I'm doing and from her admission.

"What was I doing to you?"

"Eating me," she moans. My mouth waters, wishing that I was doing exactly that right now, knowing that she tastes like pure fucking heaven.

"You want me to?"

She shakes her head and I refuse to acknowledge the disappointment that sits heavy in my stomach at the rejection. "No. I want your cock. I want it as deep in me as it'll go. Make me scream, Zach. Make me feel it for days."

Fuck. My. Life. How's a guy meant to say no to that?

"You're a dirty little bitch, aren't you, Kitten."

"Zach, please."

Wrapping my fingers around her hip, I pull her body to a better angle and fist my cock, stealing myself for the sensation that's about to zap every one of my senses when we connect.

Sucking in a breath, I find her entrance and slide in, pulling her back until I'm as deep as possible in this position.

My fingers dig into her skin as I pick up pace. It's hard enough to leave bruises, but I can't find it in me to care as I thrust into her slick pussy. It's like warm velvet. So fucking good.

"More, Zach. Need more."

"Hold on, you're getting on top."

I manage to roll on to my back and pull her over with me. She lifts off me and I miss the connection immediately, but within seconds she's sinking back down on my cock. Her eyes find mine and they hold the same desire racing through my veins right now.

Surely this time will get her out of my system. I'd hoped one taste would do it, but I only became more addicted. One fuck didn't do it either. But this one... this is it. After this, I'll be able to walk out of this flat and put her behind me. My thoughts shatter as she lifts herself up and then slams back down on me. Her head falls back, making her body arch and thrusting her tits towards me. Unable to resist, I push myself up on my hands and suck one and then the other into my mouth.

She cries out my name as I bite down, skirting the perfect line of pain to increase her pleasure.

"Zach, Zach, fuck," she chants, getting louder and louder. I know she said her mate passed out but that was hours ago—she could be one of those drinkers who wakes up perfectly fine, bright and early the next morning.

Sitting myself up, I take her arse in my hands and help her grind down on me. I'm insanely deep in her like this, our bodies connected in every way possible as she wraps her legs around my waist and threads her fingers into my hair.

"Fuck," I mutter, slamming my lips down on her to swallow her cries.

As my balls start to draw up, her pussy begins to clamp down around me. She whimpers and cries into my mouth as our dirty kiss gets even sloppier and we both race towards our releases.

Her fingers tighten to the point of pain in my hair seconds before she crashes. She squeezes me so fucking tight that I've no choice but to follow her over the edge. I drop my head into the crook of her neck and bite down on her skin as my orgasm knocks me for six.

Fuck, this woman. I can't get enough.

That thought is like a bucket of cold water over my heated skin.

This is bad. Really fucking bad.

Of all the women I've fucked, why's it got to be this one who gets under my skin?

"Zach, are you okay?" she asks, obviously sensing the shift in me.

I never spend the night with a woman. I fuck her, get what I came for, and fuck off the second I've dropped the condom into the bin. Jesus fucking Christ, we didn't even use protection. No wonder the feeling of her wrapped around me was so fucking earth-shattering.

"Uh yeah... I just... uh... need to get back."

I lift her from me and set her down on the mattress. I swing my legs over the edge and sit up, keeping my back to her. Her stare burns into my skin, calling me back, but I can't. I need to get out of here and away from what she does to me.

Pushing myself from the bed, I pull my boxers and trousers on before picking up my shoes and leaving the room in search of my t-shirt.

"Zach, don't leave like this," she pleads, but I ignore her until I'm standing in her doorway, about to make my escape.

"This was a mistake. I suggest you start looking for a new job." Her gasp of shock practically takes all the air from the room. Forcing my feet to move, I quietly close her door behind me, hoping like fuck that her friend's not awake and about to collar me on the way out.

What I need right now is to escape to my own flat to try to get my fucked-up head together. I don't need twenty questions about why I'm here and where I see my future with her friend.

I laugh at myself. I don't have a future with a woman, especially not her. My life is my business. That's where my focus should be, not worrying about when I'm next going to get the chance to be inside her again.

The bitter cold of the early morning bites my skin as I step from her building for the walk of shame. It's never felt shameful before, and I never really understood the saying seeing as I was always proud as fuck about my conquests and feeling relaxed and sated. Right now, I feel anything but that. If I'm being honest, I'm tenser than when I made the fucking stupid decision to come here last night. Part of me thought she'd slam the door in my face, if she even opened it in the first place, but a huge part of me knew something would happen. The previous times I'd touched her, she was like putty in my hands. I had no reason to believe that after a night of drinking in Pulse she would be any different.

The second I get into my flat, I strip out of my clothes and get myself in the shower. If I can't get her out of my head then at least I can get her sweet scent from my body.

All I can hope is that she took my warning seriously and doesn't return. That way I'll be able to get on with my life like she never happened.

CHAPTER NINETEEN

TABITHA

"THIS WAS A MISTAKE. *I suggest you start looking for a new job."*

Tears burn the back of my throat and sting my eyes as his words repeat over and over in my head. Of all the things that could have happened when we woke after our marathon sex session last night, him fucking me once again and then clearly expressing that it never should have happened and that he didn't ever want to see me again wasn't up there on my list.

His regretting it isn't a surprise. I knew the second I allowed him in that I'd regret it, but I was powerless to stop, especially once he had his hands on me. I might hate the arrogant prick, but even I can't deny that he's hot and got some skills.

I've never had a night like that with a man before. This right now wouldn't be so bad if the sex was terrible, but it fucking wasn't. It was amazing. Even as I think about it my pussy clenches to feel him stretching me open again.

Sorry, not happening.

Refusing to allow myself to cry over Zach fucking Abbot, I get myself out of bed. The sun has barely started rising so I'm not surprised when I look at the clock to find it's barely seven AM.

With a sigh, I plod through to my en suite. At least I had the foresight to drink some water last night so I've only got a slight twinge in my temples from the amount of alcohol we packed away.

Christ, was that only last night? As I sit on the toilet, I cast my mind back to the events of the night before. Of Summer and Diane's horrified faces when they discovered where Danni had sent us, and then Summer's pure terror when she was expected to go up on stage. If I hadn't offered, would Zach have seen me? Would this whole disaster have never happened? Is the whole thing my fault because I was helping his soon-to-be sister-in-law out?

A bitter laugh falls from my lips. At least I feel less guilty about lying to him now if he's going to continue to be the wanker I always thought him to be. I never had a look in where Zach and his idiot friends were concerned at school. I was too boring, too dull, too quiet to even feature on their radar. Maybe it's just the way it's meant to be that he got a taste of me after all this time, seeing as he seemed to make it his school mission to bed as many girls as possible. He just doesn't know he's knocked another off almost a decade later.

HATE YOU

I have the longest shower in history as I try to wash the memories of last night away, although every time I move I'm reminded of every single thing he did to me. My muscles pull and my pussy is sore from the pounding it took after months of celibacy.

I eventually emerge from my room wearing an oversized jumper, which is so big that it hangs off one of my shoulders, that I stole from one of the previous guys I was seeing but never returned, and a pair of hot pants. I'm just about to walk out of my room when something silver on my bedside table catches my eye. Walking over, I find it's the dog tag that Zach had around his neck last night.

Picking it up, I turn the piece of metal over. *Jonathon Wilson*. I know that name. It was one of his best mates at school. I've no idea what happened to him. Looking at this, I guess he joined the military at some point. Why would Zach be wearing it?

Without the caffeine I need, my brain doesn't fire correctly so I place it back down and head out to the kitchen. I'll worry about it later.

I'm standing at the coffee machine, wishing that it went faster, when a door cracking open startles me. I'd forgotten she was here.

Guilt hits me in waves, threatening to buckle my knees. What was I thinking last night? She could have come out when we were kissing. She could have heard banging in my room and walked in to check I was okay. She could have discovered that I've been lying to her since starting my new job.

Fuck. I rest back against the counter in an attempt to hold myself up. She looks rough. Maybe I was right last night and there was a very slim chance of her ever emerging.

I tell myself that, after we've both had some caffeine, I'll confess.

"Morning," I sing, much more cheerfully than I feel. "How are you feeling?"

"Fuck. Off," she grunts, making me laugh. She gets to the coffee machine right as my cup's finished brewing and swipes it from under the spout.

"Hey, that's mine."

"I need it more," she counters, carrying it over to my sofa.

"Don't you want milk?" I ask, knowing it's how she usually has it.

"No." I watch as she curls herself in the corner and hugs the mug in her hands. I think some might say that's karma for what she did to poor Summer last night.

I make myself a drink and head over to join her.

We're both silent as we sip at our too-hot coffees, desperate for the hit they're going to give us. I try to come up with the right words to say to explain that I know more about her brother than she does, but every time I open my mouth to say any of them, they die on my tongue.

His words might have seriously hurt this morning, but still, I don't feel right spilling his secret to Danni. Fucked up, I know, but I can't help it.

"So, last night was fun," I eventually say, steering well clear of anything involving my late night activities.

"You think Summer hates me?"

"I'm sure it'll be fine. She'll understand that you were just trying to allow her to go crazy."

"I knew it wasn't really her thing, but I wanted to push her a little. Make her step out of the comfort zone she and my brother live in on a daily basis," she explains.

"I get it, Dan. But maybe you should have at least

warned her. You saw what she was wearing, she had no clue what was about to hit her."

Danni chuckles. "I know, right. Did you see the look on my mum's face when the stripper came over and waved his cock in front of all of us? I thought we were going to have to ring an ambulance. You reckon that she's only been with my dad?"

"They were together young, so I'd be tempted to say yes."

"Can you imagine that? Only being with one man. Only experiencing one cock."

"I'm sure it's got its benefits," I mutter, thinking of how much being rejected sucks even if it is by a one-night stand.

"Meh, your twenties are time for oat sewing. I'm all for testing out the market before choosing my prime cut."

"I hate to break it to you, but you've not exactly been tasting the goods recently."

"Don't remind me," she groans, leaning forward to put her empty mug down and pulling her phone from her pocket. "I have got back to online dating though. Got a couple of hopefuls I'm chatting to right now."

"Oh yeah? Let's see."

Taking pity on her, I move to slide up next to her on the sofa.

"Oh he's hot," I say when she shows me the first picture. He looks just her type. Perfectly put together, in a suit, slick, styled hair. The kind of man my parents would love to see on my arm.

"Right? He's so sweet too, and so funny. I think I might suggest we meet soon."

"What does he do for a living?"

"Banking, I think."

"You think?"

"We've not really got down to the nitty gritty of boring stuff yet."

I don't argue with her, but I can't help remembering how many times she's told me that a man's job is vital when it comes to dating. She doesn't mean it in a pretentious, he-must-have-a-good-job-and-loads-of-money way, more that he needs to be motivated and hard working. I understand that and must admit that I share the sentiment.

"Ohhhh." She suddenly sits up straighter as an idea hits her. "I should invite him to the wedding, and you can invite your sexy stripper. Has he rang yet? He was proper keen." She elbows me as that part of last night comes back to me. I'd pushed it from my mind the second I'd walked away from Christian, and Zach most definitely shattered any memory of any other guy the moment he kissed me.

"I'm not inviting a stripper to a wedding, Dan. I can't imagine it's his idea of a perfect first date, can you?"

"I don't know. It's an open bar and free food. It could be worse." She's got a point, but I still don't like the idea.

"I'll message Carter now, see how he feels about it."

"Maybe you should invite him for a drink or something first. If you can't stand him in real life it'll ruin the wedding."

"Good idea. Go on then. You too."

"Oh… um… I gave him my number, remember? I have to wait for him."

She nods, her nose stuck in her own screen, smiling to herself as she asks this guy out.

"I'll order breakfast. What do you fancy?"

My mind goes straight in the gutter, thinking that a re-run of my time with Zach is exactly what I fancy. Instead, I mutter, "Pancakes?"

"Ummm... yes." She taps about on her phone before exclaiming that they'll be here in thirty minutes and that she needs more coffee.

I get up to grab us both a refill, and it's not until I sit back down next to her that she properly looks at me.

Her eyes focus on my neck, and her eyes narrow. My heart begins to race at what's she's found, my palms getting sweaty under her scrutiny. "Did I miss something last night?" She tilts her head to the side like a little puppy waiting for an answer.

Lifting my hand, I cover the bit of skin she's staring at.

"Umm..." My cheeks flush. I'm unable to stop them as I picture our bodies rolling around my bed while she was sleeping on the other side of the wall. This would be the perfect time to admit the truth. But when I speak, very different words come out. "I... uh... had a moment with some guy last night."

Her eyes go so wide I swear they might pop out. "Oh my god. Was it *him*? Please tell me it was him. The tension as he danced for you was fucking electric. Is that why he wanted your number so badly?"

I feel fucking awful, but the lie falls from my tongue too easily. "Yeah."

Danni squeals, making me wince, and claps her hands in front of her in excitement while I die slightly inside. I never lie. Okay, so I may stretch the truth to my parents from time to time, but I don't lie. Especially not to my best friend.

The pancakes are incredible, but they're not enough to make me forget. Danni doesn't miss the torment on my face, because before she gets up to leave, she suggests organising a night out with the guys after the wedding, I think in the hope it'll cheer me up a little. I agree, because I always want to spend time with our friends and it seems to get harder and harder to get everyone together these days.

As the day passes, Danni bids me farewell and the time creeps around to when I should start getting ready for work. The butterflies and dread I felt this morning only get worse. Did he really mean what he said before he left, or was it just a spur of the moment comment?

There's only one way to find out, I guess, and that's to turn up. He should know that one barked order isn't going to get rid of me. If I were that weak, I never would have returned after our first encounter. One thing's for sure when it comes to what Zach thinks about me, and that's that he underestimates me at every turn. He's not going to get rid of me that easily. I love my job at his studio, and I love the guys. So what, he's a dick? I'm sure we can learn to tolerate each other. Falling back into bed with him shouldn't be an issue, seeing as he regretted it so much after the event.

I'm halfway to work when my phone rings. Part of me expects it to be him making sure I'm not going to turn up, but when I eventually manage to juggle the coffees in my hand and pull my phone out, and find an unknown number staring back at me, my stomach drops. It can only be one person.

"Hello?" I ask hesitantly.

"Hey, Biff?"

"Yeah."

"It's Christian, from the bar the other week and then the uh... club last night," he says like I might need the reminder of the most embarrassing night of my life.

HATE YOU

"Oh, hey. How's it going?"

"Good, good. I... uh... wondered if you fancied grabbing a drink one night this week."

"Um..." I want to say no, but then the image of Zach walking away from me this morning pops into my head and a plan starts forming, causing the nerves fluttering in my belly to turn to excitement. He might want to play dirty, but he doesn't realise just who he's playing with. "Yeah, that sounds great. Monday to Wednesday would be best for me as I work the other nights."

"How about Tuesday?"

"Can you text me with a place? I'm just about to start work."

"Yeah, no worries."

I come to a stop outside Rebel Ink and spot Zach's blonde hair flash through reception and disappear towards his room. My next words are out of my mouth before I even really think of the consequences.

"I know this is a bit forward, and you're probably busy but..." I suck in a breath before just going for it. "I've got a wedding to go to next weekend and I could really do with a date. Do you fancy it? I mean, if you're free. It's got an open bar and five-star food," I ramble on, feeling like an idiot and not realising that he's laughing at me down the line.

"That sounds great. I'd love to."

"Okay, great. It's Saturday afternoon into evening, but I can give you all the details on Tuesday."

"I'm looking forward to it." I can practically hear his smile down the phone.

"Yeah... uh... me too." I hang up before he has a chance to ask why I don't sound quite as enthusiastic as him.

I could have just made the stupidest move ever. But it's too late now.

I push the door open with my butt, not allowing myself to think about what I've just done, and I instead set about delivering the guys' first coffee of the night.

"Here she is, our guardian fucking angel," Titch announces, successfully making the others emerge who eagerly accept the coffees I hand them. "Uh oh, there's only four. That mean boss man pissed you off?"

"Something like that," a deep voice booms. I was too distracted by the others to notice his door open.

My heart jumps into my throat, but I refuse to turn and look into his eyes. I don't need him to see how much he hurt me by walking away like he did this morning.

"I didn't think I'd be seeing you today, Tabitha." His voice is cold, unlike I've ever heard it before, and it makes a shiver run down my back and tears burn my eyes.

"Well... someone needs to keep these animals in line, eh?" With that said, I march back towards reception, drop my bag on my desk and race to the safety of the kitchen. Pushing the door to behind me, I blow out a breath. I need to be stronger than this. Just the sound of his voice shouldn't almost reduce me to tears. I need to show him that no matter what he says, what he threatens, he doesn't affect me.

Once I feel like I've got myself together, I hop up on one of the bar stools and sip my coffee in peace. We've got ten minutes until the open sign lights up, and I get the feeling I'm going to need every ounce of strength I possess to get through this shift.

I'm just about to get up to throw my cup in the bin when the door's pushed open. I hold my breath as I wait to find out who it is that's come to find me.

Turning to the sink quickly, I attempt to make it look like I'm busy.

"Stop pretending to wash up," he barks, making every muscle in my body tense. He moves around the room. My body is so hyperaware of his that I don't even need to look to know exactly where he stops.

"You've got something of mine." The fact that it's a statement rather than a question pisses me off.

"Do I?" I ask innocently, knowing full well that what he wants is currently sitting in my purse.

"Don't try to play me, Tabby Cat. Give me back what's mine, and if you're lucky you might get through this shift unscathed, seeing as you foolishly ignored my suggestion and turned up for it anyway."

"I don't know what you're talking about. Get off me," I screech when his warm fingers grip my shoulder and force me to spin around so I'm facing him. He stands so close that I've no choice but to look up at him to keep eye contact. His eyes are dark and angry, his chest is heaving with frustration. He doesn't let up on his painful grip even when I try to twist out of it.

"Where is it?"

I smile at him innocently, and he bares his teeth.

"I'm not fucking joking, Tabitha. Where it is?"

"Tell me why you wear it and I'll consider it."

"Fuck you," he spits, taking a step back and turning before lifting his hands so his fingers grip his hair.

"You already did, remember? It's what got us in this mess in the first place."

"Don't I fucking know it." He takes a few deep breaths. "Look, that... it just... it means a lot to me and I'd like it back."

"Is that you asking nicely?"

His shoulders rise and he drags in a long breath before blowing it back out. "Please." The word is said through clenched teeth, but I can't help but smile in achievement. "Please can I have it back?"

"I'll see what I can do." Pushing from the counter he pinned me against, I walk out into reception. I have every intention of getting it for him the second I'm at my desk, because he really does seem quite cut up about it, but there are clients waiting.

I sort them out first. The whole time Zach stands behind me, watching my every move with steam practically shooting from his ears. For my own amusement, I make sure I'm extra thorough with each client.

Titch, Spike and D all come out to get their first victims of the day, and after about ten long minutes we're once again alone.

"Well?" he asks, stepping up to me. His body heat burns into my side and his smell seeps into me. For a second I'm unable to function as memories of last night hit me like a fucking truck. My thighs press together, my knickers getting damper by the second. Man, he might be an epic prick, but fuck if I wouldn't go for another round. "Tabitha?"

"Huh? Yeah?" I look up at him, and the second he looks into my eyes, he knows. He knows exactly what I'm thinking.

"That good, huh?"

"Yeah, the pancakes I had this morning were pretty fantastic, thanks for asking."

"Right. Well..." He gestures towards my handbag.

I pick it up and pull my purse out. I'm just about to unzip the coin section to grab it when I stop.

"Why do you wear it? It's not yours."

"None of your business."

"It's clearly important to you. Who's Jonathon, and why do you have it?"

"Just hand it over and stop pissing me about, I've got work to do."

"Your client's not due for thirty minutes," I counter.

"You think that's all I do. Sit around waiting for clients. This is my fucking business. I do everything. Now hand it fucking over so I can go. I'm fed up of looking at you." His comment cuts, I can't deny that, but I try not to allow it to show on my face.

"What happened to him?"

He looks up to the ceiling as if he's praying for strength. "He died, okay? You happy now?" He shoves his hand out towards me once again.

The pain etched onto his face is enough to have me reaching for the dog tag and pulling it out. He snatches it from me before the chain even leaves my purse, sending coins scattering across the floor.

"Pick that shit up and get on with your job." The emotion in his voice is almost enough to make me follow him to make sure he's okay, but knowing that it's probably the last thing he wants, I force myself to stay where I am until the slamming of his door reverberates through me.

I'm on my hands and knees, picking up the coins which he managed to spread far and wide, when the entrance bell goes off.

Glancing up, I see a young girl by the door looking around the place. She's dressed simply in black ripped skinny jeans, a white t-shirt and a vintage looking leather jacket.

"Hi, can I help you?" I ask, climbing to my feet.

When her blue eyes find mine, I can't help but notice the hesitation in them. It's a bit like she's just realised she's walked through the wrong door.

"Oh um... I've got an appointment."

"Okay, come over." As discreetly as I can, I run my eyes over her, questioning if she's even old enough to be here. "What's your name?" I ask once the computer's woken up.

"Kassie Fox."

I find she's right and that she's booked in. "Okay, I just need you to fill this out. If you can pass it back to me when you're done, I'll let Zach know that you're here." I swear she tenses at the mention of him. "Is this your first time here?"

"It is. But I've heard good things about the place."

I nod as she steps away from my desk. "The guys are amazing."

I keep my eyes on her as she drops her tote bag onto the coffee table and then shrugs off her jacket. I have a hard time stopping my mouth from dropping open in shock when she reveals that the t-shirt I thought she was wearing is actually a vest and that both her arms are already pretty well inked. When she turns and flicks her hair, I notice that there's also ink there too. Okay, so maybe she's older than she looks, seeing as she clearly has some experience with a tattoo gun.

She fills out the form in only a matter of minutes, and she's soon handing it back over to me. I glance down to make sure she's signed it and take note of her date of birth. She's almost twenty. She sure doesn't look it.

"I'm really, really sorry to ask this. But do you have any ID?"

"I do," she says like she gets asked it on a daily basis.

She pulls her passport from her bag and passes it over. Her hands tremble as she does so, making me even more suspicious.

"Fantastic, thank you. I'm sorry to have asked."

"It's fine. I'm used to it. Comes with the territory of looking like a pre-teen." I glance down at her chest, noting that she's anything but a pre-teen in that department.

I smile softly. "You nervous?"

"Yeah. You'd think it would get easier, right?" She laughs as she lifts her arms and looks at her ink.

"You've got more experience than me, that's for sure. I'll let Zach know you're here. He shouldn't be too long."

She takes a seat while I reluctantly push my chair back and head in the direction of his room.

CHAPTER TWENTY

ZACH

I FEEL like a fucking pussy but the moment I lifted my hand and found his dog tag was missing. I felt like I'd lost a part of me. It's been there since the day his parents handed it to me at his funeral. I never take it off, so why I did last night fuck only knows. I do everything with it on, usually including fucking women. I know he's gone, he has been for quite a while now, but with it there, it makes me feel like he's still a part of this. I wouldn't be where I am now if it weren't for him, I know that for a fact.

Something settles inside me the second I wrap my fingers around the cold metal. I slip the chain over my head and drop the tag into my shirt. I almost feel as naked without it as I would if someone were to erase my tattoos.

HATE YOU

I'm just sitting down to go through some emails when there's a knock at my door.

"What?" I bark.

I'd spent all morning convincing myself that last night wasn't as mind-blowing as I remembered it to be. I told myself it was the alcohol and the fact I'd managed to bag the girl who hated me. The prize at the end of the chase. But seeing her again just now after I warned her not to come back, fuck. She took my fucking breath away.

She was standing there in her tight as fuck jeans and an oversized jumper that hid everything she has going on beneath. My cock swelled the second I saw her, and it fucking pissed me off. She was meant to be out of my system. I'd fucked her. That was meant to be it. So why was I craving another taste of her sweet pussy more than I wanted the coffee she'd forgone bringing me while handing the others theirs?

The door cracks open and her pink hair fills the gap. "Your first client's here. Try to be nice. She's really nervous."

"I'm always nice."

An insincere laugh falls from her lips as she turns back. I jump from my seat and follow her just in time to watch her arse sway as she makes her way back to her desk. Fuck, that arse. I bite down in the inside of my cheek as I remember how it felt to sink into her from behind last night. How rosy her cheek was after I slapped my palm across it.

"Zach? Zach?" My name being repeated eventually drags me from my thoughts and I look up to find Tabitha staring at me with a frown on her face and a young girl who looks like she's about to puke on my shoes.

"You old enough to be here, kid?"

"Uh..." She hesitates. I'm seconds from sending her back to the playground she came from when Tabitha pipes up that she's seen ID and everything's good.

I nod at Tabitha and take the girl's form when she hands it to me. I quickly scan it before taking in her name.

"Right then, Kassie. You ready for this?" She gives me a nervous smile but collects her jacket and bag and follows me down to my room.

"You look too well inked to be nervous," I say when I spot her hand shaking when she lowers her bag to a chair I have in the corner of my room.

"I'm... always like it. Needles," she adds with a shrug of her shoulders.

"Glutton for punishment, eh?"

"Something like that."

"Come and take a seat and we'll go through what it is you looking for."

"I've got a drawing."

"Okay." She pulls a piece of paper from her bag and hands it over. Before me are two beautifully sketched angel wings. "Wow, this is incredible. You draw it?"

She nods shyly.

"Don't be shy about this. You're really talented." She beams at my praise, and for the first time today I actually feel good about myself. "So where's it going?"

"On my back. Shoulder blades."

"Okay, well top off and lie on your front. Let's see what we're working with."

She immediately does as she's told and doesn't bat an eyelid like I'm sure most girls would at removing their top in front of a stranger. She lies down and moves her long, dark hair out of the way.

"So who did all these others, seeing as it's your first time here?"

"Loads of people. Some more talented than others." I glance down her arms and see that she's right. Some could do with a little work to tidy them up.

"Are you at art school or something?" I ask when the silence stretches out for a little too long once I've set to work.

"Or something," she mutters. "I'm just doing some bar work right now."

"Do you want to do more with your art?"

"Maybe. I've never really had the opportunity to think about it, let alone do anything about it."

"That's a shame. You don't want to waste a talent like that."

She falls silent once again, lost in her own thoughts, and I allow it as I focus on my own art.

I complete the outlines but come to a stop. Her skin is raw. It's never going to cope with me doing all the shading. "I think we need to call it a day for now. Can you book in for a few weeks' time? This needs to heal before I do any more to it."

"Sure. Can I see?"

"Of course." She gets up and stands in front of my mirror while I hold another up for her to see her back. Her breath catches at the sight.

"Happy?"

"Incredibly. You've done an amazing job."

"It's not finished yet."

She continues to stare at it in the mirror, totally enthralled by it.

"Is it for anyone special?" She lifts her eyes to mine and they hold for a few seconds. There's something within hers that I can't read, but for some fucked-up reason I feel like I should be able to.

Eventually, she shakes her head. I'm not sure if it's a no to answer my question or if she just doesn't want to talk about it.

"T-thank you so much," she says eventually, reaching for her top.

"Wait. I need to wrap it."

"Oh, of course. Sorry."

I quickly finish her off and allow her the escape she's quite obviously desperate for the second I've finished.

I follow her out of my room and to reception where she books her next appointment with Tabitha before almost running from the studio.

"What did you do? I thought she'd come out looking less scared, but if anything she was even more terrified."

"Me? I only did what she asked."

"What was that?"

"Some angel wings on her back. I think she's lost someone. Maybe it was a little emotional seeing it or something."

"Whoa, so you do have a little compassion in there somewhere."

"And to think we almost had some kind of a normal conversation there for a minute." She smirks at me. "I'm starving. Get me some lunch. And none of that vegan shit you tried palming me off with last time. I want meat, and plenty of it."

"Didn't think you played on that side of the field," she deadpans.

"Fuck off, Tabby Cat. You know full well which way I swing."

I don't realise that as I'm saying it Titch emerges with

his client. Thankfully, the client is totally oblivious to what's going on, but Titch is anything but. He grins like a Cheshire fucking cat, and as he passes me he whispers, "You tapped that?"

Growling, I turn my back on all of them and shut myself back in my room. Fuck knows why I thought it was a good idea to come out here in the first place.

CHAPTER TWENTY-ONE

TABITHA

TITCH WAS like a dog with a bone after he assumed that Zach and I had slept together Sunday night. The only thing that managed to get him off my case about it in the end was telling him all about my date tonight. The second I said the words, he looked up to where Zach was most likely still hiding in his room. It was almost as if he knew something I didn't, but I wasn't going to ask. It was clear how Zach felt about the mistake that was Saturday night, so I decided it was best left in the past. So what if it was the best sex of my life and I felt like we connected in a way I never have with anyone else? So what if he's all I can damn well think about, even if it is because I want to throttle the arrogant motherfucker. There was never a chance we'd ever be an item, anyway. He's the bad boy every girl wants to tame, he always has been, and I'm the good girl who for all these years managed to stay the hell away. What happened? Oh yeah, I took my Gran's advice and decided to be a rebel. Great plan that was, thanks Gran.

I smirk to myself, pulling out a sketchbook I found in a drawer the other day when I was feeling restless. I grab a fine liner and just see where it takes me. I've got twenty minutes before my Uber will be here to take me to the place Christian chose for tonight. My nerves for what the night might hold has me getting ready long before necessary just to have something to do. It's a bar and grill on the other side of town. I'd never heard of it until he texted the name to me, but having since looked it up online, I'm hoping it might be a place I return to.

By the time my phone alerts me to my approaching driver, I sit up straight and stare down at my drawing. It's a portrait of a guy, with tattoos obviously, but it's his back as he walks away. He's looking over his shoulder with a pained expression on his face. Well, if that doesn't tell me where my head's at with regards to Zach, then I don't know what will. Closing the book, I leave it on my coffee table and slip my feet into my shoes.

I didn't want to look like I'd made too much effort tonight, seeing as I'm not sure I really want this to go anywhere, so after rummaging through my wardrobe for a good ten minutes, I eventually decided on a simple loose black blouse over a pair of grey skinny jeans and finished off with some heavy jewellery and my leather jacket. In an attempt to waste time, I've curled my hair and pulled the front section back from my face.

I look in my hall mirror before leaving the flat, and my

heart drops a little that I'm not going to find Zach waiting for me at the bar.

Giving myself a talking to, I pull the door open and embark on whatever tonight is going to bring me.

CHRISTIAN IS WAITING outside the entrance when I arrive, wearing a black, long-sleeved t-shirt and a pair of dark jeans. I'm glad he's not made any more effort than I have. It settles something inside me. Not that he really needs to dress up. He's hot, and I already have enough knowledge of his body to know that what's hiding beneath those clothes is pretty insane too. So why doesn't he give me the butterflies?

"Biff, you look stunning, as always," he says, reaching for me and pulling me into him so he can kiss my cheek. A much more gentlemanly move than any he did on Saturday night, that's for sure.

"I'm so sorry about the other night," Christian says with a wince once we're shown to our table and handed menus. "It's not exactly how I usually tell a woman I'm dating what I do for a living."

We're dating?

"Oh... um... It's fine. I guess it's better to have it all out in the open." My cheeks flame at my choice of words. "Shit," I mutter, covering my eyes with my hand. Could this be any more awkward?

"Still, I hope you enjoyed yourself. I mean, it got you here." He looks a little smug as he sits back in his seat and runs his eyes over what he can see of me.

"Yeah, I mean, you were good, don't get me wrong, but—"

"But?" he asks, leaning his elbows on the table like I'm about to give him some serious pointers to up his game.

"It was probably the most mortifying thing I've ever experienced. I was saving the bride-to-be. Trust me when I say it's not the way I usually spend my Saturday nights."

"Good to know that I was your first." He winks, and I quietly groan, needing to move on from this mortifying conversation.

"So..." I scramble for something to change the subject to. "I thought you worked at Ted's."

"I do, I pick up shifts there when I have free nights."

"Oh, okay." I nod, an awkward silence descending over us. We both look down at our menus, pretending that it doesn't exist. Or at least I'm hoping that's what he's doing too.

The waiter thankfully comes over and breaks the weird tension that's formed.

"So what is it you do?"

Not really wanting to talk about Rebel Ink or anything to do with Zach, I focus on the other part of my life. "I'm currently studying for a Masters degree in fine art."

"Oh nice, so you can draw? Paint?"

"Yeah, both really. I'm not sure what I'm going to do once it's finished, but it's fun for now. I enjoy it."

"That's good. Um..."

I knew I should have turned him down on this date. A little voice inside me was screaming that it wasn't going to go well when he rang and asked. I'm only here because in my head I know it'll piss Zach off. Not that he even knows about it. Actually, that's probably not true because Titch will have made sure to tell him.

"This wedding on Saturday. You said you were going to give me the details."

"Oh right. I mean, don't feel like you need to come just because I mentioned it," I ramble in the hope he might change his mind.

"I wouldn't want to leave you without a date. I've got no work for Saturday right now, so your offer is as good as any. Plus you mentioned a free bar, right?"

"Yep."

"Tell me more then."

I rattle off all the details about the hotel the entire day is being held in, and he agrees that he'll pick me up so we can travel together. If it weren't for knowing that Zach's going to be there, then I might have told him not to bother, but my need for revenge keeps me moving forward with the plan. He needs to know that I know who he is and what secrets he's keeping.

"I hope they've booked a decent DJ. The last few weddings I've been to have been horrendous."

"Well, actually..." I rattle off the guy's name that Harrison and Summer have booked, and Christian's eyes light up. By the time our dinner comes it seems we've found at least one thing in common: our music taste. That conversation lasts us through to dessert.

"Do you fancy going to see a band I know? They're playing down in Camden tonight."

If he'd have asked me this during the first thirty minutes of this 'date' then I'd have quite adamantly said no, but things have most definitely turned around so I find myself agreeing and sliding from the booth after he insists on paying.

Unbelievably, by the time our Uber pulls up outside my building sometime before two AM, I've actually had a really great night with Christian. The band he took me to see were incredible, and he even introduced me to them once they'd finished their set and we sat together drinking until about twenty minutes ago when we called it a night.

"Thanks for tonight. It's been fun," I say, looking over to find him already staring at me. My stomach twists. I hope he's not expecting an invite up to my flat. We might have had a good time together, but one mistake in the bedroom in a week is enough for me.

"It has. So..." he trails off, as if that invite is going to come next.

I ignore the slight disappointment that darkens his eyes when I say something completely different. "So you'll pick me up at ten thirty on Saturday, right?" The service is at eleven thirty, so that should get us there in plenty of time. Danni has tried convincing me to get a room and stay the Friday night as well as the Saturday, but the second I discovered I was working for Zach, I point-blank refused. Saturday night was always going to be harder to get out of, but as it turns out, I want to be there to watch the fireworks.

"Oh yeah, right."

"I'm staying the night at the hotel, sharing with my friend," I add before any other idea enters his head. It's a lie—we have separate rooms booked—but he doesn't need to know that. "So you'll need to get yourself home. Is that okay? I can pay for your car."

"Oh no, t-that's totally fine. I'll see you Saturday then." His eyes bounce between mine and my lips, but I'm not going there. My head's already messed up with one man who shouldn't be up there. I don't need two duelling.

I say a goodbye, step from the car and give a little

wave. I don't need him walking me up to my door, that's for sure.

I pull my phone from my bag as I climb the stairs. I'd told Danni about meeting Christian tonight, so I already know I've got at least one message sitting on it, asking how it went and if I got lucky. When I wake it up, I find I've actually got five messages, although when I open them, there's only one asking about my date. The other four are inappropriate gifs.

I'm busy replying and digging around in the bottom of my bag for my keys, so I don't bother looking up when I get to my flat. I'm very quick to do so, however, when instead of coming to a stop in front of my door, I crash straight into a very hard and very warm body.

"Jesus fucking Christ. What the hell do you think you're doing?" I scream, his hands gripping my upper arms to steady me as my phone goes skidding across the tiled floor, probably shattering into a million pieces. I narrow my eyes at him, waiting for him to explain himself. My breath catches at the dark and haunted look in his eyes, but I refuse to say any more until I know why he's waiting here for me like a fucking stalker.

I don't have to wait much longer, because his hand finds the back of my head and his lips slam down on my own. His tongue is almost instantly in my mouth, searching out mine and demanding it joins in.

My back hits the doorframe as he takes the keys from my hands and fumbles about for the lock. At no point does he take his lips from mine, yet somehow he manages to find the right key and open the door.

He begins to guide me inside with his hands on my waist and his dark blue eyes boring down into mine, rendering me speechless and not allowing me a chance to think properly. He bends down at the last minute and retrieves my phone from the floor before dropping it into my bag. Then his focus is purely on me once again.

The front door slams closed as he kicks it shut, both his hands sliding up my body, pushing my jacket off. It lands on the floor with a thud, and he continues until his fingers twist in my hair and tug, allowing him the access to my neck he wants. He bites on the exact spot he did before, and a bolt of heat heads straight for my core. My stomach summersaults in a way it's not done all night while I've been with Christian, making it even more obvious that there's nothing between us. Nothing like this, anyway.

"Oh god," I whimper when he palms my breast and pinches my nipple through the fabric.

My breaths come out in needy pants as his hands roam, desperate to find some skin. He backs us into the kitchen, and as my back hits the counter, his fingers slip under my blouse, finding the heated skin of my stomach.

"Arms up," he groans in my ears, and I'm powerless but to do as he says.

The fabric is gone and on the floor in a flash, as is my bra not a second later. My breasts are heavy as they're released, but he takes their weight, sucking one nipple and then the other into his mouth, his eyes on mine the entire time.

I somehow manage to find some sense in all this madness. "We shouldn't be doing this. You shouldn't be here."

"And you shouldn't have been on a date." His lips trail down my stomach until he's on his haunches in front of me. He makes quick work of popping open my jeans and pulling both them and my knickers off my legs. My shoes come off too and drop to the floor with a bang.

"Fuck, I need you on my tongue."

"Oh god. Oh god," I chant as he runs his finger through my wetness.

"I think we've already determined that I'm not him."

"T-that's right, You're... you're the fucking devil."

The smirk he graces me with tells me that he fucking loves it too.

"Tell me, Kitten. Was it *him* that made you this wet? Or was it me?"

The temptation to lie is high, but when I open my mouth the truth falls out. "You. Only you."

"Right answer, Pussy Cat."

He lifts me so I'm sitting on my counter. The cold marble bites into my arse, but the warmth of his hands brushing down my thighs is a welcome distraction.

"Lie back." I do as he instructs and wince when my back hits the cold.

He parts my legs and blows a stream of air against my exposed centre. I shudder from that alone.

"It's only been three days, Kitten. You that desperate for me already?"

"Zach, please," I beg, desperate to feel him against me once again. "I need your mouth on me now." A part of me thinks he's just come to punish me and that he'll leave without ever really touching me, but thankfully I'm wrong because the tip of his tongue connects with me and I cry out in delight as his teeth graze over my clit.

"Yes, yes, yes," I cry, my hands finding his hair and dragging him closer.

He eats at me like a man possessed, licking, sucking

and biting like he's been starved of me. My back arches against the counter as I get closer and closer to my release.

Sliding two fingers deep inside me, he stretches me open and finds my g-spot. He teases it relentlessly with his fingertips while assaulting my clit with his tongue and teeth. In seconds I'm racing towards the light as it begins to flash behind my eyes.

"Zach, fuck. Zach, Zach, Zach," I cry, my release crashing into me, halting my breaths and pulling every single one of my muscles tight as I fly. "Fuuuuuuk," I groan as my body convulses beneath his touch.

My skin's covered in a sheen of sweat and my lungs push out ragged breaths as I come down from the high. Wiping his mouth with the back of his hand, Zach stands, a smug as fuck smirk on his face, but I'm so dazed that I don't give about shit how proud he is right now. All I know is that I need more. That might have been earth-shattering, but it was only the starter. I can see that in his eyes.

His hands go to his fly and in seconds he's got his hard cock in his hand. He strokes a few times, the muscles in his neck straining with his need to push inside me. The sight of how much he needs me right now makes me feel more empowered than I think I ever have.

I bite down on my bottom lip as I watch him, wondering what's keeping him.

"What's wrong? Changed your mind?" I tilt my head to the side, taunting him. He's standing there fully dressed while I'm stripped bare on my kitchen worktop, yet right now I feel like the one with all the power.

"Never." He thrusts forward and fills me. I cry out at the invasion and he stills to give me a second before dragging my arse over the edge of the counter, pulling almost all the way out, and slamming back into me.

He's so deep. So fucking deep it makes my head spin.

"Fuck," he grunts, feeling it too.

His fingers dig into the flesh of my arse, and the sting of pain tells me that I'll have his prints bruised there in the morning. A reminder of yet another mistake when it comes to this infuriating man between my legs.

Sweat beads his brow as he continues to fuck me into oblivion. The finesse he showed the other night has long gone. He's just a frenzy of thrusts and grunts as he pushes us both towards the releases we need.

"Come, Kitten," he demands. "Come. Now." My muscles contract on cue as he roars his release, his cock twitching deep inside me, leaving me full of his seed.

Almost immediately he pulls out of me and slides my body so my arse is back on the counter. His palms land either side of my thighs and he hangs his head, his eyes squeezed shut tightly.

"Zach?" I ask softly, running my fingers through the hair that's fallen onto his brow.

"Don't," he barks, backing away and looking anywhere but at me.

"Zach," I warn, knowing what's about to happen but ready to beg it doesn't, even though I know it's probably the wrong thing to do.

"You're mine, Pussy Cat. You need to remember that." With that warning hanging heavy in the air, he storms from my flat.

The slam from the door makes my body jolt. Pushing myself up, I look around, trying to make sense of what just happened.

He knew I had a date. He waited for me to get home

and fucked me like an animal, claiming that I'm his, yet he doesn't want me. Not really.

I sit there for the longest time in a puddle of our own making before I eventually drag my aching body towards my shower to once again wash the scent of him from my skin.

CHAPTER TWENTY-TWO

ZACH

TITCH DELIGHTED in telling me all about the fact that Tabitha had a date. He grinned like a fucking Cheshire cat the entire time while my jaw popped with frustration. I had no idea who the fucker was she was going out with, but the idea of anyone putting their hands on what's mine very nearly sent me over the edge.

It's how it should be. I knew that, but it didn't stop my imagination running on overdrive since the second he gave me all the details. I'm not sure what he was hoping to achieve by telling me the time and place they were meeting, but if it was for me to turn up and publicly claim her then he was going to be bitterly disappointed because that wasn't fucking happening. Or at least I didn't think it was.

Thankfully, I guess, I get a text from my brother Tuesday morning which means at least I won't be sitting around like a moron while she's on her date, driving myself insane wondering how they're getting on and if he's going to satisfy her quite like I did.

Harrison: Mum + Dad's tonight. Suit to try on. Be there. No excuses.

Rolling my eyes at the phone, I send back a quick reply saying that I'll be there and slide it back into my pocket. I've only got one client booked in today. He's coming in for his second session on an intricate back piece that we've been working towards for some time, so at least I know I'll be able to focus on that all afternoon and not my impending family time, and certainly not *her* and her date.

Before I know it, I'm pushing through Mum and Dad's front door and making my way down towards the kitchen where I already know everyone will be.

"Whoa, you were right, he is still alive," Dad says with a laugh when he spots me first.

"I'm sure you'd have heard if I weren't." He pulls me into a man hug and slaps me on the back. I'm kind of embarrassed by the fact that I've no idea when I was last here. All I know is that it's probably been too long seeing as they're really pretty great parents. It's my fucked-up issues that keep me away.

Mum leaves whatever she's stirring on the stove and comes over to hug me. "I've missed you," she whispers in my ear, making my guilt over not visiting quadruple.

Dad hands me a beer and I pull out a stool from under the breakfast bar.

"Have you sorted a date for the wedding yet? Summer needs her name."

I roll my eyes as Mum turns her back to the dinner. Of course I've not got a date. I only said I'd bring a plus one to shut her up about me needing to settle down.

"I've got a couple of options." Dad almost chokes on his beer.

He pats me on the shoulder as he comes to sit beside me. "So what have you been up to? Where have you been?" Dad starts like they do every time I appear after a long absence.

"Just here and there. Spent some time in America a few weeks ago. Not much to tell really." It's a lie, obviously, and like most times I'm here the truth is right on the tip of my tongue. But I can't help feeling that I've kept everything hidden for so long now that confessing everything will hurt them more, knowing that I felt like I couldn't confide in them from the beginning.

Thankfully, Harrison, Summer, and my niece and nephew arrive before Mum and Dad really get a chance to start digging. After a short and sharp welcome from my brother and a hug from my soon-to-be sister-in-law, Harrison thrusts a suit bag into my hands and all but drags me up the stairs so I can make sure it fits. I rustle both Alfie and Cass' hair as I pass them, much to their irritation.

He drops down onto the bed in my childhood room after following me inside and crosses his arms. As usual he's dressed in one of his flashy suits, making the differences between us as stark as ever with me in a ripped pair of stonewash jeans and a black t-shirt with my ink on display. His dark hair is perfectly styled and swept back from his freshly shaven face, whereas my blonde mop is a mess and I've not shaved in at least two days.

"Nice of you to show your face for this," he barks, his eyes holding mine.

"I'm not going to miss your wedding."

"Forgive me for not having all that much confidence after you bailed on my stag."

"It was golf," I groan, stripping off and pulling on the insanely expensive suit I'm being forced to wear to this thing. I hate suits. I hate how restrictive they are, and I hate how boring they are, although the hot pink lining this one is sporting does give it a bit of character, I must admit.

It fits perfectly—unsurprisingly as it's been tailored for me. My measurements were requested weeks ago so I had little doubt it wouldn't fit.

"It okay?"

"As far as a suit goes, it's great, I guess."

"Can you be at least a little excited about this? I don't want your miserable fucking face in our photographs."

"I'll smile, I promise," I mutter, giving him a flash of the fakest one I can muster.

"Such a pain in the arse." He pushes from the bed. "I know this is going to fall on deaf ears, but for the love of god, will you visit Mum and Dad a little more often? They worry about you."

"They don't need to."

"They're our parents, Zach. It's their job. You'll understand when you have your own."

"Yeah, that's not happening."

"You can't be a fucking nomad forever."

"I'm not. I have a home and a life. None of which involve me having kids."

"You say that now. Just wait until you meet the one."

"Are you even listening to me?"

He stops at the doorway, looks back over his shoulder and laughs. "Oh, I'm listening. You're just forgetting who the oldest and more experienced out of us is. It will happen, Zach. And she'll knock you on your fucking arse, mate." With that, he leaves me to remove the damn suit from my body.

I avoid the adults when I eventually head back down in favour of discovering what Alfie's playing on the PlayStation set up in the family room.

Falling down beside him, I watch him race his Audi around the track a few times before he spins it.

"Let the master have a go."

After changing the settings so it's two player, he hands me a controller and off we go.

"How's it going, Cass?" I ask my niece who's sitting on the other sofa with her head stuck in her phone.

"Fine."

I nod, taking Alfie out on a corner. "How's school?"

"Boring."

"Looking forward to the wedding?"

She groans. "I guess."

"Wow, I do love our stimulating conversations." This gets her eyes on me. Not that I'm paying that much attention seeing as I'm winning, but I feel them drilling into the side of my head.

"Well maybe if you were around a little more you'd already know the answers." Her footsteps sound out on the polished oak flooring before she storms from the room.

"Smooth," Alfie chuckles.

"You got something to say too?"

"Nope, you do what you gotta do."

I smile to myself. At least someone under this roof gets me. Even if he is a teenager.

Dinner is tolerable at best, but once Danni arrives and blends in with the rest of the family, I again feel like the outsider as they all sit and discuss the family business and mention people I've never heard of. I know that I bring a lot of this on myself by being distant, but I couldn't imagine anything worse than spending my days working with antiques.

I eat, I drink, I make a few noises at the right time, and then the second I'm able to escape I do with the promise of seeing everyone Friday night at the hotel where the wedding is being held. I tried to tell them all that I'm not needed until Saturday morning, but Mum got this look on her face, her bottom lip trembled, and her eyes watered, and I knew that I didn't stand a chance.

My intention is to go straight home. The Uber I ordered drops me at the studio. It would be so easy to let myself in and go up to my flat, but that's the opposite of what happens. Instead I head to a bar in the hope of drowning my sorrows.

One whisky soon turns into a few more, and eventually I find myself surrounded by the guys as we all shoot the shit and get off-our-arses drunk. I spot Titch looking at me inquisitively a number of times, but thankfully at no point does he even mutter her name. I'm grateful because I might be trying to play it cool, but the reality is that I'm picturing her taking him back to her flat. I'm imagining just how he might touch her, how he'll make her feel.

When my frustration gets the better of me, I knock back my current drink and stand from the seat I'm in.

"I'm done. Laters."

My name's called a few times behind me at my sudden departure, but I ignore them all. I've got a destination in mind, and no fucker is going to talk me down right now.

The walk to her place is short, and in no time I'm slipping my way into her building and hammering my fist on her door in an attempt to break up whatever's happening inside.

I guess you could say I'm lucky that no one's home. At least if she's gone back to his then I can't continue to keep picturing them in her bedroom.

Not knowing what to do, I slide my arse down the wall and rest my head back. I only intend to stay there for a few minutes before making the journey home but it's only a few seconds later that the sound of her heels click up the stairs. I could jump in the lift and disappear before she sees me but that's the opposite of what I do.

The relief I feel when she appears and I discover she's alone is greater than I'll ever admit. The sight of her all dressed up and swaying slightly after a long night stirs something inside, and it's strong enough to ensure I stay exactly where I am and take what I came here for. Her.

I step up to her and I'm no longer in control of my actions. My need, my desire for the woman takes over everything, and it's not until she's crying out my name and pulsating around my cock impossibly tightly that my senses start to slip back in.

Fuck.

My heart pounds erratically in my chest as I pull out and step back from her. She's laid out on her kitchen counter, looking every bit the seductress she is, and I panic.

My need to take her in my arms and carry her to bed

so we can continue is almost all-consuming, but I know I can't. This woman isn't mine. She can't be mine. We're wrong on so many levels and spending this evening with my family is just a reminder of everything I don't want. Yet I can't help myself when it comes to Tabitha.

I intend on walking out without saying a word, but as I step back a warning falls from my lips which I fear gives too much away about how I'm feeling. There's no fucking way I'm sticking around to find out though. The faster I get away the better.

THE REST of the week is fucking torture, and it only gets worse Thursday night knowing that she's out at the reception desk and almost within touching distance. It would be so easy to go out there and take her, to tell her the things that have been running through my head the last two days that involve things I never, ever thought I'd think, let alone ever consider saying aloud. If it weren't for this bloody wedding, I'd have fucked off by now, not able to cope with everything that's building inside me. I'm going to blow at some point. The only question is when.

CHAPTER TWENTY-THREE

TABITHA

I KNEW I only had to put up with him for one night at work. I was fully aware he was spending from Friday lunchtime at the hotel for the rehearsal and family meal, but that didn't mean I wasn't a nervous wreck walking into the studio Thursday afternoon. I'd heard nothing from him, not that I was really expecting to. But the warning he gave before walking out of my flat is still on repeat in my head, and something kept telling me that he'd be back or get in touch. As it is, it's been radio silence. I hate to admit it, but it's driving me crazy. Every time I hear someone walk down the hallway outside my front door, my heart jumps into my chest thinking it's him. Every time there's a creak or a bang I assume it's him somehow letting himself in. But nothing. No contact, no visits.

I've no idea what to expect tonight. He's been so hard to predict this far, so who knows what side of Zach Abbot I'm going to get. I can only hope it's not the arsehole, although I can't help thinking that him being a knobhead will help convince my body that we don't need him.

As it turns out, I see him once all night. He appears from his room at some point towards the end of my shift to use the toilet, and that's the only time he emerges. Equally, I don't bother delivering him any food or drinks, assuming that if he wanted something he would ask.

I might hear the door open, but I don't need to. I can feel the second his eyes land on me. My skin burns and something beneath begins to tingle. He's not even in touching distance and it's like he has total control of my body.

I fight the pull, but eventually it gets too much and I'm forced to look up. Only, when I do look to where I know he is, he's moved and has his back to me as he walks away.

My stomach drops at not being able to look into his eyes and know how he's feeling. I need to know if this thing between us is driving him as insane as it is me.

My entire life I've wanted to stay as far away from guys like Zach as possible, but right now, he's consuming every moment of my life. It doesn't matter if it's day or night, he's there in my head, taunting me, teasing me, reminding me of just how electric we are together.

I let out a sigh as he disappears behind the door to the bathroom and drag myself to the kitchen so I'm not still sitting there when he comes out. I don't want him to think he's having any effect on me or that his cold shoulder isn't making me scheme up ways to get us alone just so I can get what my body's craving.

As frustrating as Thursday night is knowing that he's only the other side of the wall, it's got nothing on Friday night. The studio without him is just wrong. The second I step into the building it's like there's something missing. I know we might avoid each other on the best of days, but even still, his presence is here. But today the place just feels cold. It's not helped that it's also an unusually quiet night, so my hours drag. I end up pulling my sketchpad from my bag and mindlessly doodling when I find myself unable to focus on any meaningful task.

"Damn, Biff baby. I think you're sitting in the wrong room with skills like that." I slam my book closed at hearing Titch's voice behind me. I was so lost in my own head that I didn't hear or see him appear from his room.

"It's nothing," I wave off, pushing the book away from me and waking up the computer.

"That was not nothing. Let me look."

"Really, I was just messing about. I'm away with the fairies tonight, I can't seem to get my head on straight."

"Aw, you missing him already?"

"Um... what?" I splutter.

"Oh, come off it. You think I can't see that you want him as bad as he does you. I'm still trying to get to the bottom of if you've already bumped uglies. Zach won't tell me fuck all. But you... you seem much more... open. Up for a bit of gossip if you will," he says with a smirk as he rests his arse against the edge of the desk beside me. His eyes bore into mine as I look up at him.

"Haven't you got some work to do?"

"Yeah... detective work."

I can't help but chuckle when he wiggles his eyebrows at me.

"There's nothing to tell," I lie. "I hate him. He hates me. End of."

"Titch, stop giving the girl grief. You piss her off and she might cut all of us off the coffee deliveries like she has the boss," Spike says, walking through with a handful of mugs.

"Nah, man. She loves me too much to cut me off, right, Biff baby?"

"I wouldn't use those words exactly," I mutter as I smile at Spike in a way of a thanking him for rescuing me from Titch's incessant questions.

Thankfully, the phone starts ringing on the desk. I turn my back on both the guys and lift it to my ear.

"Good evening, Rebel Ink. How can I help?"

"Hey, Biff, it's Corey. Big Man in tonight?"

"Sorry, no. He's at his brothers' wedding."

"Damn, that come around already? Shit," he says. I've only spoken to Corey a few times but he seems like a decent guy. He must be if Zach trusts him enough to set him up a studio in LA of all places.

"Time flies when you're having fun," I mutter.

"He still giving you grief?"

"Um..." I pause, wondering if I'd given him an inkling in the past that we don't get on. "What makes you say that?"

"Shit, er... nothing. Listen, I've gotta go. Client just walked in. I'll try him again after the weekend. I'm sure he's in his element right now, I'd hate to interrupt." He laughs, proving that he knows Zach pretty well because I'd put money on him hating every minute of this weekend.

"Okay, no worries. If I can do anything to help, I'm here," I offer in case it's of any use.

"Cheers, Biff, but I think you've already got your hands full over there."

By the time I hang up, I'm alone again. Letting out a sigh, I drag my sketchbook back over and attempt to drown out the silence with the pen hitting the paper.

I BARELY GET a wink of sleep as I toss and turn, trying to imagine what tomorrow might bring. By the time I drag my arse out of bed at the crack of dawn to get to the salon, I've pretty much decided that I'm going to cancel on Christian. I know it's last minute and it's a dick move, but I'm not sure I can go through with it.

I pull on a pair of leggings and a jumper dress before leaving the flat. It's a cold morning, but the sky is a stunning clear blue and a smile creeps on to my lips knowing that Summer will wake up this morning to weather she could only dream of for her big day.

I'm the first at the salon—no surprise there, seeing as it's seven AM on a Saturday morning. I'm booked in for the full works so I look like I'm prepared for the day on the outside, even if my insides are a fucking mess.

"Coffee?" Alice, my hairdresser, asks the second I step through the door.

"Do you even need to ask?" She laughs as she heads out back to make me one.

I take a seat at the chair she's pulled out for me and let my hair down from the messy bun I shoved it in when I got up.

"So, all ready for the big day?" she asks, placing the mug on the shelf and running her fingers through my hair.

"Can I get your opinion on something?" I don't know why I ask, it's not like I want to talk about it... about him, but the words fall from my lips nonetheless.

"Shoot." I've known Alice for years. This was the first salon I walked into after the one my mum took me to all my life refused to do something as simple as put some highlights through my hair. Much to my mum's horror, I got up and walked out. I found this place not ten minutes later and Alice happened to have a free slot. The rest, as they say, is history. Although we've never spent any time together outside of this salon, I consider us to be friends, and seeing as she's not really involved in my life, per se, I consider her opinion to be impartial.

I explain all while she twists and twirls my hair. I sent her some images a few days ago but really, as long as it looks pretty and works with the fascinator I bought, I'm not all that bothered what she does. I trust her.

"So your best friend has no idea you're slamming her brother?"

I groan. "Do you need to say it so bluntly?"

"Just checking I've got all my facts straight," she says with an innocent smile that makes me roll my eyes.

"So do I cancel on my date?"

She blows out a breath and slides a few more grips into place. "I want to say yes because he's no idea what he's about to walk into and there's a good chance he doesn't deserve it, but man, Zach sounds like he needs to be taught a lesson, and turning up today with a hot date on your arm could be exactly what he needs."

"But he's also going to find out I've been lying. What the hell have I been thinking?" I drop my head into my hands, forcing Alice to release a lock of my hair. I should have just been honest with everyone in the first place. When all this is out in the open, I'm the only one who's potentially going to lose. Danni might never forgive me, and Zach, well, I know I probably shouldn't really be all that concerned about what he thinks, but I am.

"You had your reasons. Plus, if he's kept everything from his family like you say, then he'll probably only be grateful you didn't spill everything."

"Yeah, I guess."

"And Danni will understand that in a kinda fucked-up way you were protecting him."

I blow out a long breath and reach for my coffee, wishing it were something stronger.

By the time my hair is done and Alice and I have talked each other in circles, I get up and head to the beauty part of the salon to have my nails and make-up done.

I don't reveal my inner turmoil to the therapists who work their magic on me. I've met them both a few times, but we're not friendly enough for all that. Plus, after spending my entire hair appointment discussing it, I'm done. All I feel now is dread. Whether or not I take Christian seems almost a moot point right now. As long as I turn up, the shit's going to hit the fan and I've most definitely left it too late to back out now.

By the time I'm standing at my flat window, waiting for a car to pull up outside, I'm a nervous wreck. I nearly cancelled on Christian at least ten times on the journey back from the salon alone. But the thought of walking into that ceremony room with no one standing beside me terrifies me.

A silver Mercedes comes to a stop right out the front, and my stomach turns over.

Fuck. Fuck. Fuck.

I slide my palms down the soft fabric of my dress and attempt to calm my racing heart. Knowing that I need to get down there before I lock myself in the bathroom and never leave the flat again, I take a step back from the window, grab my clutch and the wedding gift that's sitting on my coffee table and my small overnight bag, and leave the flat on shaky legs.

"Whoa, Biff, you look... wow," Christian says when he meets me in the entrance to my building. His eyes run the length of me but even now, I don't get the tingles I probably should when he does it.

"You don't scrub up too bad yourself." I take a moment to appreciate him dressed to the nines in a sharp grey suit. No one would ever guess the bad boy stripper that's hiding beneath right now. A little excitement hits me that at least I'm going to be walking around this wedding knowing that the guy every single lady in the room will be eyeing up spends most of his weekends getting his kit off. I suddenly panic that some of the hens might recognise him, but when I lift my eyes to his once again and find his neatly styled hair, it settles. He looks like a different person. They were all way too drunk to notice.

"You ready?"

"Yes, let's do this." He holds the door open for me and I slide in before he joins me.

"Your hands are shaking."

"I'm... uh... just excited to see the bride," I lie.

Our drive to the hotel is mostly in silence, thank god. I'm grateful that Christian didn't try to spark up too much of a conversation, because I'm so bloody nervous right now that there's no way I'll be able to concentrate.

We end up getting stuck in some weekend roadwork traffic, and when the car finally pulls up in front of the hotel it seems that everyone's already made their way into the ceremony room.

I breathe a sigh of relief that I've got at least another hour before Zach spots me.

With Christian's hand resting in the small of my back, we make our way through the hotel and find ourselves seats toward the back of the room. Everyone around us talks amicably, the excitement in the room palpable as they wait for their bride.

Harrison looks out over the crowd, appearing as cool and calm as ever with his son by his side, but I wonder if that's how he's really feeling on the inside.

I run my eyes over the heads in front of us, searching out a certain blonde one. On the first pass, I don't see him and I start to wonder if he decided against a day of forced family time, but as I move my eyes back once again I find the bright tips of his hair. My spine stiffens and everything stops. My temperature starts to soar to the point that I wonder if I'm going to pass out as I just stare at the back of his head.

"Biff, are you okay? You're as white as a sheet."

Unable to drag my eyes away now I've found him, I mumble, "I'm good," to Christian and hope this thing gets started soon as a distraction.

"I know you said it was going to be a lavish affair, but this is beyond what I was imagining. How many guests have they got attending?"

"Um... like, two hundred now, and something crazy like five hundred this evening." Totally unnecessary if you ask me, seeing as they're already married, but each to their own.

"Whoa. I'm not sure I know that many people, let alone want them at my wedding," he whispers.

"Right? Not sure I'd be up for this, to be honest," I admit, although I'm sure it's exactly what my parents imagine when they think about my wedding day, if I ever have one.

"I thought all women wanted this?"

"Not on this scale."

I want to say more, but Zach turns in his seat and looks towards the back of the room. My breath catches in my throat that he's going to have felt me looking at him, that he knows I'm here. It's crazy, I know, but my irrational mind won't stop picturing him marching right up here and throwing me out in front of everyone.

But as I should expect, he never actually looks at me. Instead, he just winks at someone behind me and turns back around.

I'm desperate to see more of him, but all I get is his face in the crowd. I want to get a look at a suited and booted Zach before he realises I'm here. I've only ever met the bad boy, I want to experience this other side of him that he hates so much.

Before long, everyone has found themselves a seat and the music changes. Harrison turns so his back is to us, but the tension in his shoulders is obvious as he waits for his bride.

After an excruciating minute or two, the doors behind us open and in walks Summer's bridesmaids, Danni, her American cousin, and her soon-to-be stepdaughter, all dressed in stunning pink gowns.

All heads turn toward them before looking at the

door. A gasp fills the room the second Summer appears, but I don't turn to look. I keep my eyes on Harrison. He looks down at his feet as he attempts to keep it together and not turn around, but when Summer is halfway down the aisle, he loses his fight. His eyes find her immediately, and the love that oozes from them has tears burning my own. He watches her as if she's the only other person in the room. It's mesmerising to see, and just like every other single woman in the room, my yearning for that to happen to me only grows ever stronger. I want someone who looks at me like I'm his whole world, like I'm his reason for living.

An unsteady sigh passes my lips as I watch her final steps. I jolt like I've been shot when Christian's warm hand lands on my thigh.

He leans in and whispers, "You're a bit of a romantic, aren't you?"

"Who isn't when they witness that?" I whisper back, not taking my eyes from the couple at the front of the room.

For the whole ceremony I can't drag my eyes away from them. The little looks they give each other, the slightest of contact as they make their vows... it makes my heart ache. I'm so happy for them, but fuck, I can't deny the jealousy that's raging within me.

I forget all about where we are and what's probably going to happen very soon as they embark on the next part of their lives together.

It feels like no time when they're announcing the new Mr. and Mrs. Abbot, and cheers and congratulations erupt from the crowd and the ecstatic bride and groom make their way towards the back of the room.

"The bride and groom would like to invite you to join them for an aperitif in the great room."

Everyone starts moving in the direction the wedding party has all left in. The row we're sitting in empties yet I stay put, suddenly terrified of what comes next.

Danni winked at me as she walked out, so she knows I'm here. She's going to be waiting for me out there, I know it. But... but... fuck.

"Is everything okay?" Christian asks, also noticing that we're the only ones left sitting here.

"Yeah, yeah. Let's go and get a drink."

This whole thing was a mistake. Being here is a mistake. I should have made some excuse, claimed I got food poisoning from a dodgy take-out last night or something. Anything that would mean I'd be anywhere but here right now.

CHAPTER TWENTY-FOUR

ZACH

I'LL BE the first to admit that this is not how I enjoy spending my Saturdays, but I also can't deny that watching as my big brother said 'I do' to Summer didn't make me smile on the inside and stirred something in my chest. Is this something I want for myself? Absolutely not. I've only been on the periphery of this wedding planning that Mum's been so obsessed with over the past few months, but that's enough to know that I've not got the patience for any of it.

With the most important part of today over, I start to wonder how long I've got to stick around for before it'll be deemed acceptable for me to disappear to my room for a bit. I fucking hate small talk, and that is all that's going to be happening the second we step out of this room. I'll be hit with the same questions I get every fucking time we have a gathering. "Have you found a woman to straighten you out yet?" "When are you going to join the family business? I'm sure you'll be an asset somewhere." All of them just add fuel to the already smouldering fire that's in the pit of my stomach whenever I'm forced to spend time with these people. My parents might have at last realised that I'm a free spirit and do as I please no matter what they say, but it's about time everyone else did. They all learned long ago that I don't fit the Abbot mould. I don't conform to their ideals. What the fuck ever. I'm me, and they either like it or they fucking lump it, because I'm not changing for no fucker.

By the time everyone else has left the room, I'm damn near desperate for a drink, but that doesn't mean I accept the fancy looking cocktail a young waitress waves under my nose.

"I don't think so, sweetheart. Fancy getting me a whisky instead?" Her cheeks flush at my use of the word 'sweetheart', just like I'd hoped, and she goes rushing off, hopefully in the direction of the nearest bar. She's cute, and I can't help but stare at her arse in her skirt as she rushes away. Maybe she could make today better.

"You know, you could find it in you to at least look at little happy about today," Lana says, wrapping her hand around my arm as she settles into my side.

"I am." She lifts a perfectly sculpted brow at me. "Fine, how's this?" I give her a fake smile and she laughs.

"Yeah, you pull that smile in the photos and you're likely to be cut out."

"Suits me."

"Talking about suits, I'd forgotten how well you'd filled one out." The reminder of the last time she saw me in one is like someone throwing a bucket of ice cold water over me. "Shit, fuck. Forget I said anything." Her eyes fill with tears as similar thoughts fill her head.

"It's okay. Let's just get through this, and we can go and get shitfaced, eh?"

"Sounds like the perfect plan." She plucks one of the fancy drinks from a tray when another server passes. "You want one?"

"No, I've placed a special order. And here it comes right now." We both watch as the girl returns with a single glass of whisky sitting in the centre of her tray.

"The drink or the girl?"

"Both." I wink at her before turning towards the girl. "Thank you, you've no idea how badly I need this." I lift the glass to my lips, and as I expected she stands and watches as I swallow the amber liquid.

"A-Another?" she stutters, her cheeks still amusingly pink.

"Make it two, and we've got a deal."

"Will you leave her alone? She's too young for you."

"She's serving alcohol. She's old enough."

Lana tsks before turning her attention to the room. "We're getting fed soon, right?"

"Fuck knows. You think I was listening when they laid out the schedule?" I tug at my collar, totally uncomfortable in this bloody suit and already desperate to replace it with jeans and a t-shirt.

"You're useless. I only came because you promised me decent food," she teases.

My aunt and uncle wander over and ask me all the usual questions, I answer them as politely as possible, knowing that they'll be the first of many. Lana joins in where necessary, playing the part of my date perfectly, but the second I introduce her my aunt and uncle know exactly who she is.

They soon bid me farewell and head off to give someone else twenty questions.

"You know, you could have great fun making shit up. No one has a clue who you really are, so they'd probably believe anything at this point." I consider her suggestion, but I'm not really sure I have the energy for it, even though it would probably be a laugh to convince all these rich snobs that I was an astronaut or something equally as unbelievable. "The money that's in this room right now in clothes and jewellery is insane, you know that right?"

I mumble some kind of agreement. Lana knows how much I hate this scene, how uncomfortable I feel surrounded by it all. She doesn't need to remind me.

"Whoa, that dress is stunning. I wonder *who* it is." Rolling my eyes, a couple of my Mum and sister's favourite designers on the tip of my tongue, I follow Lana's stare.

The dress she's talking about is a simple navy slim dress with bright pink flowers around the waist. It's nothing amazing, I'm actually surprised that out of all the dresses here that it's the one she's picked out. I run my eyes over the woman's curves that the dress displays perfectly, and my cock stirs at the thought of having them beneath my hands as I make my way up her neck and to her... wait a fucking minute... pink hair. Pink?

My heart slams against my chest.

No, no, no. It can't be.

I take a step back, successfully backing into a waiter and sending his tray full of drinks crashing to the floor.

"Fuck," I bark, going to help him but being denied as another waiter comes over to assist.

"What's wrong?" Lana asks, following my stare and finding the woman in the dress once again. Only now she's staring right at me. "I recognise her." I barely register Lana's words because there's something exploding inside me. I try to remind myself of where I am and that the last thing I need to do right now is make even more of a scene, but as the fire blazes I'm afraid I've got no power over what comes next.

Her eyes are wide, like a rabbit caught in headlights, but there's not as much shock on her face as there should be, and that's when it dawns.

She's always known.

"Fuck."

Every muscle in my body screams at me to march over to her and drag her from the room so I can demand the answers I need, but when my legs move, they go in the opposite direction.

"Zach?" Lana calls, the clicking of her heels following my escape.

My steps don't falter until I've thrown open a set of double doors and raced down the steps into the garden.

"Zach? What the hell? Who is she?"

My chest heaves and I fight to drag in the breaths I need.

A bitter laugh falls from my lips. "I don't know," I admit. I thought I had her all figured out. The posh girl wanting to be a rebel. Well, I was right about one thing: she is the posh girl. I just had no idea she was somehow directly connected with the posh people I try to avoid at all costs.

I never should have fucking touched her.

My fists clench as memories of my time with her slam into me. Even now, when I can barely see through the red haze of anger that's descended around me, I can't forget how fucking electric we are together.

But why is she here? How does she know your family?

Summer's a student. So is Tabitha. I tell myself that that is it. She's friends with Summer and had no idea I was connected to her. This is just a coincidence. *Only, it's not.* I remember the look in her eyes as she stared at me. She was expecting me. That look in her eyes wasn't shock. It was fear. Fear because I'd just figured her out.

"Zach, where the hell are you going?" Lana shouts as I storm back toward the hotel. Scene or not, I need to hear the truth from her lips before I put an end to anything that might have been between us for good. I ignore her repeated question as I push back through the doors and find the room exactly as it was before my world imploded.

I search for her in the crowd but come up short. My nails dig into my palms with my need to hear her beg for reprieve when I get my fucking hands on her. My teeth grind with my need to hurt her.

A man clears his throat at the other side of the room, earning him all the attention. "The bride and groom would like the wedding party to join them outside for photos."

"Come on, arsewipe. Let's go," Danni says, suddenly appearing at my side and linking her arms through mine.

I allow her to drag me from the room because I'm not sure what else to do right at this very moment.

We're almost outside when I spot her. She's at reception, taking a room key from the member of staff behind the desk.

She's staying the night. Good. That means she's got nowhere to run.

CHAPTER TWENTY-FIVE

TABITHA

MY STOMACH TURNS over the second our eyes connect. Anger radiates from him the second he realises it's me.

"Shit."

"Oh, it's Zach," Christian says, shocking the fuck out of me. Dragging my eyes away from Zach, I look over at my date. It's all the excuse he needs, because the next time I look up he's practically running from the room.

"You... you know him?"

"Yeah, he does my ink."

"Oh, fucking hell. This isn't fucking happening."

"What's wrong?"

"I... I need to go and get some air. Can you—"

"I can come. You look like you're about to be sick."

"I might," I admit, "but please, just stay here and please don't tell anyone you know Zach and certainly don't mention what he does for a living." Christian's brows pull together in confusion, but I don't have it in me right now to explain. "I... I just need a minute. Get me a white wine, yeah?"

He nods as I turn and run from the room as fast as my heels will allow.

"Fuck." My back hits the wall of the hallway when I stop to take a breath. I've no idea how I wanted today to play out, but that certainly wasn't it. "Jesus, fuck, fuck," I whisper to myself, trying to stop my head from spinning.

Seeing the hotel's reception in the distance, I push from the wall and head over to try my luck.

"Good afternoon. How can I help you?"

"I've got a room booked for tonight. I know it's still a little early for check in, but I just wondered if—"

"What was the name?"

"Tabitha Anderson." The guy clicks about on his computer a little before a smile pulls at his lips.

"You're in luck, it seems your room is all ready."

I'm not sure luck is a word I use to describe any part of today but if it means I get my room and somewhere to hide then I'll take it.

He hands me a key card after a few seconds and gives me directions. "Room five-one-four. Take the lift to the fifth floor and your room is down the corridor and to the left. Please call if you need anything. Have a wonderful stay."

I can't take it from his hand fast enough. In the blink of an eye I'm in the lift and heading for the peace of my room to attempt to get my head on straight.

It takes me three attempts to get the door to open. I'm

on the verge of tears by the time the little green light flashes with frustration.

I push inside, drop my clutch on the side and fall down onto the end of my bed. I don't notice anything about the room aside from the fact it's got a bed.

This was such a fucking stupid thing to do. I never should have come. Seeing the fire in his eyes even from that distance was enough to know how badly I've fucked all this up.

I can't be sitting there more than two minutes when there's a knock at my door.

How the fuck has he found me already?

I shake my hands out at my sides as I stand in an attempt to lose some of the tension pulling at my body, but it does little to help.

The door's knocked again, and despite not wanting to allow whoever it is to know I'm inside, my own voice betrays me. "Just give me a minute."

Glancing at myself in the mirror, I wipe at the smudged make-up under my eyes and drag in a breath that I hope is full of confidence.

I walk towards the door, my legs so unsteady I would think I'd had a skinful, not just a sip of whatever that drink was they were handing out downstairs.

Putting my eye to the peep hole, I almost sigh with relief.

Pulling the door open, my eyes land on what's in his hand. A very large glass of white wine.

"Come in." Christian hands it to me before following me inside. "How'd you find me?"

"I followed you out to reception to make sure you were okay. I overheard your room number."

"I can't really complain," I say, lifting the glass and taking a less-than-lady-like mouthful.

"What's going on, Biff?"

I blow out a breath and try to figure out where to start.

"I work at Rebel Ink. I'm the new receptionist."

"Oh?"

"None of Zach's family knows what he does. He's kept Rebel a secret from them all."

"Why?"

"I don't know for sure. He doesn't know that I know, and he wasn't expecting me here today. His sister is actually my best friend and—"

"And you've been sleeping with him."

I drop my head into my hands. "This is such a fucking mess."

"You've got that right. So you invited me here to what, exactly? Make him jealous?"

"No," I say truthfully. "I just needed someone beside me when the shit hit the fan, and I'm sorry it's you. I had no idea you knew each other. I never would have—"

"It's okay," he says, taking my hand in his. "I believe you."

"I doubt Zach and Danni will be so forgiving."

"Wow. Okay, so correct me if I've got any of this wrong. Your best friend, Zach's sister, has no idea you're sleeping with him. Zach also has no idea, and his whole family don't know he tattoos?"

"Something like that. I knew Zach from school, but he doesn't remember me. I didn't know he owned Rebel when I went for an interview. But then he turned up and I'd heard so much about him from Danni so I just played along and kept his secret. Nothing was meant to happen between us. We hate each other." He raises a brow. "No, really. And after this, he's really going to hate me. Danni too."

"So what now? You can't exactly hide up here for the rest of the wedding."

"Can't I?" I ask hopefully, and he laughs.

"You need to talk to both of them before things get out of hand."

"And what about you?"

"What about me? I'm here as your date, and it seemed that Zach was also here with one, if the leggy brunette beside him was anything to go by."

My stomach turns again at the thought of Zach bringing a date.

"I don't want to ruin Summer's day."

"Well maybe don't do it in the middle of the wedding breakfast then, eh?"

I laugh, and it feels good after what my day's been like. "Thank you."

"I like you, Biff," Christian admits, looking down at his feet. "You're... different. A breath of fresh air. But I can settle for friends." My chest aches as he looks back up at me, still a little hope shining in his eyes.

"You can leave if you want. I'm so sorry for dragging you into all this."

"Hey, you said free booze and fancy food. I'm going nowhere until those two promises are fulfilled."

"Okay." I stand and square my shoulders. "Let's do this then," I say with much more enthusiasm than I feel. I drain the last of my wine and slam it down on the dresser.

I'm Tabitha Anderson the woman. I no longer hide away from guys like Zach fucking Abbot.

With my head held high and my arm linked through Christian's, we head back down to the wedding together.

All the while my stomach's in knots and my heart's damn near beating out of my chest.

Thankfully the wedding party still seems to be absent when we walk back into the room.

"Bar?" Christian asks.

"I thought you'd never ask."

He orders us both a drink while my eyes scan the room, waiting for the moment they all start reappearing.

Eventually, I start to relax a little. Hopefully that'll only continue as the wine settles into my system. I'm lost in a conversation with Christian when a shiver runs down my back.

"Fuck. He's just walked in, hasn't he?"

Christian looks over my shoulder. I don't need to hear his answer—his face says it all.

"He's—" He doesn't get any more words out before warm fingers wrap around my wrist and I'm none too gently pulled from my spot.

"Let's go," Zach growls in my ear before forcing me out of the room.

He pulls me to a stop and pushes me up against the wall. His eyes are wild with his fury as he stares at me, his chest heaving and his breaths racing over my face. His hand rests against the wall beside my head. He might be on the edge of losing control, but I can't help noticing just how hot he looks in his fancy suit. It fits him like a second skin and makes him look like the posh boy that he really is deep down. That doesn't mean that his eyes and jaw line don't scream rebel. I see more than what he's willing to give, and I think that could be one of the reasons he hates me so much.

"I'm fucking waiting."

"Bus stop's outside, *boss*," I sass. His hand slaps against the wall and I flinch in shock.

"Why the fuck are you here?"

"Because I was invited." I know I should just explain everything, but there's something about him that makes my defiant streak undeniable.

"Stop being a smart arse. Who are you?"

I open my mouth to tell him the truth, but another voice sounds out around us. Zach has no choice but to move away from me, but his eyes still hold mine. The hatred in them makes my insides quiver, but it's not an unwelcome or scared feeling. Very much the opposite.

"What's going on here?"

"Nothing," Zach barks, still refusing to look at his sister.

"O-Okay. Zach, this is Tabitha, my best friend." His chin drops as a missing piece of this puzzle falls into place. "Although it seems you must remember her."

"Remember her?" It's only now that he turns to Danni. "From where?"

"School, you idiot. Tabitha was in your year."

He rears back like she's just slapped him. "Right, yeah. School."

Danni waves him off. "See, I told you he's not really changed."

"You got that right. Once an arsehole always an arsehole." Danni's eyes widen at my bluntness, but she laughs in amusement. Zach mostly looks impressed by my lack of filter.

"Come on, I need a drink," Danni complains.

"I've actually already got one. It's with my date." Zach bristles at my statement.

"Okay, well let's go drink it then."

"No," Zach barks. "I need to talk to Tabitha."

"Right, fine," she fumes before storming off.

"Tabitha Anderson," he says, as if saying it will help summon up some long-lost memory. "Nope, can't say I remember you."

"That's not a surprise. I was one of the girls that guys like you didn't even think were in the room."

"Guys like me?" His lips press into a thin line as he steps closer once again. His scent fills my nose and makes my brain misfire.

"Yeah, self-proclaimed god's gift to women. Arrogant, pig-headed arseholes who got whatever it was they wanted."

I expect him to be angry at my description of his younger self, but instead he just smiles.

"Whoa, now I get it." He lifts his hand and takes my chin between his thumb and finger. "You wanted me and I saw straight through you."

"Ha. You wish. No, I hated you then and I hate you now."

His eyes narrow. "The feeling's fucking mutual, Kitten." He releases me and takes a huge step away. "Watch your fucking back, Tabby Cat." And with that he's gone, leaving me wondering what the fuck just happened. He vanishes in the opposite direction that his sister went, and when I look down the corridor, I see a flash of pink that could only have belonged to her.

"Fuck."

CHAPTER TWENTY-SIX

ZACH

BLOOD RACES PAST MY EARS, successfully cutting anything else off. I've no fucking clue if anyone calls for me as I storm through the room where everyone's gathered. My only focus is getting away from her and removing any thoughts of her from my head. What I want to do is wrap my hand around her fucking neck while I fuck my frustration out on her. The temptation to drag her to some unused room in this hotel and do just that only moments ago was so strong that it almost happened. Had it not been for my sister's interruption then I might have.

She's my sister's best friend. I went to school with her. How do I not know any of this?

I fall down onto a bench that's sitting in the shadows

and rest my head back against the wall of the hotel as I try to catch my breath.

I didn't want to be here today, but I never could have imagined this.

I should remember her.

I rack my brain for any hint of a memory of Tabitha from all my years at school, but I have nothing. Absolutely nothing. The fact that I can't remember only adds to the anger that's just about to bubble over. I can't lose my shit, not today.

I focus on my breathing, but nothing helps. Nothing but ploughing into her fucking body is going to help right now.

She's got a date.

"Fuck," I shout into the silence around me.

I rest my elbows on my knees and hang my head.

The sound of footsteps approaching should make me look up, but when I see the colour of the shoes, I don't bother because I know what's coming.

"You've been fucking my best mate."

"Apparently so." There's no point denying it. I knew she was watching our interaction. She'll have seen the spark that seems to always be between us, even when I want to fucking kill her with my own bare hands.

"You know, if you actually bothered with your family, like ever, then you might have a clue who we're all friends with and know who to steer clear of."

"I don't need a fucking lecture, Dan."

"No? Well you're getting one."

She doesn't bother sitting with me. Instead she stands with her hands on her hips as she rants about my life choices. Choices she only assumes because she doesn't actually know anything about my life.

It dawns on me that Tabitha could have told her everything about me, about my life, my business, about everything, yet she hasn't. Why? She says she hates me, so wouldn't the perfect revenge be to tell all my secrets to those I keep them from? She could have sold me out to Danni in a heartbeat, but she hasn't.

"I haven't got time for this." I push from the seat and take a step away from her.

"You fucking hurt her and I'll kill you."

Spinning on my heels, I pin her with a look that would make most people cower, but not my feisty little sister. "She's been lying to you this whole time, Dan. Maybe it should be her you're ripping into right now."

"Oh, don't worry. She's firmly on my shit list."

I walk off before Danni has the chance to say any more. I need a fucking drink.

Ignoring everyone, I march straight up to the bar and order myself two whiskys.

"Two at once. You must be really enjoying yourself," Lana laughs, hopping up onto a vacant stool next to me.

"You have no fucking idea."

"Try me."

"I've been..." I try to come up with the right term to use to describe what Tabitha and I have been doing, but it eludes me.

"Fucking?" she helpfully adds when I say no more.

"Something like that. Well... she's here, and it turns out she's friends with my sister."

"Oh. That's... interesting. So, this fuck buddy—" I cringe at her use of that term. There's most definitely nothing serious between Tabitha and me, but why does hearing those words just feel wrong? "She know who you really are?"

HATE YOU

"She my receptionist," I mutter into my glass.

"Shut the fuck up. The one with the pink hair?"

"Yeah, how'd you—"

"I left something at your flat the last time I was there. You were elsewhere when I came back for it so she let me up. Let me tell you, she was jealous as fuck that I'd spent the previous night up there with you." A wicked smile curls at Lana's lips.

"What did you do, Lan?"

"I might have mentioned something about the pack of condoms that were sitting on the side to make her think we'd been, you know." She waves her hand about instead of saying the words, but I hear them loud and clear. My lip curls at the thought "You don't need to look so offended. I'll have you know that I'm an awesome lay."

"I don't need to hear shit like that. You're practically my sister." She shrugs and orders herself a drink when the barman stops in front of us.

"And another two for him. I think he needs it."

Lana and I had never really had anything to do with each other in all the years I'd been around her family, with her being three years younger we were always interested in different things. Then after Jon died, we became close. Never that kind of close, though. We both leaned on each other as we got through our grief. We've been pretty solid ever since despite our differences. He brought us together, and I'll forever be grateful because she's been a great friend to me.

"So... let's summarise. You're fucking your receptionist, who also happens to be your sister's bestie, and she's here today."

"She was also in my year at school and I had no idea. And I hate her."

"You hate her. She's got you this twisted up because you hate her."

"The fact that she's here and was even invited should tell you that she's not exactly my type."

"Zach," she breathes. "I know you don't want to be in this world, but I've got news for you, buddy. Your last name means that it's where you belong whether you like it or not. Have you ever considered that she might feel the same? She's working in your studio, for fuck's sake. She might want to rebel from all this just like you do. She might actually be your perfect woman."

"Shut the fuck up, Lana."

I lift my new glass to my lips as an accomplished smile spreads across hers.

"So where is she?" Lana asks, spinning so she can take in the room.

"There," I mutter, tilting my head in her direction without even looking up from the wooden bar top in front of me.

"Ah yes." She's silent as she watches, I assume Tabitha, for a few minutes. "So, how do you want to play this?"

I consider her question for a few minutes, but I don't get a chance to come up with an answer because my parents come over.

I don't hear a word of what they ask Lana. Instead I scan the crowd. I don't want to know where she is, not really, but the temptation to look at her is too strong to ignore.

I find her immediately over Dad's shoulder. She looks perfectly put together as she laughs at something someone says before taking a sip of her drink while I'm over here feeling like I'm about to erupt at any moment.

The second my dad moves slightly, that moment seems to happen.

"What the fuck?" All the conversations stop around me as I take in the man she's standing with. *Fucking Christian.*

I push from the bar stool I'm leaning up against, sending it crashing to the floor. All eyes are on me as I storm across the room.

My fingers wrap around her upper arm and I twist her until she has no choice but to face me.

"He's your fucking date? What the fuck are you playing at? Do you find this fucking funny? Was this your plan all along?"

"What? Zach, no. I had no idea that—"

"If you would all like to begin making your way to the grand room, the wedding breakfast will be served shortly," someone behind me says, cutting off whatever Tabitha's pathetic excuse was about to me.

"Zach, come on. Everyone's looking. Deal with this later," Lana whispers in my ear. She wraps her arm around my waist and tries to move me.

"You," Tabitha says, locking eyes on Lana.

"Nice to meet you again," Lana says politely to Tabitha who looks about ready to throttle her. "Zach, move now."

She none too gently tries to drag me in the other direction. When I eventually pull my eyes from Tabitha's stormy grey ones, I notice that everyone else is also heading that way. Well, those of them who aren't staring at us.

"This isn't over." I pin her with a look before allowing Lana to pull me away. I spot Danni standing in the corner of the room, doing her bridesmaid duty and encouraging everyone to move in the right direction.

"You need to get through today and then you can cause whatever kind of scene you wish. Do not ruin today for Harrison or your parents, please," Lana begs as we move through the huge room to find our table.

I keep my head down and refuse to look back to see if they're following us.

Of all people, she's here with fucking Christian. Crazy thoughts fill my head. *"Have they been seeing each other since the night at Pulse? Are they a couple?* Then comes the even worse one. *"What does this mean for us?"* I shake that final one from my head, because it really doesn't need to be there. It doesn't mean anything for us because there is no us.

CHAPTER TWENTY-SEVEN

TABITHA

"I CAN'T DO THIS," I say, my chest heaving as I watch Zach and his date's backs as they walk away from us. "I can't be here. Not with him, and certainly not with her."

"It's okay," Christian says, placing a comforting hand on my shoulder.

"No, it's not. Me being here right now is ruining everything. I should leave."

"And have Summer notice two empty seats at her wedding breakfast? She's more likely to notice that than a little animosity between you and her new brother-in-law."

"A little?"

"Okay, so a lot. Just take a moment, breathe, and then get your arse in there and celebrate your friend's wedding like you should be. Put everything else aside for a few hours. You've got plenty of time to deal with all of that later."

I nod, knowing that he's right but not really wanting to accept it.

Sucking in a deep breath, I pray it'll give me some strength and I take a step towards the room. We're almost the only ones left in here now, so when a pink dress appears in my periphery, I know there's only one person it can belong to.

"Danni, I—"

"Don't," she barks, and I still at the harshness in her tone. I've always known it's been there, but I've never been on the receiving end of it and fuck, if it doesn't sting. It's the least of what I deserve though.

A huge ball climbs up my throat, and I have to really fight to stop the tears that want to so desperately escape from filling my eyes.

I allow Christian to escort me into the room, and we quickly find our seats. It's not hard seeing as almost all the others are taken. And just because karma wants to fuck with me today, obviously I'm sitting so Zach is right in my eyeline.

My eyes lock on to him the second I look up. He looks breath-taking with his sharp suit, his cleanly shaved face and his now messed-up hair. It was perfectly styled when I first saw him only a couple of hours ago but now, thanks to me, it looks like he's run his hands through it a million times in the last ten minutes alone.

Like he can feel my stare, he drags his focus away from the man across the table he's talking to and looks directly at me. The coldness in his eyes is like a spear through my heart.

"I'm sorry," I mouth, hoping it will help even just a tiny bit.

He shakes his head and turns away. I'm so close to sitting there and sobbing as a guy with a microphone announces the arrival of Mr and Mrs Abbot and everyone around me stands and starts clapping. I join in, but I hardly see the happy couple through the tears filling my eyes.

How did I make such a mess of all this? All I was trying to do was follow Gran's advice and find a life of my own. All I seem to have achieved is to ruin the lives of those I love. I gasp. Love? No. I hate him. Hate. Him.

The meal is probably the best one of my life but equally the worst. The food is out of this world, and even better than I sold to Christian apparently, but I struggle to eat and then really taste any of it. All I want to do is run, yet I'm forced to sit surrounded by people I don't know and talk about my parents because although I may not know these people, it seems they all know who I am and are keen for me to remember them to my parents. Like that's going to happen. I get question after question thrown at me about when I'm going to join the family business and continue the empire that's been built for me. I make all the right noises about wanting to get some life experience first and all that kind of bullshit, anything but tell the truth which is that I'm going nowhere near it, even with a bargepole.

By the time the coffees are served I feel like I could go up to my room and sleep for a week. It's definitely preferable to spending the rest of the day with this fake arse smile on my face.

Not once through the entire meal did Zach so much lift his head to look at me. His date, however... she was lapping that shit up. It was almost like she was trying to figure me out. I've no idea if she's just his usual go-to girl or if there's more there. Fuck, my chest aches at just the thought of him seeing someone else.

"I need to have a few minutes to myself. I totally understand if you want to leave. Actually, I think you probably should."

Christian's eyes flick around my face as he tries to decide what he should do.

"You do what you need to do, I'll be here when you get back."

"Christian, I—" It's that moment that I notice he's not really looking at me but at someone over my shoulder. Following his line of sight, I find a woman that I don't recognise staring back. "Oh, I see. Well, I guess one of us should at least get laid tonight." A bitter laugh falls from my lips and Christian's eyes come back to me.

"Shit, if you don't want—"

"No, you go and have fun. It's what should happen at these things, right?"

"You sure you're okay?"

"I will be." Leaning in, I place a quick kiss to his cheek and stand. "Go get 'em, hot shot." With a wink, I walk away from the table and thankfully through the crowds of people who are also leaving the room in favour of the bar without being interrupted. I have no clue where Zach is. He disappeared the second he thought it was acceptable. Danni has been busy with her duties but I've no doubt she'll find me the second she gets a chance.

The moment I close my hotel room door behind me, I rest my back on it and blow out a very long breath.

I stay there for the longest time, running the events of today over and over in my mind. It doesn't help. I still feel like a fucking idiot for putting us all in this fucked-up situation.

I'm lost in my own head when there's a loud click behind me and then someone's trying to push the door open.

I jump forward to allow whoever it is to enter.

"Can I hel—" My words falter when I see who it is.

Danni steps inside the room and closes the door.

It's not until she takes a step towards me that she looks up. Her eyes, like mine, are full of unshed tears.

"Danni, I'm so—"

"Don't," she barks, holding up her hand to ensure I seal my lips. "How long? How long have you been lying to me for? And don't even think about doing it again."

"Just a couple of weeks," I whisper, ashamed that I've lied to her at all.

"Just? So you think that *just* because it's a short amount of time it's okay? When were you planning on telling me exactly?" I open my mouth to respond, but she must be able to read something in my expression. "Wait. You were going to tell me, right?"

"It's... it's more complicated than that, Dan."

"How is it complicated exactly? All you had to do was tell me you'd met him. Tell me you liked him. But no, you went behind my back when you know full well that I'd have supported you no matter what. Because I would, you know. If you'd have come to me and explained you liked him then I'd have said good luck, see if you can tame the fucker. But no. You decided to lie, time and time again if the connection between the two of you is anything to go by."

"That's just it, though. I don't like him. I fucking hate him."

She rears back like I've just slapped her. "But—"

"It's complicated. But I need you to know that he's not been lying to you. He had no idea who I was. Until you pointed it out downstairs, he had no idea we went to school together."

"Right, okay." I sit down on the edge of my bed while she paces back and forth, trying to make sense of all this. "So where did you meet him?"

"You really need to be talking to him about this, not me."

"No, Tabitha." My jaw drops at her use of my full name. "I'm asking you. I'm standing here asking for my best friend to be honest with me."

"I know, and I get it. But there are things that aren't for me to explain. Zach is..." I trail off, trying to think of the correct way to describe him.

"Zach is..." she prompts.

"Complicated."

"Yeah, you said that word already. Twice in fact. I understand you think it's complicated, but I'm asking for you to break it down for me. I don't understand what's so important that you'd keep it from me."

"You know Zach's secretive about what he does."

"So he's made you keep his secret."

"No, he had no idea I could— ugh... none of that matters right now. I'll tell you everything you want to know, but you've got to speak to him first." It physically pains me to do this, and the look on Danni's face damn near breaks my heart. I know my loyalty should be with her and that I should spill all Zach's secrets in a heartbeat after everything, but I can't. Some weird little fucked-up part of me still feels the need to protect his secret.

She stops pacing and comes to a stop in front of me. "You're fucking serious, aren't you?" I nod. "Why the fuck are you protecting him after the way he treated you downstairs?" The tears that were pooling in my eyes spill over at last.

"Because they're his secrets to tell, not mine."

"Even to me?" The pain in her voice is palpable as her own tears drop.

"I'm sorry. I'm so sorry," I sob.

She opens her mouth to say something but decides against it. She takes two steps back towards my door. "Fuck you, Biff. I hope he was fucking worth it."

A sob rips from my throat at the same moment she pulls the door open and runs through it.

Falling back on the bed, I take the lid off everything I've been holding inside today.

WHEN I EVENTUALLY DRAG MY exhausted arse from the bed, both my hair and makeup need a total redo. Finding my phone at the bottom of my bag, I shoot a quick message to Christian to make sure he's still okay. It takes a few minutes but eventually I get a reply that's a huge smiley face. Well, at least one of us is having a good day.

After rummaging through my overnight bag, I remove all my make up and start again, followed by my hair. Neither are as sophisticated as when I first arrived, but it'll have to do.

When I wrap my fingers around the door handle, I don't feel even the slightest bit prepared for what tonight might hold. I desperately want to stay hidden up here, but if by any chance Summer does look for me then I'll never forgive myself.

The party is in full swing by the time I get to the great room once more. All the tables from this afternoon have been cleared out and there's now a dancefloor in front of a massive DJ set up with loads of lights and gigantic speakers.

The lights have been dimmed slightly so it takes a second for me to spot Christian, but when I do I find him sitting alone.

"Hey, how's it going?"

"It's good. She'd had to go off to mingle."

"Who is she?"

"Friend of the family, I think."

"You think? What the hell have you been talking about all this time?"

"She's a dancer."

"One that keeps their clothes on or..."

"You're funny. How are you feeling?"

"Like I've been hit by a truck. Never been better."

"Wine?"

"Please."

I watch as he gets up and walks to the bar. I look around the room once more but I see neither Danni nor Zach and my heart drops.

CHAPTER TWENTY-EIGHT

ZACH

"SHE TOLD me to speak to you. So here I am. What the fuck am I missing here, Zach?"

"Not here," I say, dragging my sister out of earshot of other guests.

"Well?" she prompts once we're alone.

"Now isn't the place or the time to dive into my life. If you really cared you'd have asked before now," I snap.

"Now, that's not fair. I always ask what you've been up to. I'm curious as fuck as to what you do with your time. Aside from banging my best friend it seems and making her keep your secrets."

"Yeah, well they're my secrets. Just like she'd keep any of yours from me. She's fucking loyal, thank fuck."

"What the hell is that meant to mean?"

"Nothing. Look, I'll tell you whatever you want." Her eyes light up. "But not today. Let's just do what we've got to do today then you can interrogate me tomorrow."

"Really?"

"Really," I agree with a sigh. "Now can you drop it?"

"Sure," she sulks. "I'm still pissed at you, though."

"When aren't you?"

She slaps me in the chest before I turn to walk away. I almost immediately find the happy couple and Harrison pulls me in for a brotherly hug, not something that happens all that often.

"Congrats, you two. Has it been everything you hoped it would be?"

"Better," Summer swoons before she's distracted by my sister.

"What the fuck is going on?" Harrison asks, his tone brisk and cool, much like I imagine him to be at work.

"It's nothing."

"It better bloody not be, because if you ruin any part of—"

"Chill. It's not going to happen. I've got it under control."

"When have you ever had anything under control before?"

"I'm more capable than you want to believe," I say, hoping like fuck it's true.

The second I saw Christian sitting with the daughter of my parents' friends not so long ago instead of his *date*, I almost lost my shit. Fuck knows why I care, though. He can do whatever the fuck he wants, and if it hurts Tabitha, all the better.

Leaving Harrison with his new bride, I walk towards

the bar. It's been at least thirty minutes since some alcohol passed my lips.

"Well, well, well, look who it is," I say, sliding in next to Christian.

"Zach, man. I had no idea this was your brother's wedding, I swear to you." I look at him and raise a brow. "Or that you and Biff have a—"

"Have a what?" I interrupt, suddenly desperate to hear what she's told him about this whole clusterfuck.

"A... uh... thing going on."

"There's no thing. I fucked her a couple of times, that's all. Really, I can't fucking stand her. It's a good fucking job she's a stellar lay because I wouldn't keep her around otherwise." I don't see his fist coming until it's too late.

"Ow fuck." My hand comes up to my lip, and it starts swelling almost instantly. "You fucking..." I fly at him, but hands landing on my waist from behind stop me.

"What the fuck did you just promise me, bro?" Harrison growls in my ear. "Sort your shit out or fucking leave."

I take a deep breath, holding eye contact with Christian, letting him know that he'd be on the floor by now if I had my way.

"We good?" Harrison asks and hesitantly releases me.

"Whisky. Make it very large," I bark at the waiter when he appears from nowhere in front of me.

"Coming right up, Sir."

I can feel Christian staring daggers into me, but I refuse to look at him until I've had a drink. I'm too sober to deal with this shit right now.

"I had no idea she even worked for you until today. She wasn't in last weekend."

"No, she was too busy at Summer's hen do it seems. I should have put two and two together that night. But you said there were like, four hen dos, so I just didn't think."

"Why would you? Did you see her there?" he asks with a wince.

"You mean, did I see you gyrating your naked arse in her face? Then yeah, I fucking did."

"Sorry, man. It's just my job."

"Really? Because it seems it got you an invite here."

"I met her before that night, actually. That night just gave me the chance to ask her out again."

"It was you she was with Tuesday night." I don't ask it as a question. I already know the answer. "It couldn't have been a very good date."

"What makes you say that?"

I down my drink and lean over. "Because she ended the night with *my* cock inside her." If he looks shocked, he doesn't show it. It doesn't mean I still don't look smug as shit, though.

I push my glass towards the barman, gesturing for another, and stand.

"You don't stand a chance with her, so if you feel like continuing things, then I strongly suggest you stop. You won't win."

"And you will?"

"Nah. I don't want her." Even before the words have left my lips they feel like a lie, but it still doesn't stop me, and it won't stop me showing her just how angry I am with what she's done either. "But I sure as shit don't want you having her."

With that, I pick up my new drink and walk away. Sadly, the second I do, she walks into the room.

She's fucking beautiful, and I hate that I've come to

know her well enough to know she's on the verge of breaking down. She clearly stood up for me with Danni, seeing as she's since come to me for the answers she wants. But even knowing both of those things, as our stare holds, my blue to her tormented grey, I can't help but need to show her exactly how angry I am with her.

Her eyes drop to my lip and concern flickers through them, but it's not enough to make her ask about it.

My grip on the glass tightens, and my cock swells with the need to drive into her hard and fast. To feel her body trembling beneath mine.

My jaw grinds and the muscle in my neck pulses with every thump of my heart. I hope she can see how close to the fucking edge I am right now.

"Come on, let's dance," a familiar deep voice says behind me before Tabitha lifts her hand and slips it into Christian's. The fucker has the audacity to wink at me before he pulls what is mine to the dancefloor.

I tell myself to walk away, to find a dark corner where I can hide and get shitfaced, but my legs don't comply and I'm forced to stand and watch as he pulls her body into his and together they start moving to the music.

If he's trying to get a rise out of me, then he's going to be bitterly disappointed. I have every intention of showing Tabitha who she belongs to, but I also have every intention of doing it when we're in private, where she has no one to come to her rescue.

I'm eventually distracted when some fucker I don't recognise calls my name and starts gushing about what a beautiful day it's been and asking when it's my turn.

I just about manage to hold in the 'fuck off' that's right on the tip of my tongue.

No sooner has whoever the fuck he is disappears than

another couple turns to me. They give me the 'wow, haven't you grown' speech that I really don't fucking need. Apparently, the last time they saw me I was seven, seeing as they couldn't come to Harrison's first wedding. I manage to refrain from pointing out that seeing as twenty years have passed since then, it shouldn't be a fucking shock that I've grown.

As the night passes, so do the people who insist on sparking up a conversation with me. I start to think it's a game. They must be able to see that I'm balancing the fine line between sanity and losing my shit, but still they insist on asking me the same bullshit questions again and again.

The only good thing about the many nosey visitors I get is that they pay attention to what I'm drinking and almost always arrive with a glass. It does help with my quest to drink today out of my system.

There's a break in people as Harrison and Summer take to the dancefloor for their first dance and I take the opportunity to visit the empty bar and convince the guy to just give me the fucking bottle.

I forgo the clean glass he tries to give me and take the bottle outside. I am done with this.

The loud bass of the music soon starts thumping through the wall, making me even surer that I made the right decision to escape. I see a couple of others who venture out to smoke, but mostly they're guys wanting a little peace as well so no one really says much as I continue drinking from my bottle.

When I eventually head back inside, the bottle is long empty, my legs are a little unsteady, and it seems that the party has come to an end. There's a whispered little voice in the back of my head that tells me I'll be in the shit with my parents for bunking off the rest of the party and not saying goodbye to everyone, but why would anyone care? It's not my fucking wedding.

Spotting my sister propping up the bar, I head over.

"Where is she?" I slur, slamming my hand down on the bar and making her jump.

She looks over, her eyes running down the length of me. "Fucking hell, Zach. You're wasted."

"I think I have every right to be after what that bitch has done." Danni's chest puffs out as if she's about to defend her, but at the last minute she must remember all the lies and keeps her mouth shut.

"I'm not telling you."

"What the fuck is wrong with you? She fucking lied to you."

"That doesn't mean I'm going to feed her to you, arsehole."

"What will it cost me?" Her brows draw together in confusion before the penny drops. Now the thought of being inside her hotel room and being able to get my hands on her has filled my mind, I won't stop until it's happening.

She considers my question for a few seconds. "Tell me where you met her."

"She works for me. She came to me for a job and one of my dumb arse colleagues thought it was a good idea."

"She works for you? What the fuck, Zach?"

"Surprise, Pipsqueak. I'm not just a fucking dumb arse who pisses his trust fund up the wall. I'm a fucking businessman, and a fucking good one at that. Now tell me where the fuck she is."

Danni looks at me as if she's suddenly seeing an entirely different person. "You... you have employees?"

"Where the fuck is she?" I ask again, ignoring her question.

"R-room five-one-four." I turn, but her voice stops me.

"I might not like her very much right now, but my warning still stands. You hurt her and I'll hurt you."

I salute her before walking away and directly into the open lift.

My heart pounds faster and faster the closer I get. It's been hours since I've had her alone, and even longer since we've been in private. I've got plenty I want to say to her, but I feel that on this occasion actions might speak louder.

I'm not the kind of guy people lie to and are able to get away with it. I haven't got where I have by allowing people to walk over me. Especially pussy cats like Tabitha. She's chosen the wrong man to go into battle with, and she's about to discover what a fucking mistake she's made crossing me.

I lift my hand to her door and something inside me settles. This ends now, Tabby Cat.

CHAPTER TWENTY-NINE

TABITHA

I'M STARING at myself in the bathroom mirror, about to take my make-up off when the knock sounds out. It's so hard it makes my bones rattle. I knew it was coming, and that was almost enough to have me calling an Uber and heading home. But I didn't. I need to face the music and it seems that he's chosen right now as the perfect time.

Holding on to the marble top, I count to ten in an attempt to calm my racing heart enough to be able to deal with him. To be able to rationally explain why I did what I did without breaking down, or worse, caving to the control he seems to have over my body when he's in the same room as me.

"Open the fucking door, Tabitha, or I'll knock the fucking thing down." The rough slur to his voice does things to my insides that it really shouldn't. He's angry, understandably so, but it shouldn't turn me on quite like it does. There's a fucking door between us yet my knickers are already getting a little damp.

His loud knock sounds out once more, and I force my legs to move before he gets us both kicked out of the damn hotel.

"Tabi—" His loud voice is cut off the second I pull the door open. His hand lands on the wood, and he pushes so hard that I have no choice but to step back or be crushed like a fly behind it.

I take one look at him with his loosened tie and messy hair and I know I'm in for a rough ride. I guess the question is, just how rough can I take?

I've never been with a guy like Zach before. All my previous partners have been a gentleman both in and out of the bed. But Zach... He's no gentleman inside or out of the bedroom, or kitchen counter, and he's got more passion and skill than all of my previous guys put together.

He says nothing as he slams the door behind him and stalks towards me. His chest heaves under his fitted shirt and my mouth waters at knowing what's hiding beneath the fabric.

"Zach?" My voice is soft and breathy, exactly what I didn't want it to be, but the effect he has that I was afraid of is hitting me full force.

His blue eyes are electric as they stare into mine. They're full of something I've never seen before—promises or threats, I'm not sure.

My stomach tumbles in anticipation of what he's going to do.

"Turn around," he demands and my body reacts on its own.

I expect him to undo my dress, to run the zip down my back, driving me crazy, but he doesn't do that. Instead when his fingers find the fabric at the nape of my neck he pulls. Hard. The sound of ripping fabric fills the room and I cry out. "Zach, what the hell?" My dress falls to my feet, totally ruined. I don't get a chance to dwell on it, because his hand lands on me.

The warmth of his palm and fingers wrap around my neck as he pulls me back into him. I gasp when he squeezes a little too tightly and his rock hard cock presses into my arse.

"You've been fucking lying to me since the day I found you in my business. You've looked me in the eye knowing exactly who I am, exactly what I'm hiding, and you've said nothing. Not only that but you've lied to my sister. I may not come across like a family orientated kind of guy, but don't be fooled. You wrong them, and I'm fucking coming for you."

"Zach, what are you—"

"The time for you to talk is over, Pussy Cat. You had your chance and you betrayed me, betrayed us. You want to know what I do to people who betray me?"

The whisky on his breath fills my nose, but his words... they do little to scare me off. It's going to take more than a few threats from a guy I know better than he thinks I do.

I shake my head slightly, wanting to know what he's got to say.

His other hand lifts and brushes my hair away from my ear. My entire body shudders at his soft touch before his breath skates across my skin as he speaks.

"I ruin them, Kitten. Ruin. Them."

A squeal falls from my lips when he spins us and pushes me up against the wall.

His cold angry eyes bore into mine, but there's more than that in their depth. There's lust. Pure, unfiltered lust. I might be scared right now if that weren't there, but it is, and fuck if I'm not prepared for whatever it is he has in mind for me.

His hands cage me in and his eyes drop from mine. He takes his time running them over my almost naked body. By removing my dress, he's revealed my navy lace lingerie, including garter belt and stockings.

"I'm going to really enjoy this," he whispers menacingly before reaching out and tucking his finger in the small piece of fabric between the cups of my bra and tugging harshly. It doesn't immediately rip under his force, but it doesn't hold out all that long before the fabric is falling free of my body and the cool air of the room is making my nipples pucker.

"You wear this thing for me?" I don't answer, just tilt my chin in defiance. If he thinks he's going to intimidate me then he's got another think coming. I know him better than he thinks I do, and I'm not scared of him or the words he might spit while he's drunk and angry. He wants to take all this out on me, then fine. I deserve it for lying to him. I'll take whatever he has. "Did you think that I'd take one look at you like this and forget all about the lies, the deceit?"

"I wore it for him," I taunt, enjoying the straining of the muscles in his neck and the purse of his lips at the thought.

"You just can't help yourself, can you? Lies, that's all you're capable of."

"Me? You're the one who's been lying to those who love you for years. So what I didn't tell you everything, but I also kept your fucking secret, didn't I?"

His fingers grip my chin.

"Did I fucking ask you to?" I hold his stare, but I don't respond. We both know that he would have if he knew I was friends with his sister.

Without thinking, I lift my hand with the intention of wrapping it around his neck and pulling his lips down to mine. He's so fucking close, his scent is filling my nose and his body heat is burning into me. I need his taste too.

"No," he barks. "You don't get to take what you want tonight."

His fingers wrap around my waist and I'm turned once again until my heated breasts are pushed up against the cool wall. I gasp in shock as he takes both my hands in his. The sound of fabric moving behind me has butterflies erupting in my belly before the soft fabric of his tie is wrapped around my wrists. Heat floods my core that I'm about to be totally at his mercy. He might be in a bad place right now, but fuck if I want to be anywhere else.

There's some more rustling and then the heat of his bare skin presses against my arms, my bound fingers just coming into contact with his still covered cock. It's rock hard and straining against the fabric. He growls when he feels me teasing him, but he doesn't move.

"You're at my mercy from now on, you got that?" I nod, turning my head to the side in the hope I can see him, see the desire that I know is going to be darkening his eyes.

His fingers run up my arm, dance over my shoulder and up my neck before they thread into my hair. He grips almost painfully hard and tips my head to the angle he wants. Dropping his lips to the slope of my neck, his teeth graze my skin and I shudder.

"You're a kinky little bitch under that posh exterior, aren't you, Kitten?" If he'd asked me that before him, I'd have adamantly denied it, but this isn't the first time he's said something like that and I can't help but thinking he might be right. The moisture between my legs is starting to run down my thighs as he pins me here. I'm so desperate for his touch right now that I'd probably do just about anything.

"For you, yes."

"Fuck," he grunts at my response.

His hand slips around the front of me. He pulls me back into him slightly so he can palm my breast. I keep my fingers wrapped around his cock, and if it's possible it gets even harder as he teases me.

"Fuck, Zach." My head falls back against his shoulder as he pinches one nipple and then the next almost to the point of pain. It does nothing to relieve the situation I've got going on in my knickers.

"You're in for a long night, Tabby Cat."

"Yes, yes," I cry as his hand skims down my stomach and slips into the lace.

"Hmmm," he hums in my ear when he finds me freshly waxed before dipping lower and parting my lips. "Fuck. You're enjoying this too much." He finds me slick and ready for him, embarrassingly so.

His fingers find my throbbing clit and he circles it a few times. I'm already so worked up that in mere seconds I can feel my impending orgasm making itself known.

Just when I'm about to begin the final climb towards the mind-numbing pleasure I know Zach is capable of, his fingers are gone and I'm left with my head spinning and my muscles clutching at something that no longer exists.

"Get. On. Your. Knees," he demands slowly, and with each word my mouth waters more at the thought of getting a taste of him. He's been down on me a number of times, but as of yet, I've not had a chance to return the favour. Right now, I'm more excited about it than I probably should be.

With his help, I turn and lower myself in front of his still fully clothed bottom half. The outline of his cock is visible beneath the fabric, and I lean forward and run the tip of my nose up it.

My eyes flick up to his just in time to see his lower at the sensation. I might have my hands bound right now, but there's no denying that I'm very much the one in control in this moment.

I sit back on my heels, my chest heaving, and bite down on my bottom lip as I wait for him.

He takes two steps back and looks at me, really looks at me. It's as if he's memorising every single part of this moment.

Getting impatient, I squirm, hoping to gain a little friction, but he notices and arches a brow. It doesn't have any effect on me, I'm more than happy to defy him. But the second his hands go to his waistband, I stop all movement in favour of watching him undress.

He drops his trousers, quickly followed by his boxers, and kicks them along with his shoes and socks off into the room somewhere.

"Now, where were we?" He takes a step forward and my eyes drop to his cock. The tip's glistening, he's right on the edge just like I am.

Leaning forward, I lick up the precum and his entire body tenses at my simple touch.

He moves closer still and gives me a little more to work with. I lick around his head, revelling in the unique taste of him before he threads his fingers into my hair and forces me to take him in my mouth. I suck him as deep as I can before pulling back. He allows me to take as much as I can, but as his fingers start tightening and his length swells even more, I know his control is about to snap.

"Kitten," he grunts, pushing that bit deeper. When I take it he growls and pushes deeper still. I'm so fucking full of him that my eyes begin to water as I fight the need to gag around his size.

"Fuck, fuck. I fucking hate you, Kitten. Hate you." His words are groaned at best as his cock twitches and he empties himself down my throat. His grip tightens and the sting added to everything else today has thrown at me has a tear dropping from each of my closed eyes.

After a couple of seconds, Zach pulls back and looks down at me. I feel the heat of his stare, but I keep my eyes closed and refuse to look up at him.

"Kitten?" I stay where I am, afraid of what I'll do or say the second I look into his eyes.

After a beat, his hands land on my waist and I'm pulled up from my position on the floor.

"Tabitha?" The concern that laces his voice has me looking at him. He takes in my tear-stained cheeks and his eyes soften in a way I don't want or need. He might be looking at me right now thinking that he's broken me, or *ruined* me in his words, and I guess he has in one way because I know for a fact that he's ruined me for anyone else.

My heart aches as I stare at his concerned eyes and I

realise for the first time that as much as I might tell myself that I hate this man in front of me, the way I actually feel about him is very, very much the opposite. But I also know that nothing good can come out of me feeling that way. Zach is an enigma. He lives his life as he wants, he follows no rules and attaches himself to no one. There's no way he'd ever return the feelings. He's got everything he wants.

Hasn't he?

I hate that little bit of hope that creeps in. If he had everything then why does he keep coming back, claiming that I'm his or whatever bullshit he spews when he's high on lust?

Two more tears fall as I realise that this is all I'll ever get of Zach Abbot. I guess I've had more than anyone else. *Other than his date?*

"Who is she?" The question is out of my mouth before I even blink.

"Wh–oh. Lana, she's a friend." I'm a little taken back that he's answered me so honestly.

"So she's not... you're not–"

"Never."

His hand lifts and he cups my cheek. I suck in a surprised breath at his sudden tenderness. His eyes bounce between mine as if he's trying to figure something out, trying to read me.

"I'm so fucking mad at you." He drops his forehead to mine and blows out a whisky-scented breath. His other hand grips on to my hip, his fingers tensing. "I so badly need to..."

"Need to what?" I encourage when he trails off.

His eyes open and find mine. They're dark, heated and haunted all at the same time. I can see his inner turmoil. He wants to hurt me. To punish me for what I did. But he can't do it.

"I..." Instead of finishing that thought, he pulls my hair so I have no choice but to look up and offer my lips to him. His slam down on mine and his tongue invades my mouth. His other hand makes quick work of undoing the ties keeping my hands bound, and in seconds they're free and my back is once again against the wall. He lifts me, my legs immediately wrapping around his waist, and before I've had a chance to register what's happening, he's inside me.

His fingers dig into my arse as he thrusts up into me.

"Oh god," I cry as my head hits back against the wall, but I feel nothing aside from what he's doing to me.

"Nah, devil, remember?" I laugh at his comment. "Oh fuck," he groans when my muscles squeeze him tighter. He drops his head onto my shoulder and sucks on the sensitive skin below my ear. "Come for me, Kitten."

I follow as ordered, my body desperate for the release. My arms wrap tighter around his wide shoulders as I prepare for what's about to hit me.

He thrusts, one, two, three more times and I detonate, his name a loud cry on my lips, ensuring that our neighbours know what to call him in the morning.

"Holy shit." My words are barely above a whisper as I fight to get them out between my heaving breaths.

"Fuck. Can't get e-fucking-nough, Kitten." My chest swells at his admission as he pulls me from the wall and carries me to the bed, still inside me and still impossibly hard.

He lowers me down with much more care than I'm sure he would have done when he first barged into this room not so long ago.

He settles himself between my thighs and wraps my legs around his hips. His eyes run over the lace that's still around my waist and down my thighs. His fingertips follow the edges, making my skin erupt in goosebumps.

"You should wear stuff like this all the time."

"Really?" I ask, amusement dancing in my eyes. "I thought you hated all this fancy kind of shit."

"This," he says, snapping one of the straps against my thigh, "this is different. This is hidden for only me to see. This *shit* can be as fancy and as expensive as you damn well please."

"I've got plenty," I admit, making his eyes light up in delight. "If you're lucky you might get to find out."

"Hmmm, I like the sound of that." He leans forward and takes my lips as his hips slowly tease me.

I'm just wondering where his fight has gone when I'm suddenly flipped over and his hand connects with my bare arse cheek.

His cock impales me from behind and I once again cry out, already desperate for another release. He fucks me, just like he promised, until I'm full of him. My body is lax and ready to pass out after the stress of the day, but one look in his eyes when I flip back over and I know it's not going to happen anytime soon.

And it doesn't. I don't get to pass out until the sun is almost up and we've fucked on every single surface of that hotel room. At some point he ordered us drinks and we made our way through a bottle of wine, some of which is now soaked into the sheets after he tried drinking it from my bellybutton.

Both still wet from the shower we shared, we fall on to the bed, my hair dripping over my shoulders, but I'm too exhausted to care.

Zach pulls the sheets up over our naked bodies, and pulls me into him. Somehow his cock is hard again, but I ignore it this time. I need a few hours at least.

His hand lands on my cheek as he stares into my eyes.

"Why didn't you tell them?"

"It's not my secret to tell."

"Why didn't you tell me?"

"Why would I? You made it clear you hated me and wanted nothing to do with me."

"Did I really?" he asks, poking me in the stomach with his cock.

"Hmmm. Yeah, well, I felt like it was too late by the time that happened."

"It's never too late to tell me the truth, Kitten."

I bite down on my bottom lip, desperately trying to keep my thoughts to myself.

"Spill," he says, amusement covering his tired face that's soon wiped away when he registers what my words really mean.

"I... I think I'm falling out of hate with you."

His mouth opens and closes before he swallows and pulls me towards him to rest his lips on my forehead.

Fuck.

CHAPTER THIRTY

ZACH

"I... I think I'm falling out of hate with you."

The second those words hit my ears, I'm suddenly wide awake.

I came here with the intention of teaching her a lesson for lying to me, for pretending to be something she's not, and it was all fine until I got one look at those fucking tears. They fucking broke me. The thought of pushing her too far damn near ruined me, let alone her. Suddenly everything seemed a little pointless, my revenge mission felt pathetic. No one had been hurt, and I'm sure she had her reasons for doing what she did, and at the end of the day I can't forget that she kept my secret. She protected me. I'd been asking myself why all day and I think I might have just got my answer.

There have only ever been a couple of women I've been with more than once over the years, and all of them are ones who share my need to stay unattached. We work because we use each other for the pleasure we need before going about our lives. That is, until her. Until Tabitha. Everything changed the day I walked into the studio and found her there looking like a member of the royal fucking family. I told myself she didn't fit, but is the reality of the situation that she fits there, in my life, more than I ever could have expected? My studio has been my sanctuary for as long as I can remember, even before I owned it, but suddenly with her there, it's different. And when she's now not there, fuck, I don't want to be either, and that's something I never thought I'd say.

Her breathing evens out, telling me that she's succumbed to her exhaustion after the epic session I put her through. It was nothing like I was planning when I forced my way into this room but fuck, it was probably better than that.

Her tear-stained face pops into my head again. It mixes with her admission and I panic.

If she doesn't hate me anymore then that means... no, I can't even go there.

As gently and as silently as I can, I get myself out of her bed and scramble around the room to gather up my clothes. I feel like the walls are closing in on me, and I need to get the fuck out of here.

I still when I pull the door open and it creaks, but there's no noise or movement from the bed so I run.

My room is on the floor above. Dressed in just my boxers, I run up the stairs and pray I don't bump into anyone who gets up at the arsecrack of dawn.

Thankfully the hallways are empty and no sooner am

I inside my room than I'm dressed in my normal clothes and shoving everything else into my bag. I can't be here. I can't walk down to breakfast in a few hours and look at her when I know she's going to wake up and find me gone. I just can't do any of it.

With my bag in hand, I take off. I check out with the half-asleep member of staff behind the desk and get the fuck out of that hotel and away from this side of town. I need my space. I need my home. I need the security of my normal life. Of my secret life.

I run all the way back. My legs ache and my lungs burn as I pull my keys from my pocket and let myself inside the studio.

I leave all the lights off and go straight for my flat. A place she's never been. But... shit. She has, Lana said she'd come here. I might not have seen it with my own eyes but that doesn't mean I don't picture her here. Her scent is still in my nose, on my skin. If I didn't know any better, I would think I could turn around and find her standing in the bedroom doorway, waiting for me.

Fuck. My head's a fucking mess.

I turn the coffee machine on and drop my phone to the side before stripping out of my clothes once again and heading for the shower. One that's not full of her products and her scent.

I scrub every inch of my skin in my attempt to forget. To forget the broken look on her face. The way her shoulders sagged in defeat. The way my heart damn near burst out of my chest as I stared down at her, having achieved what I set out to. I was meant to feel better for teaching her a lesson, but all I felt was regret. I'd hurt the one person who means something to me, the only woman to have been more to me than a quick fuck.

"Fuck," I scream into the confines of my shower, slamming my palms against the tiles in frustration.

I can't have fucking feelings for the woman. She's everything I don't want. She's from a life I want to forget, not dive straight back into.

Lana's words come back to me. *"Have you ever considered that she might feel the same? She's working in your studio, for fuck's sake. She might want to rebel from all this just like you. She might actually be your perfect woman."*

"No, no, no." I bang my head down again and again, hoping it'll remove these kinds of thoughts from my mind. I don't fucking need this. I don't need a distraction, I don't need a woman, and I certainly don't need to hand my fucking bollocks over to one for her to squeeze whenever the fuck she wants to. I've seen it happen time and time again with friends. I want to be me, live my life, not one that some woman dictates.

When I eventually make it back to the kitchen, I forgo the coffee and head straight for the bottle of whisky in the cupboard. Hair of the dog, I tell myself, pretending that it's not the ache still pulling at my chest from leaving her that I'm trying to numb.

My phone's been angrily vibrating on the kitchen counter as I lie on the sofa, nursing my bottle. I know it's my mum going crazy because I bailed on the family breakfast that had been arranged for this morning before Harrison and Summer headed off on their honeymoon, but quite frankly, I couldn't give a shit.

I ignore it the best I can as I run through everything that happened in the last twenty-four hours. I do everything I can to keep my life as drama free as possible. I knew the moment I laid eyes on Tabitha that she was going to be trouble. It's why I tried to get rid of her.

I sit up, remembering something from last night. My need to discover who she really was has me swiping my phone from the side, ordering an Uber and pulling my shoes on.

I'm down at the door, waiting for the car before it pulls up. Now I've had the idea I'm desperate to try to jog my memory.

My parents' house is empty, as I was expecting. They're probably still smoozing the guests that stayed the night at the hotel. I push the front door closed behind me, but I don't look back to see if it's shut or not. Instead I head for the stairs. Taking two at a time, I feel like a teenager again, running away from being told off for not towing the family line. Again.

I push through my bedroom door. It's exactly as it was the day I moved out. I expected Mum and Dad to do something with it, not just shut the door and forget about it.

I pull open my wardrobe door and find a stack of books like I remember and rummage through until I find the one I want.

Our school yearbook.

The photographs are in alphabetical order, so I don't need to go far past my own to find an image of a nondescript mousy brown-haired girl, who I still don't recognise, named Tabitha Anderson.

"Jesus." I rub at my rough jaw as I stare into a pair of grey eyes that have become so familiar. My heart twists looking into them, despite her only being sixteen in this photograph.

I sit back on my bed with the book on my lap as I

continue staring, desperately trying to drag up some old memory of her. But there's nothing.

Guilt pulls at my insides that I don't remember this girl. This girl who's turned into a woman who means more to me than I'm willing to admit.

"You're a fucking arsehole," I tell myself.

I've treated her like nothing but shit. All the while she's known exactly who I am and not told a soul my secret.

It's a good job I can't bring myself to admit how I feel, because even if I did, I wouldn't deserve her. She needs a decent guy. One who will treat her the way she deserves, not one who goes storming into her hotel room with the intention of getting revenge for something that doesn't really mean much in the grand scheme of things. My stomach turns over. She would be much better with Christian. He's a decent guy. He was decent enough to escort Tabitha to yesterday's wedding having only had one date. That's a man who knows how to treat a woman, right there.

At some point I must give in to my exhaustion, because the next thing I know I'm being woken to the sound of my dad shouting through the house, asking if anyone's there before feet pound up the stairs.

"Hello? Is there anyone–"

"Zach," Mum says on a sigh when she pokes her head around my door and finds me half asleep on my bed.

"What the hell are you doing here? We thought we'd been bloody robbed," Dad barks while Mum must notice the expression on my face and places her hand on Dad's forearm to stop him before she comes to sit beside me.

"Go and make us all a coffee, yeah?" she instructs

Dad, who immediately follows her order like he always does.

Once he's gone, she turns her soft, kind eyes on me before briefly glancing down at what's in my hands.

"Whoa, it's been a few years since I've seen one of these," she says, taking it from me and looking at the photographs. "Aw, you were so handsome, even back then." She makes it sound like it was a million years ago. Mind you, considering I've been very intimate with a girl I went to school with yet I don't remember, maybe it was a million years ago.

"Tabitha was there yesterday, wasn't she? Did you get a chance to catch up with her?"

I blow out a long breath as I try to figure out exactly how to answer that question.

"I really need to get going."

"What's going on, Zach? You missed breakfast this morning and now this? Talk to me, please," she begs, her eyes soft and beginning to fill with tears. Unable to watch someone else I care about cry in front of me, I get up from the bed.

"It's... nothing. I just couldn't remember who she was is all. Fancied a trip down memory lane."

"Do you want some food before you go?"

"No, I'm good. I just need to..." I trail off, not really having an answer, just needing to get the hell out of here.

"Okay, well. We're here if you need us," Mum says sadly.

I nod. It's all I'm capable of as I once again walk away from both my parents and the house. Why do I find it so hard to confide in them? Why do I keep this wall up between us like I'm trying to use it to protect myself?

I stop at the shop on the way home for some food, but

most importantly, some more whisky. I'm not working tonight so I intend on getting wasted in the hope I can forget all this bullshit ever happened.

My next client isn't until Wednesday night, so as I lock the door behind me, I vow not to step foot back through it, or even open it again until I'm needed downstairs.

CHAPTER THIRTY-ONE

TABITHA

I'M EXPECTING IT, but still, waking to find the other side of the bed cold fills me with dread. I knew I'd ruined everything the moment those words slipped past my lips. It's his fault. He told me to be honest, so that's what I did. It's not my fault he couldn't handle the truth.

I roll onto my back and wonder at what point everything went so wrong. I think it might have been the night I let him into my flat while Danni was sleeping in my guest room.

I lie there for the longest time before I drag my arse from the bed to find out that the breakfast that's been booked for all the staying guests starts in thirty minutes. That's assuming I'm brave enough to show my face. Both

Zach and Danni will be there, and I'm guessing neither will want me to join them.

After swallowing a couple of painkillers to hopefully numb my pounding head, I have the most depressing shower of my life as I remember vividly what happened in here only hours ago.

I rinse the lingering scent of him from my body before quickly blow drying my hair and applying just enough make up to cover the evidence of my serious lack of sleep last night.

Wearing a pair of jeans and a violet jumper, I head down to where the breakfast is being served. As I expected everyone is already seated and tucking into their food, which I can't deny smells incredible.

I look around at all the happy faces as they relive yesterday's events before I find the happy couple. They look like they're on top of the world. Beside them, Zach's parents look equally as thrilled. Danni, however, just stares down at her plate while poking at whatever's sitting there uneaten. She must feel my stare because after only a few seconds, she glances up at me. Our eyes hold. Everything I want to say to her, all the apologies I need to give her are right on the end of my tongue. I manage to pull my eyes away and find the seat next to hers is empty. Is that where he should be sitting? And if so, where is he? I assumed he'd gone back to his room, wherever it is, but has he run further than that? My heart sinks.

I look back to Danni who shakes her head at me in disappointment. My feet move, but they don't take me the way I need to go. Instead I find myself heading back up to my room with a lump in my throat the size of a fucking basketball. I pack up my few belongings and get the hell out of that hotel, thankfully without bumping into any of the wedding guests, or at least any I recognise. My Uber is waiting right outside the entrance for me. I jump in and confirm my address before sitting back and wishing I could rewind time.

"Would you be able to pull over here please?" I ask when he heads toward a corner shop by my house. "I'll just be a couple of seconds."

He doesn't look happy about it but he agrees and pulls over. I hop out and race around the shop to grab what I need.

Thirty minutes later, I'm sitting on my sofa, one of my favourite old films playing on the TV, wearing a pair of leggings and an oversized shirt, and I'm digging onto a huge tub of cookie dough ice cream. I'd usually accompany it with a bottle of wine, but seeing as I consumed enough to stock a small bar last night, and it's not even midday yet, I forgo it. For now at least.

I think back over last night. Zach looked wild when he first pushed himself into my room, and I can't deny that even now, the memory of his dark eyes has flutters erupting in my belly.

I shove another spoonful of cold goodness into my mouth. The moment I realised just what I felt for him hit me like a fucking truck at exactly the wrong time. He was trying to hurt me for lying to him. He wanted to break me, and I guess in a way he did. One moment I realised that I'd fallen in love with him and the next my heart was shattering because I knew he'd never feel the same. He came to hurt me, for fuck's sake.

But something happened in those next few moments. Something that had my heart racing and for the mask that he'd pulled on to slip. He went from a monster on a mission to the Zach I've had little glimpses at over the past few weeks. The softer side, the one who isn't always in charge of everything, isn't always untouchable. In just those couple of moments, I thought I had him. The way he touched me, the way he kissed me, the way our bodies moved together. It's something, something special, something more than just two people coming together in the heat of the moment. When he looked into my eyes as he told me to be honest, there was more there. There were promises he was terrified to make, a future he was terrified to think about, I'm sure of it. And then I went and opened my big fucking mouth and ruined everything we'd built in the last few hours.

Getting up, I dig my phone out from the bottom out of my bag, hoping that I might have something from him, or Danni, but the only name that stares back at me is another that I only feel guilty about.

Christian.

I never should have invited him yesterday. Not that I could have ever imagined that he knew Zach and was going to make the situation a million times worse. I don't think I could have chosen a worse fake date if I'd tried.

Swiping my phone, I stare down at his words.

Christian: I hope everything worked out ok after I left.

My thumb hovers over the keyboard as I try to come up with something positive to say. Seeing him leave with the woman he'd been chatting to most of the night made me felt a little less guilty about dragging him into my mess in the first place. At least he might have got something out of yesterday, even if I'm sitting here with a gaping hole in my chest.

Tabitha: Everything worked out as it should be. I hope you had a great night.

Christian: It was great, thank you ;-)

I can't help but smile at his winky face. He's a good guy and deserves a good woman in his life, one who's not going to use him like I did.

While I've got my phone in my hand, I send a message to Danni. I've got no idea what to say, so I keep it simple and just send, *I'm sorry*. I offer to explain all, but I'm not expecting for her rush over here to hear me out.

I spend the rest of the day digging to the bottom of my tub of ice cream before pulling up an app on my phone and ordering myself Chinese for dinner. If I'm going to wallow in self-pity, I may as well do it with unhealthy, fatty food.

When I eventually fall into bed, I'm numb. It's exactly what I need, but the second I fall asleep, I'm assaulted by dreams of him and what could never be.

I DON'T STEP foot out of my flat for the next six days. I put off the meeting I'm meant to have with my lecturer at uni. I unplug my home phone, not that it ever rings aside from nonsense calls about the accident I've never been in, and I keep my mobile on silent. The couple of times I've checked it, no one wanted me. Until Thursday night when I didn't show up to my shift at Rebel Ink. I debated it, a lot. I could turn up, hold my head high, and like all the other times, pretend nothing had happened. Or I could accept my fate. Zach doesn't want me there, he never has. So now's as good a time as any to finally listen to all the times he's not so bluntly told me to leave and I do just that. Silently.

Thursday and Friday night, my phone is almost constantly alight with messages and calls from both Titch and D, but I refuse to answer any of them, deciding, with the help of a bottle of wine each night, that they're better off without me. Zach wants nothing to do with me and nor does Danni. I'm sure they'll only agree with them once they discover the truth.

The only good thing about my week in solitude is that I complete the uni project I've been working on for forever.

I sit back on the old sofa in my studio and stare at the three canvases, finally happy with the outcome.

I sip at my wine and look over every inch of the paint before me as thoughts about my future enter my mind. Soon I'll be finished and I'll no longer be able to say I'm a student. Sure, I could do more, but even I'm starting to think my parents are right and that I'm just using this as an excuse to waste time. I love art, I love doing it, looking at it, learning about it, but really, what am I going to do next? Going to join my dad in a successful company where I can make a good life for myself would be the easiest option, but it's an option I still have no desire for.

I think back to that final conversation with my gran. *"Follow your heart and just breathe. Spread your wings and fly, Tabby Cat."*

I blow out a long breath as I try to figure out what that means for me now. I may have those words tattooed on my body, but I'm no closer to figuring out what I should do once I've taken that breath. My heart still beats with *him* inside it, but I'm not stupid enough to know that running after that dream would only lead me to a dead end. He's made it clear time after time that there's no future for the two of us. There wasn't really a past, if I'm being honest. Just a girl who got swept away by the bad boy. Fucking hell, I'm such a cliché.

My buzzer going off drags me from my thoughts, and I push myself up from the sofa to see who's here. I've ordered dinner but I'm not expecting it to be here yet. My only other thought is that it's my parents after realising that I've disappeared off the face of the earth, but I find that hard to believe. We can go months without talking, a few days is a drop in the ocean.

I push the button to talk to whoever it is. "Who is it?"

"It's me," a soft, familiar voice says. "I think we need to talk." My heart pounds in my chest as I let my best friend up into my flat. I've reached out to her a couple of times this week, but all my messages have gone unanswered.

I open the door to allow her inside before turning to get a glass of wine.

"Hey," she says awkwardly as she joins me in the kitchen.

"Hey." I lift my arm to pass her the glass, but she shocks me by walking straight up to me, her eyes full of unshed tears. I have no choice but to put the glass to the counter as she wraps her arms around me.

CHAPTER THIRTY-TWO

ZACH

WEDNESDAY AFTERNOON COMES AROUND ALL TOO quick. I've spent a solid three days inside my flat. I've got up to date with the boring part of my business that involves invoicing, health and safety and insurances that have been hanging around on my to do list for too long. But mostly I've drunk and I've drawn. I've been so busy since... well, since I first took over this place that aside from time sitting on flights back and forth to the US I've not had time to sit and do what I love. Draw. I end up with a sketchbook full of tattoo ideas, both for me and others, and I hate to admit it, but most have been sketched with her in mind. No matter how much I tell myself that walking away from her was the right thing to do, she's right there at the forefront of my mind taunting me and telling me that I made a mistake.

I've picked up my phone to call her more times than I want to admit. And every time my phone's vibrated signalling an incoming call or text my heart's jumped into my throat, thinking that it's her. I don't even care at this point that she'll be contacting me to give me a tongue-lashing for my behaviour. Actually, the thought gets me quite excited.

Rearranging myself in my trousers at the thought of getting the chance to argue with her, I push myself from the sofa and prepare to go and meet my client. The young woman's coming back so I can complete her angel wings. With a coffee in hand, I make my way down to the studio.

It seems I'm not the first one here because the lights are already on and there's a faint buzzing coming from Titch's room.

"Morning, boss," comes from the kitchen as I'm standing staring at Tabitha's desk like a fucking loser.

I tip my chin at D in greeting, but he frowns as he takes me in.

"Everything okay?"

"Yeah, never better," I lie. "Got a busy day?"

"Nah, just a couple this afternoon then I'm off early."

I nod, give him a smile that I don't feel and head for my room. D's been a part of my life for too long now. He adopted me into this life pretty early on and he's been there for me like family ever since.

"Zach," he calls when I've got my hand on the handle of my door. I look back to find him not far behind me. "I'm here, yeah. If you need anything."

I nod again, unable to say any words for fear of the

truth about how I'm feeling to come tumbling out. I shut myself in my room to get prepped.

The ding of the front door being pushed open sounds out only twenty minutes later, and I head out to greet her.

I find her sitting on the edge of one of the sofas, chewing on her nails. If it's possible, she looks even more nervous than last time.

"You know, I'm pretty sure it's meant to get easier each time," I say, leaning my hip against the wall as I study her. Her blue eyes fly up to mine and her lips part in shock like she didn't hear me coming.

"Oh... um... yeah, you're probably right. I've never been one to do things the way I should though."

I smile at her, knowing the feeling well. "Right, well... are you ready to get this over with then?"

She nods, and I turn to head back to my room, but not before I swear I hear her mutter that it's about time.

I ignore her, assuming it's just her fear talking, and hold the door open for her to join me.

"You know what to do." I gesture for the bed and move to grab my stool. As she lifts her top to give me access to her back, I notice that her entire body is trembling with fear. "We don't have to do this today if you're not ready," I offer, worried about her state of mind right now.

"No. I need to get this over with."

"Okay. If you need me to stop, all you need to do is say." She nods and gets herself into position.

I hesitantly get started, expecting her to call me off any second, but she just lies there as I do my worst.

I'm getting toward the end when I feel eyes on me. Looking up, I find her staring over her shoulder at me, but she's so lost to whatever it is that's in her head, she doesn't even notice my attention. I allow myself a second to take her in. Her eyes are light blue, but her hair is so dark it's almost black. She looks much younger than she is, if her ID was to be believed, and although she's pretty I'd be more tempted to describe her as cute seeing as she looks so young.

She eventually comes back to herself and gasps in shock when she finds me studying her. For someone so small and cute, it's impossible to miss the strength she has. There's something in those blue eyes which tells me she's not the naïve young woman some people might mistake her for. I'm under no illusion that all this ink is her armour, and one she wears very well.

"Sorry," I mutter, focusing back on what I should be doing.

Suddenly I have this almost uncontrollable need to ask her questions. Real questions about her life and how she's found herself here, but I bite my tongue. That's not how I usually operate, I do my thing and only talk if my client is the one who sparks up a conversation.

While I'm working, the time seems to drag, but the second I pull back from her body, I realise it was over in a flash.

"Okay, you are done." A sad smile curls at her lips as she lies there. "You want to see before I wrap it?"

She nods and scoots off the bed so she can stand in front of the mirror. I hold another up before her so she can see. Her breath catches the second she locks eyes on it, and they immediately fill with tears.

"WHO'S IT FOR?" I don't mean to ask, it's none of my business, but the words fall from my lips without permission.

Her eyes find mine in the mirror and all the colour drains from her face. She sucks in a long breath before cursing.

"I'm so sorry. I never wanted it to be this way."

"What are you talking about?"

"The wings. They're for... they're for our mum."

Silence fills the room, but neither of us breaks our eye contact in the mirror as her words settle around us.

Our mum.

Our mum?

I laugh. "What the hell are you talking about?"

She spins, and the second I get a look at the fear on her face everything inside me clenches. My fists curl and my short nails dig into my palms. My first instinct is to kick her out, forcibly if it means she leaves, but for some reason my body doesn't react. My heart races and my head spins as I continue staring into her apprehensive eyes.

"I'm so sorry," she whispers. "I didn't want to do it like this. But I..."

"Fuck," I shout, my hands coming up to grip my hair as Kas jumps back like I'm about to hit her. *What the fuck?*

I look up at her. Her eyes are wide, her arms wrapped around her chest protectively as if I'm about to lash out. It's enough to drag me from my own head for a second.

The silence aside from our heavy breathing is suffocating as we stare at each other, her eyes begging me to believe her and my head not knowing what the fuck is going on.

Things I've heard my whole life start to run through my head. It's been a running joke between me and Harrison for as long as I can remember that I'm the milkman's kid, seeing as I'm the only one with less than zero interest in the family business. Where everyone else has dark eyes and hair, here I am with blonde and baby blues. No one's ever confirmed anything and my parents have loved me the same as the others, but there's always been that slight seed of doubt in my mind. But as Kas stands here waiting for my response, I can't help that seed suddenly exploding to a full-blown fucking tree inside me.

I don't need to hear any more to know she's telling the truth. I feel it. There was something about her the first time she turned up, how scared she was, the way she studied me when she thought I wasn't watching

I stumble back and fall down onto the chair as I try to process what she just said.

Our mum.

Our mum.

"Zach, I'm—"

"My sister?" I finish for her, my brows draw together in confusion as I try to process all this.

She nods. "I know this is a shock but I... I couldn't be alone any longer." Her voice cracks and when I look up I'm struck with just how hard all of this must be for her. Whether what she's saying is true or not, she's fucking drowning, and I feel like I'm watching it happen. Standing, I pull her into my arms and hold her tightly while she cries.

My heart thunders as she trembles against me.

"I'm sorry," she whispers. "I can't... I can't do this."

Before I've registered what's going on, she's out of my arms and running from my studio.

"Kas, wait," I call, but it's no use. She's too fast. The front door slams, and by the time I get out there I've no clue which way she's gone.

As I stand in reception alone, the weight of what she just told me really hits me.

"Motherfucker," I shout, kicking the coat stand that's in the corner. I watch it sway and crash to the floor seconds later. Not satisfied with that, I clear everything from the top of Tabitha's desk and send a bookcase full of magazines crashing to the floor.

"What the fu—" Titch and D come racing from their rooms at the same time and come to a stop side by side in the entrance to the reception. "Zach?"

I roar in frustration, as I storm towards the door to my flat. "Leave me the fuck alone," I bark over my shoulder, successfully stopping them from following me.

My chest is heaving like I've just run a fucking marathon when I fall back against the inside of my door. My life is falling apart and connecting in equal measures as I think over my life and how I've never felt like I've fitted in.

Pulling my phone from my pocket, I find my parents' number and hit call. I've no clue which one of them might answer, or if they're even in, but I don't give a fuck right now. I just need an answer.

"Hello?" My dad's voice booms down the line, and it's like a knife to the chest. I just about keep myself standing, knowing the conversation that's about to commence.

"Were you ever going to tell me?" My voice is much steadier than I was expecting.

"Tell you what, son?" he asks innocently, but I don't

miss the slight waver in his voice. It's all I need to confirm what I already know. *She was telling the truth.*

My knees give, and I slide down the door until I'm on my arse.

"Did you think I'd never find out? That your lies would never catch up with you?"

"Zach." The way he says my name, the softness to it, has a lump forming in my throat. "I think maybe you should come here and we can talk about this in person."

Red hot anger like I've never experienced before explodes in my belly. "You've been lying to me my whole fucking life. I'm not listening to a fucking word you've got to say, let alone following your damn orders. Who was she?" I demand.

"Zach, please. I'm not doing this down the phone. Tell me where you are and I'll come to you."

"Fuck you, old man. Fuck. You."

The phone in my hand goes flying across the room and shatters against the wall. Who the fuck does he think he is to start making demands when he's the one who's spent the last twenty-seven fucking years lying?

I'm up off the floor before I've realised I've moved, and the washing up that was sitting on the drainer flies off in all directions as I sweep my arm along the counter. Glasses and plates smash, but the sound isn't satisfying in the least, not like I hoped. Ripping the door open to where I've got alcohol, I pull out a bottle, not even noticing what it is. Twisting the top, I take a long pull. The strength of it burns my throat as I swallow, but it's not enough to stop me having more.

CHAPTER THIRTY-THREE

TABITHA

"I'M SO SORRY," Danni says between sniffs when she pulls back from me. "Is that for me?" She nods at the glass of wine and I push it towards her, confused as to how this is going to go down. I thought she was going to turn up and shout at me.

I watch as she drinks half the wine in one go. "You've got some explaining to do."

I follow her as she walks toward my sofas with her wine in hand. She takes the left-hand one, curling her legs beneath her and getting comfortable so I take the right.

"Start at the beginning," she demands, and so I do.

I forget all about any fucked-up loyalty I had for Zach and I tell her everything about his business and what he does with his life. Pride fills her eyes as I explain the success he's had and how his business is thriving not only here but in his American studios as well.

"Well, fuck me. I didn't think he had it in him," she says, downing the last of her wine before getting up to retrieve the bottle I stupidly left in the kitchen.

"He's got a lot in him that you probably don't know about," I mutter, more to myself than her, my cheeks heating as I think of some of the time we spend together.

"So about that. How'd you end up..." she waves her hand around, not wanting to say the words.

I cringe as I think about our first time, but this is time for me to be honest so I decide not to hold back on any details.

"I was in the next fucking room. You dirty bitch," Danni squeals.

"I just can't—couldn't," I correct when I remember that it's over, "help myself." I sigh, remembering his touch like it was only yesterday. Craving it like I might get to experience it again. But he's made his choice, and I'm not the kind of woman who goes crawling after a man who clearly doesn't want her, no matter how good the orgasms are.

The whole time we're talking, my phone is going crazy. "Are you going to get that at any point?" Danni asks, looking over to where it's vibrating against the kitchen counter.

"It's just the guys wanting to know why I didn't come back to work."

"You didn't tell them you were done?"

"No, I thought I'd leave it up to the boss to explain how he fucked up."

"Fair enough. Seems like they miss you."

I blow out a breath. "I miss them too. I loved working

there, spending time with the guys. Something about it just felt so right."

"And you're allowing my dickhead of a brother to ruin that for you? I thought you were stronger than that."

"I'm not going back there when he clearly doesn't want me."

Silence falls between us, but the concern that's been on Danni's face since the moment she walked into my flat is still there.

"My parents are worried. Something's going on. They won't tell me what, but they've fallen out and they can't reach him."

A bitter laugh bubbles up my throat. "So that's why you're being so nice all of a sudden? You need me to get to him." I realise my mistake the second the words are out of my mouth, because her face drops.

"Biff, no. I was angry on Saturday night, unbelievably so, but it was a crazy day and emotions were running high. I've had a few days to think and I've realised that I might have jumped off the deep end slightly. Zach's always been... mysterious. He's never given himself to us completely and always held such a huge part of himself back. I shouldn't have expected you to sell him out the second you learned the truth. I know you're a better friend than that. Of course it hurts that you kept secrets from me, but I understand. I get why you did it, and I know I shouldn't hold it against you. Fucking him while I was in the next room though... that's an entirely different situation." She can't hold her smile in and after a second it curls at her lips.

She goes to say more but is interrupted by my buzzer ringing.

"That'll be my dinner. There's enough to share if you want some."

"Yep, I'm starving."

I get up to allow the delivery in, pressing my finger on the button without bothering to speak. I don't think anything of it until a thundering knock sounds out on my front door.

"Biff, open up," a familiar voice booms.

My brows draw together. I know they want me to come back, but I'm not really sure a home visit on a busy Friday night is necessary.

Knowing I can't ignore him when he's standing the other side of my front door, I walk over and pull it open.

Titch comes barrelling inside before I've even said a word.

"I need you to come to the studio," he demands without so much as looking around.

"I'm sorry, but I'm done. He's—"

"A fucking mess, Biff. I can't get him to come out of his flat. He's been in there since fucking shit up in the studio on Wednesday. He won't listen to us. But I have a feeling he'll listen to you."

My heart starts to race as I put Titch's words together with what Danni just said. "What's happened?"

I don't hear Danni's footsteps until she's right behind me.

"What's going— *You*, what the fuck are you doing here?" I look over my shoulder to find her staring daggers at Titch. Her voice, which was concerned, suddenly turned to ice when she realised who I was talking to.

I look back to Titch, whose eyes are wide and lips parted in shock. "Dan—"

"Don't," she barks in a tone I've never heard from her

before. I look back and forth between them, expecting one of them to fill in the blanks for me, but neither does as they just stare at each other, their bodies set as if they're about to fight any second.

"Err... what the fuck is going on right now?"

"Nothing," Danni snaps, dragging her eyes from Titch and back to me. They soften and wordlessly beg me not to keep prying.

Titch seems to snap himself out of his trance without Danni's eyes on him, and he remembers why he's here.

"Will you please just come and try to talk to him? He'll listen to you."

I shake my head. "He won't. He doesn't want anything to do with me."

"Do you really believe that?" he asks, shaking his head in disbelief. "Zach's been with a lot of women over the years. Sorry," he adds when the colour drains from my face at the thought. "But I've never seen him like he was with you."

"You only saw us arguing."

"Exactly. He cared enough to keep you around to argue with. He could have got rid of you that first day he found you, but he didn't." I keep my mouth firmly shut instead of pointing out that he would have done if I weren't so damn stubborn and insisted on going back. "Please, Biff. He needs you, I know it."

I look at Danni. "You should go. Everyone's clearly worried."

I blow out a frustrated breath that after the way he's treated me I'm still willing to go and drag him out of whatever mess he's found himself in. "Fine," I mutter. "You coming?" I ask Danni as I grab a pair of boots from the hall cupboard and tug them on.

She looks to Titch and then back to me. "I'll... uh... wait here, if that's okay? Wait for you to get back."

"You just want the dinner," I joke. I can tell by the look on her face that she's as concerned about her brother as Titch is right now.

"Call me if you need me to leave, or need anything." She hands my phone over. I take it and slip it into my pocket.

"Let's go before I change my mind."

I follow Titch out. Silence hangs heavy between us as we make the short walk to the studio.

"What's happened?" I ask again when we're almost there.

"I have no idea. He had a client Wednesday afternoon and freaked the fuck out the second she left. He's been weird since the wedding, but things went nuclear on Wednesday."

"The wedding was my fault," I admit.

"Why?"

"I was there. He realised that I'd been lying to him since we met."

"Go on," Titch encourages, anger tinging his usually calm voice.

"We went to school together. He just didn't remember me."

"Oh shit, girl. No wonder he hated you and wanted you gone." He sounds more shocked than he should be.

I sigh, sadly unable to disagree with him. I was a threat and although he didn't know the severity of it until Saturday, something within him understood.

The studio is all lit up and open as if nothing out of the ordinary is going on inside. Titch pushes the front door open, and the familiar ding of the bell fills my ears.

It's been a week since I was here last, but even still I'm hit with a wave of nostalgia. No matter what happens from here on out, this place has given me something I never thought I'd get to experience. It allowed me to be me for the first time. I think it's the reason Zach and I connected the way we did. The two of us aren't so different with wanting to break away from our families, he just had no clue I was just like him.

Titch walks us straight through reception and I get a little taste of what he was talking about. My desk is empty, and a pile of magazines and books sit where an old bookcase used to be. He doesn't stop until we're at the top of the stairs and standing before the door keeping me from Zach.

"Go on..." Titch whispers.

I bite down on my bottom lip as I try to figure out what the hell I'm meant to say. Having a clue as to why he's locked himself in here in the first place would help.

Sucking in a breath, I lift my hand to knock.

The silence continues for a few seconds, so I try again. That seems to wake the beast.

"Fuck. Off." A pang hits me in the chest at the pain in his voice. It might have only been two angry words, but I heard it nonetheless.

"Zach, it's me. Tabitha."

Silence. Yet I can't help but think he's listening.

"Everyone's worried about you. *I'm* worried about you."

Silence.

"If this is about Saturday, I'm sorry. I never meant to hurt you. I know I should have told you but I knew... I knew you'd hate me." I laugh. "More than you already did, more than you already do." I sigh. "Could you just let me in? We need to know you're okay."

Silence.

"Zach, I swear to fucking god that if you don't open this door then I'm going to get D to break it the fuck down," Titch barks, clearly losing patience with his best friend's antics.

"Do what the fuck you like, I don't give a shit."

"Now we're getting somewhere," Titch says so only I can hear.

"Haven't you got a spare key or something?"

"Yeah, but he's double locked it from the inside. It does fuck all."

I try begging for a few more minutes, but it's pointless. He's not going to open the door for me or anyone.

"Go and get D," I demand loud enough for Zach to hear, getting more and more concerned the longer I stand here. The few words he has said don't sound anything like him. I'm not leaving this place until I see him, and I don't give a shit if that means we take this door off.

"Don't say we didn't fucking warn you," Titch bellows, thundering down the stairs to get reinforcements.

The second he's gone, I hear movement. "Zach, it's just me. Please, open the door. Let me see you. Let me touch you," I add, trying for a different angle.

The click of a lock turning is so loud in the empty space around me that it makes me jump. Seconds later, the door cracks open. He pulls it just wide enough for me to slip inside before slamming it shut once again.

The flat is in darkness with only a small side light on in the corner, but that's not the most noticeable thing. The entire place is trashed.

"Fuck, Zach. What's—" My words falter when I get a look at him. "Fuck." He's wearing only a pair of grey joggers, his sculpted chest and abs on full display, but I don't pay attention like I usually would because it's his eyes that draw me in. The usually glistening blue is hard and cold. Deep frown lines mar his forehead. His hair is a mess like he's spent the past week running his fingers through it, and he's grown almost a full on beard. My eyes flick over the rest of him before stopping on his bruised and bloodstained knuckles.

Reaching out, I take one of his hands into mine inspect the damage. His breath catches at my contact, and I look back up to his sad face.

I take a step forward until his body heat hits mine and run my palm up his chest until it comes to a rest, cupping his cheek. He leans into my touch, and it's in that moment that I know I've got him.

Our eyes hold, his breaths increasing with just our innocent contact. In that moment, I can't help feeling like I'm his lifeline. It's a heady feeling, knowing that I can have such an effect on such an enigma.

He stiffens at the sound of footsteps heading up the stairs. "It's okay," I whisper, afraid that he's going to freak out and kick me back out.

"Tabitha?" Titch calls.

"It's okay. I'm inside. Go back to work. I've got this."

"You sure?"

"More than sure. I'll let you know if we need anything."

He still stands frozen to the spot until the sound of the door shutting to the studio downstairs echoes around us. Then it all happens at once. His hands land on my waist, his lips press to mine, and I'm guided back until he finds a surface to press me up against.

His hands are everywhere as if he can't get enough of me as his mouth desperately assaults mine. His tongue pushes past my lips, searching mine, and I hungrily suck it deeper, craving his taste, his touch, just as much as he is mine.

I've no clue what's happened to put that look on his face, but I already know that I'll do whatever it takes to help wipe it away.

"Tabby Cat," he groans, almost in amazement as he brushes kisses across my jaw.

"I'm here. I'm here," I repeat, lightly grazing my nails up and down his back so he feels me.

"I need you. I need you so fucking bad." The honesty in his tone knocks the wind out of me.

"I'm here. Take what you need." I'm not sure I've ever said more honest words. Anything I can do right now to make whatever is eating him better, I will.

"Fuck. I don't deserve this... you."

"I'm here. Stop questioning it."

He pulls back and looks into my eyes for a beat. For a second, I think he's going to pull away, but then he blinks and I get a look at the Zach I know, the Zach I've fallen too hard for despite everything. His eyes alight with excitement and a cocky smirk pulls at his lips.

"Fuck," he grunts before his lips find mine once again. His tongue plunges into my mouth and he kisses me like it's our first. Like he's exploring me for the first time, and I lap it up.

His hand finds its way under the hem of my oversized hoodie and he groans in delight when he finds I'm only wearing a thin crop top beneath. His fingers dive under the elastic band, and in seconds he's cupping my breast in his palm.

A loud sigh falls from my lips before he pinches my nipple and a spark shoots down between my legs.

"God, I need to be inside you. I need to feel you against me, feel you coming around me." His words are like fuel to my already out of control flames.

"Yes, yes."

I pull my hand around from his back and find his hard length. I rub him over the fabric and delight in watching his eyes shutter with pleasure.

"It's been too long since I've had you, Kitten. Too. Fucking. Long."

His hand leaves my breast in favour of dropping lower. He makes quick work of pushing past my waistband, and before I get a chance to breathe, he's parting me and dipping his fingers into my heat.

"So fucking wet. So fucking addictive." He plunges two fingers deep inside me. He finds my g-spot almost instantly, and before I know what's happening, he's teasing me closer and closer to release.

"No," he barks, startling me. And then his fingers are gone. "When you come, it's around my cock."

I nod eagerly, loving the image he paints.

"What are you waiting for?"

"For you to change your mind."

His moment of honesty is like a bucket of cold water.

"W-what?" I look at him, really look at him. All his barriers are down. He's standing before me, naked and scared as fuck. Scared to feel this thing between us. Scared to believe it's real, that I can really be standing here giving him a lifeline while he's going through whatever it is that's happened in the last few days.

I close the space between us, lifting my hands to his rough cheeks, and stare into his eyes. "I'm not backing down if you don't."

"Fucking hell, Kitten. You fucking rip me wide open, you know that?"

I shake my head. "Show me." I squeal when he reaches down, grabs my arse and lifts me.

His hand finds its way into my hair and he tips my head to expose my neck. He kisses, licks and sucks his way along the sensitive skin as he carries me toward his bedroom.

"Oh god," I moan, his kiss alone building me back up. My hips thrust against him, trying to find some friction to ease the unbearable ache he's causing.

Releasing my legs, he allows me to slide down his body. His hands run up from my hips, over my waist and brush over my breasts as he lifts my hoodie over my head and drops it to the floor. My crop top follows. No sooner has the fabric passed my breasts than his lips are wrapping around one of my nipples and sucking it deep into his mouth.

My head falls back as I focus on the feeling of his mouth and hands on me. It's a feeling I'm never going to tire of, I already know that.

He releases my nipple with a pop before kissing down my stomach, curling his fingers in the waistband of my leggings and pulling them and my knickers down my thighs.

They're still around my ankles when he gently pushes against my hips until I fall down to the bed behind me. He pulls the fabric free before parting my ankles as wide as they'll go and licking up the length of me.

My hips buck from the bed as the sensation hits all my nerve endings. "Zach, fuck."

My words of encouragement spur him on. Two fingers slip inside me as he ups the ante on my clit. My fingers delve into his hair and pull, keeping him exactly where he is.

He doesn't let up until I'm about to fall over the edge, but unlike last time, I'm expecting him to pull away, and I can't argue because if his reasoning for doing it before was true, then I'm about to get something even better.

He stands from between my thighs, wipes his mouth with the back of his hand and pushes his thumbs into the waistband of his joggers.

My eyes drop down and take in every line and indentation of his body before he drops the fabric and reveals his steel length. My mouth waters as I remember just how he tasted when he was deep inside my mouth. Right now, I might need him between my legs more than my next breath, but fuck if I don't want to do that again.

"Fuck, you're remembering what it was like to have me in your mouth, aren't you?" My eyes fly up to his, shocked that my thoughts must be written all over my face.

My cheeks heating are my only response. He crawls onto the end of the bed, and I'm unable to do anything but watch as he settles between my thighs and takes himself in his hand.

The muscles in his neck strain as he works himself.

"Zach, please. Please, I need to feel you."

His eyes darken at my demand. "Feel me where?"

"Inside me, stretching me, filling m—" I don't get to finish because he thrusts forward, filling me to the hilt in one quick movement.

I cling onto his shoulders, my nails digging into his skin as he embarks on a punishing rhythm that has me soaring towards release in mere seconds.

His fingers dig into my hips and he thrusts into me again and again as he chases his demons away.

"Fuck, fuck, Tabby cat," he groans. Sweat beads his brow as he releases one hand and presses his thumb to my clit. "Come," he demands, and I can't do anything but follow orders when he slams into me one more time.

I cry out his name as pleasure detonates within me and spreads all the way to my fingers and toes. He doesn't let up his movement for a few more seconds, then his entire body stills before he growls out his release and his cock twitches violently inside me, filling me with everything he has.

He almost immediately falls down onto me and tucks his head into my shoulder. His breaths rush out against me making goosebumps prick my already heated skin.

With my hands trailing up and down his back, he stays there for the longest time. Having his weight on me feels incredible but as amazing as it might be, us lying here isn't going to solve whatever it is that has him locked up in here while he takes his anger out on the furniture and his fists.

"Zach," I whisper, not wanting to startle him in case he's starting to drift, although from the amount he seems to have on his mind, I highly doubt it.

"Yeah, Kitten," he whispers back, making me shudder with the soft way he says my nickname.

"You need to start talking."

Unfortunately, he rolls off me. I miss his weight almost instantly when he falls onto his back and stares up at the ceiling. Not liking the distance he's just put between us, I roll onto my side and rest myself on his chest. His eyes close as he accepts my support, and after a few seconds his arms come around me.

He takes a few deep breaths before his quiet voice fills the space around us. "You know that girl who came in for a tattoo a few weeks ago?" I open my mouth to get him to elaborate, but he beats me to it. "The one you had to ID to make sure she was old enough?" I nod, not wanting to distract him. "Well, she came back for her second session on Wednesday."

I tense as I wait to hear what she's got to do with this current situation. "She was even more nervous than the first time, which seemed really odd. She kept looking at me, like, really looking at me. It was weird." My brow creases as I try to put two and two together and get nowhere. He can't be telling me that she's suddenly the love of his life, because I'm currently naked in his arms.

"Okay," I say when he seems to come to a stop.

His body is once again tense as he recalls whatever happened. Lifting one of my hands, I start trailing my fingertips over the roses inked on his pecs in the hope it reminds him that I'm here and willing to listen to anything he needs to tell me.

"She's my sister." I suck in a breath, at first thinking that I've misheard him.

"She's you..." I trail off, trying to figure it out.

"Head fuck, right?"

"Um... I don't even know what to say."

"No, nor did I. But as I looked at her, I just knew. There was something about her."

"Okay so—"

"I called my dad. He confirmed it in not so many words. They've been lying to me my whole fucking life."

Every muscle in his body pulls tight at his admission. "I've always felt like the outsider, and now I know why. Whenever Harrison joked about me not being of the same blood, he was fucking right. I don't even know what to think. I don't know who the fuck I am right now."

My heart bleeds for the lost look on his face. I know he feels unattached to his family at the best of times, being so different to them, but this has really knocked him for six.

"Zach," I breathe, not knowing where to start to try to make him realise that none of what he's just said affects who he is as a person. I lift my hand to his cheek and encourage him to look at me. His haunted eyes find mine and I suck in a breath, wishing I could fix this. "You are you. An incredibly talented artist, a pretty awesome businessman, a great friend—you know, based on the fact you have a lot of them," I say with a laugh because it's not like we've ever actually been friends. The smallest of smiles twitches at his lips, telling me that he understands. "You're an arrogant prick who knows exactly where his skills lie and ensures that everyone knows exactly how good you are. You make women fall at your feet on a daily basis and have men looking at you wishing they had even half of your charm."

His smirk grows the longer I talk. "Women fall at my feet. Is that right?"

"Oh come on, hotshot. You can't tell me you're oblivious to your charms."

"I don't remember you falling anywhere near me."

"That's because I'm different."

"Oh yeah?" He reaches out and tucks a lock of hair behind my ear, and the gentle brush of his skin against mine has butterflies waking up in my belly.

"Yeah. I did the opposite. I said no. But look where I ended up anyway. Even though I hate you."

His fingers trail down my neck and over my shoulder. Goosebumps follow their movement, my nipples pebbling against him.

"Hmmm... if I remember correctly, you admitted to falling out of hate with me the other night."

"I was pretty drunk."

"Is that right?"

"Yeah. I say all sorts of shit I don't mean when I'm drunk." I can't fight the smile that wants to break, and the second it does, I'm glad because a genuine one lights up Zach's face.

"Maybe I should remind you what made you say it." He rolls me onto my back and captures my nipple in his mouth as his hard length presses against my thigh.

His fingers find me wet and willing once again, but instead of teasing me until I'm begging, he quickly moves so he's once again at home between my legs. Only this time, once he starts kissing me, he never lets up. His hips move almost leisurely as he mimics the movement of his tongue. His fingers trail teasingly down my body. His actions are so tender that they make tears burn the back of my eyes. I keep them shut, thankful that he's kissing me and unable to see the emotional wreck he's turning me into.

He releases my lips in favour of my jaw and, when he gets to my ear, he whispers my name, followed by an admission that rocks me to my core. "I'm pretty sure I've fallen out of hate with you too."

CHAPTER THIRTY-FOUR

ZACH

WHEN I WAKE NOT LONG LATER from my impromptu nap, it's with Tabitha in my arms and the memories of her turning up here earlier. I've been a fucking mess since that phone call with my dad Wednesday night. But I did not see that coming, or the fact he was basically going to tell me it was true.

Rolling over, I pull her closer and bury my nose in her hair. Just having her here settles everything inside me that's been rioting over the past few days. I knew it would, but my stubborn arse was never going to call her. I'd fucked up when I left her in that hotel room, I knew that the second the door shut behind me. The last thing she needed after that was me turning up like a fucking head case and needing to lose myself in her. But she came, and she allowed me to take what I needed.

"Did you just sniff me?"

"Yeah, I did. Problem?"

She turns in my arms and looks up at me from under her lashes. My cock twitches again. Will I ever get enough of this woman?

"I sure hope not," she says with a coy smile.

"Shit, did I say that out loud?"

"You only said what I'm thinking."

I lean forward to kiss her, but her hand on my chest stops me. My brow creases and my lips curl in a pout.

"Cute. But I'm pretty sure we didn't actually finish talking earlier, and I got dragged away from my dinner date and I'm starving." I tense at the mention of a date. "Don't get your knickers in a twist. It was with your sister… Danni," she adds just to confirm, and I hate that it allows a little bit of my reality to creep back in. "Speaking of, did you know she and Titch know each other?"

"No. As far as I'm aware Titch has never met any of my family, why?" I lie back with my hands behind my head as she scoots to the end of the bed. I take in the soft curves of her slim waist and full hips as my cock goes full mast. She stands and bends to grab something from the floor. "You're fucking killing me here, you know that right?"

She keeps her back to me but looks over her shoulder once she's back at full height and winks as she leisurely runs her eyes down the length of me until she finds my cock.

"There's time for that later. Right now, I need feeding, and looking at the state of this place, I'm thinking there's no food." She pulls one of my discarded t-shirts over her head and I can't help noticing how much better it looks on her than it ever has on me, especially when I know that there's absolutely nothing underneath it.

Her mentioning the disaster that is my flat has reality crashing down around me. "I shouldn't have let you in with it like this." I'm not sure if it's my words or my tone that has her stopping before she gets to the door.

In a second, she's back on the bed with my face in her hands. "Never apologise for needing someone."

"I didn't need someone, Kitten. I needed you." I press my lips to hers for a quick kiss, but knowing everything I've got to deal with, I don't allow myself to linger like I want.

"I'll attempt to tidy up and you can order whatever you want."

She watches me from the doorway as I swing my legs from the bed and pull on a clean pair of boxers.

"Keep looking at me like that and the only thing I'm going to be eating tonight is you." She squirms at my words and my cock swells once again.

Walking up to her, I grip onto the back of her head and pull her lips to mine. My tongue sweeps into her mouth and tangles with hers. It might have only been minutes ago I had her, but I'm desperate once again.

"You're so fucking addictive," I murmur against her lips when I pull back a fraction. My hand skims down her body and pulls her soft curves against the hard lines of mine. She gasps at our contact, letting me know that my touch affects her like hers does.

Resting my forehead against hers, I allow myself a few minutes to breathe her in. "Thank you," I whisper, my lips gently brushing hers.

She doesn't say anything, instead just absorbs my

gratitude for her forcing her way in here, into my flat, into my heart, before her stomach grumbles so loudly I can't help but bark out a laugh. "Come on, I think we need to feed you."

"Should I tell Danni that I won't be back?"

"Why, did you want to go home to her instead of being here with me?" I ask over my shoulder as I head for the bathroom.

When her answer doesn't come right away, I look back and smile. Her eyes are locked on my arse, her teeth attacking her bottom lip.

"Sorry, did you say something?"

"Order us some damn dinner, woman."

When I emerge from the bathroom only a few minutes later, Tabitha's phone sits on the counter but she's on her hands and knees in the kitchen, picking up what remains of my shattered plates and glasses. Guilt hits me, watching her tidy up my mess. My heart constricts that she feels the need to do this when I'm the one who fucked everything up.

"Leave that." The demand comes out harsher than I intend, and she stills immediately with her hand reaching for another shattered piece of ceramic. After sucking in a breath, she looks back at me. She looks so innocent, so delicate, and so fucking at home dressed in only my shirt and in my flat. "Sorry," I whisper. "You go and sit down. I'll sort this."

"It's okay, let me help," she says, standing amidst the chaos that is my life right now. She's like a fucking angel trying to drag me from my demons. The only light amongst all my dark. And fuck if she doesn't call to me. *Walk toward the light, Zach.*

Stepping over the mess, I do just that. My hands skirt

around her waist until they grip onto her arse and pull her into me. My cheek brushes hers as I move my lips to her ear. "You've done enough."

"Zach, I—" I silence her with a finger on her lips.

"Go and sit down." With a smack to the arse, she hops over the mess and does as she's told, although her eyes never leave me as I continue the job she started. My skin burns with her attention, making me wish I never allowed her out of the bedroom in the first place.

I've just about got everything swept up when the buzzer goes off. She's up off the sofa in a flash and heading for the door.

"What the fuck do you think you're doing?" I bark, halting her movements.

"Um… getting the dinner."

"Like fuck you are." Throwing the tea towel to the counter, I stalk over. "The only man who sees you dressed like that is me. You got that?"

A lopsided smile pulls at her lips. She wants to chastise me for my macho bullshit, I can see it in her eyes, but equally, she loves that I've taken possession of her.

With my fingers in her hair, I tug her head back. "You're mine. No one else gets to see what belongs to me." Her eyes hold mine, sparkling with pleasure which only gets more intense when I lift the edge of my shirt and run my finger through her wet folds. A groan of pleasure rumbles up the back of my throat. "Mine," I repeat, plunging two fingers inside her. "Understood?"

She nods but no words escape. Instead, she gasps when I find the spot that makes her scream before the buzzer goes off again, forcing me to move. Lifting my fingers, I suck them into my mouth. Tabitha watches my every move, and I know she's only getting wetter and wetter. I make myself to walk to the door to get the dinner before I take her again.

When I get back, she's laid up the coffee table with the only items she could find for us to eat off. She's got a small side plate while I've got a standard plate with a huge chunk missing, and we've got water in travel mugs.

"I think you might need to go shopping," she says with a shrug as I drop the bag down.

"What I was going to eat off wasn't top of my priority list at the time." I feel like an idiot for allowing my emotions over this whole thing to get the better of me. I was already beating myself up about how I left things with Tabitha, I really didn't need that bombshell on top of it as well.

Her warm hand lands on mine. "It is what it is, Zach. You needed to blow off steam, I get that. You can use me from now on." A smile makes its way to my lips.

"Yeah?"

"Whatever you need." I nod at her, wondering what the fuck I did to deserve this right now, as she reaches for the takeout bag and starts dishing up.

I can't remember the last time I've eaten, but the second she pulls the lid off the Chinese I'm suddenly ravenous. Glancing at all the tubs, I wonder if she suspected as much because she's ordered enough to feed the five thousand.

We sit on the floor around my coffee table and I can't help but wonder if it's the best meal of my life.

"Why are you looking at me like that?" she asks, when she notices that my attention is on her and not my plate.

"I'm sorry for how things went down on Saturday. You didn't deserve any of that."

"You were hurt, understandably. You were right, I should have been honest with you from the start."

"I'm pretty sure that if you were, we wouldn't be here right now. So as fucked up as everything is, it got us here."

She smiles at me and I relax. "Maybe you're right. You hated me on sight as it was, you didn't need the knowledge of me knowing your family on top of that. You never would have kept me."

The mention of family has my muscles locking up. Are they even that now? Reaching over, I take her hand. "Can I keep you now?"

She laughs. "If you want me."

Pulling her over the coffee table, I lean into her ear. "Always."

I allow her to sit back to finish eating. She stays silent for a few minutes, but I know she's got a million questions on the tip of her tongue.

"Spit it out, Kitten."

"What did your dad say exactly?"

"Not much. Some bullshit that we should talk about it in person."

"So you've not actually talked yet?"

I shake my head, remembering just how fucking angry I was when he confirmed what Kas had said.

"You really need to talk to them." I sigh. I know she's right, but I'm not really sure I can face it. "You need to know the truth, Zach. It might be the right time for you to be completely honest with them too, about who you are."

I mull over her words. So many times over the years I've almost told them everything, but something's always held me back. On some level I've always known there was something different about me, and I can't help but wonder if that's why.

"Will you come with me?" The words are out of my mouth before I've even really thought about them, but I know without a doubt that I want her there. If she's going to be a part of my future, which I'm hoping she is, then she needs to be by my side.

"Whatever you need."

"You. Just you."

A smile lights up her face. She reaches for my phone that's half fallen down the sofa cushion. "Organise it for tomorrow morning. It's time to get everything out in the open."

I take a long breath before sending everyone a message to meet me at my parents'. The confirmations come back almost immediately, and my nerves hit me.

"They'll be so proud of you, Zach. You've built something incredible here. You're going to blow them away."

As I look at her soft, beautiful face, it dawns on me just how much I crave their approval with what I've been doing. It's always been easier for them just to assume I'm a huge fuck-up than to risk them disapproving of everything I've worked towards since I was fourteen.

"Now," she says, getting onto her hands and knees and crawling toward me. "We've got a few hours to waste before then." She stops beside me and pulls my shirt up and over her head, exposing her sexy curves to me. "And I've got a few ideas for what we can do to pass the time."

"Oh yeah?" She throws one leg over my waist and settles herself on top of me.

"We may as well mess this place up a little more before putting everything back together."

"Hmmm," I groan as I watch her fingertip trail over

the stars on my shoulder, my cock thickening against the confines of my boxers.

"And I think we should start right now." Her hand skims down my abs before disappearing inside my boxers to reveal my length. Taking it in her hand, she lifts herself up before sinking down on me. We both groan in pleasure as she ever so slowly takes me. "Lie back, relax. I've got this."

I fall back onto my elbows and watch her body move against mine. It's one of the best things I've ever fucking seen, and one I'd like to repeat as often as physically possible.

CHAPTER THIRTY-FIVE

TABITHA

ZACH'S HAND holds mine impossibly tight as we walk up toward his parents' front door the next morning. We did as I suggested last night and fucked on every surface we could in his flat before falling exhausted into his bed sometime in the early hours.

As I walk, my muscles pull and my core aches, but it's the most delicious feeling, especially with him still standing beside me.

Part of me was worried about what I'd find when I woke this morning, but much to my delight, Zach just pulled me tighter into his body and held me like he never wanted to let go.

"You okay?" I ask as we come to a stop at the door. His

hand trembles slightly in mine, and when I glance over at him, his features are pulled tight with tension.

He nods once. I know it's his way of saying no but not wanting to verbalise it. We might have only really known each other a few weeks, but already I can read him unlike most others.

He lifts his hand to open the door, but at the last minute he hesitates and looks at the doorbell.

"Just do what you normally do. No matter what they've got to tell you, they still love you."

He nods again and goes back to the handle. Behind the door is a home much like my own parents', but instead of the cold and unhomely space I'm used to this one is filled with family and love. Everywhere I look there are photos that span over thirty years. I can't help but smile, already feeling at ease, and I've only walked through the entrance hall.

"They'll be in the kitchen."

"Let's go then."

Every head turns toward us as we step into the kitchen.

"Zach," his mum breathes as she rushes for him. Her arms wrap around his shoulders and she holds him like she's not seen him in years, not only a week. "I'm so sorry," she whispers quietly in his ear. "I love you so much, I always have. I need you to know that."

Zach stands as still as a fucking rock while she falls apart around him.

After a few more seconds she pulls back and wipes at her eyes. "Tabitha, what a nice surprise."

I smile at her, not really knowing what to say in this situation, before his dad sweeps her into his arms.

When I look up, I find Danni smiling at me from the

breakfast bar. I give Zach's hand a squeeze and take a step over to her, but I'm pulled back into his side. He shakes his head ever so slightly. The look in his eyes pulls at my heart. He's so close to the edge right now, and the fact that he needs me beside him means more to me than I think he'll ever believe.

"Would you both like a drink?" Zach's dad asks us.

When Zach makes no move to say anything, I answer for both of us. "Coffee would be great, thank you."

With our hands still joined, I lead a silent and tense Zach over to where Danni and Harrison are sitting and pull us out a stool.

"Good night?" Danni asks with a wink.

"Fantastic, thank you. I'm surprised you want details."

"I don't, what I'm seeing right now is enough." She makes a fake gagging gesture as she looks between the two of us, but she can't help the small smile on her lips at the same time. "Seriously though, if you're happy and he treats you right," her eyes drill into Zach's, "then I'm happy for you. Just... think twice the next time I'm only the other side of the wall, eh?"

Zach's hand tightens in mine. "Motherfucker," he grunts. "*She* was your friend that night?"

"Lucky for you, I was so drunk that I didn't hear a thing."

"I'm not sure that makes it any better." Hearing the lightness in Zach's tone as he jokes with his sister fills me with hope that he's also going to be able to walk out of here with a smile on his face once everyone has had their say.

"Here we go." Two steaming mugs are placed in front of us before Zach's parents join us all. "Zach, I'm so sorry that you had to find out like you did. It was never our intention to—"

"Before we do that. I've got some things I need to say first."

"Okay," his parents say in unison, while Harrison also leans forward slightly to hear what his younger brother has to say. Danni just sips on her tea, seeing as I've already filled her in on Zach's mystery life.

"While we're all being honest, I need you all to know that I'm not the waste-of-space fuck-up you think I am who lives on his trust fund and is doing nothing with his life."

"Son, that's not what—"

"Yes it is. I can see it in your eyes, your disappointment that I've never made anything of my life like the rest of you. But actually, that's not true." Everyone leans in that little bit more as Zach prepares to rock their world slightly. "I own and run a chain of tattoo studios."

His mother gasps, her hand covering her mouth in shock. His dad's chin drops, and pride fills Harrison's eyes.

"He doesn't just mean a couple here in London either," I add, needing them to fully understand and to break the silence. "He has studios in the US as well. He's building an empire."

My chest swells with pride at the look on their faces.

Silence falls around us as everyone absorbs what he just said.

"That's awesome, bro. I'm proud of you," Harrison says, getting up to slap his brother lovingly on the back.

"Thanks, man."

His mum and dad follow suit before everyone is once

again silent as the weight of the impending conversation presses down on everyone.

"Zach," his dad starts. Zach visibly flinches beside me, his hand tightening in mine as he stares at the counter in front of him instead of his father's eyes. "What you... what you discovered this week. It's true. Kassie is your sister—your half-sister. I'm not proud of the mistake I made back then, but equally, I can't regret it because it gave me you, and that's not something I'd change for the world. After we had Harrison, your mum was desperate for another, but for whatever reason, it wasn't happening. Years passed and still nothing. Neither of us were in a good place. Fertility help wasn't available as easily back then as it is now, and it was taking a toll on our relationship. Watching your mum suffer was the worst thing I've ever experienced." We all watch as he takes his wife's hand and squeezes gently, as if he's apologising for taking her back to that time. "She was so desperate to carry another baby. She was—is— an incredible mum, and the fact it wasn't happening was devastating.

"I went out with some friends one night. I didn't want to go, but they were adamant that I let my hair down. They could see things weren't good at home and that I needed a breather. I had more to drink than I usually would, enjoying the freedom I suddenly had, and one thing led to another and—" A collective gasp sounds out around the room.

"You cheated on Mum?" Harrison growls, anger filling his voice as he stares daggers at his father. Zach sits straight, his eyes boring into his dad's, his fingers clenching in mine with his need to do something.

"I did." All the air rushes from their dad's lungs as he admits his mistake. His eyes glisten with emotion and regret, and if it weren't for the vice-like grip Zach's holding my hand with, I'd get up and hug him. Just talking about it all these years later is ripping him apart—I can only imagine how bad it must have been at the time.

"She was young, and I was stupid. I can give you all the excuses under the sun, but at the end of the day, I fucked up. I knew the moment I did it that it was the wrong thing to do. I loved your mother with all my heart, but things hadn't been easy. But I knew then that I'd spend the rest of my life making up for that one mistake. She's the only one for me." He wraps his arm around his wife as the tears filling his eyes finally drop.

"I came home, admitted everything, and after a very, very long time in the dog house, she thankfully gave me a second chance.

"I thought no more of it, just grateful not to have lost my family. At no point did I consider that a few months later there would be a knock at my door and a familiar, pregnant woman would be standing on the other side.

"As I said, she was young, she didn't have a very desirable lifestyle—"

"She was a hooker, wasn't she?" Zach suddenly asks, his cold voice startling me. I've never heard him sound so cut off. It's like he's just a shell of the man I know as he listens to this heart-wrenching story that shatters everything he thought he knew about his life.

His dad looks at the table, allowing everyone to assume his answer, although after a few seconds he gives one of his own. "I didn't pay her, if that's what you mean."

"No, you gave her something much more meaningful," Zach snaps. I squeeze his hand in support when I fear he's about to let go of the final bit of restraint he's desperately clutching at right now.

"I did, and I wouldn't change him for the world. Anyway, like I said, she was young, her life was a mess. When she told me—told us—that she was pregnant and that it was mine, we offered to help her, but she was adamant that she wasn't capable of bringing up a baby. We tried to support her, we got her into a rehab and organised some counselling. It worked while she was pregnant. She did what she needed to do to ensure you were looked after and brought into the world as you deserved to be. But the day she had you, she told us that she wouldn't be your mother. That you had a family who could love you in a way she wasn't able to. It was heartbreaking to watch, but none of us could deny that she was right.

"When you left that hospital, it was in your mother's arms." Zach's mum sobs on her husband's shoulder as he retells the heart wrenching story. My chest aches for what they all went through, for the woman who was selfless enough to do the right thing for her baby.

I glance from his emotional parents to Zach. His lips are pressed into a thin line and his jaw works as he grinds his teeth. I can't imagine how hard it must be to hear all this. How you even go about accepting it.

"She was a good person, Zach. She was just in a bad place in her life. Fallen in with the wrong people. She desperately wanted better for you."

"Wha—" His voice cracks, and it causes my eyes to burn knowing how much this is hurting him to hear right now. "What happened to her."

"I kept tabs on her for a long time. It's how we know she went on to have Kassie. She seemed to be in a better place with a stable relationship. Seeing that she'd rebuilt her life, we took a step back. It wasn't our job to keep an eye on her. She was a fully-grown woman. But it gave us peace of mind that she'd turned things around."

"She's dead." His voice is cold and empty. I desperately want to crawl onto his lap and hold him.

His parents suck in sharp breaths. They had no idea.

"It's what brought Kas to the studio. She wanted a tattoo to remember her."

"Fucking hell. I'm so sorry, son."

Zach drops his eyes from his father's and to the table, his head shaking back and forth slowly. "Does she have any other family?"

"I'm sorry, but I don't know."

"Fuck," he barks, suddenly pushing the stool out behind him with such force it crashes to the floor.

"Zach?" I ask, my eyes wide with panic. His chest is puffed out like he's about to fight, and I'm terrified of what might happen next.

He looks at me and everything about his demeanour softens. "It's okay," he mouths, and I nod. Our eyes hold for a beat before he turns back to his parents. "Thank you for…" he trails off, lost in thought. "Thank you for everything. I'm sorry it had to come out this way." He digs his hand into his pocket and pulls his wallet out. "Here. This is where I am. I live in the flat above the studio if you ever want to… err… visit—"

"Or get a tattoo," Danni throws in from behind me, her attempt to lighten the mood.

His parents smile sadly, standing with him. His mum moves first and rushes around the table to embrace him.

I don't hear the hushed words she says to him, but the tears that fill his eyes almost break me. Since the moment I first met him as a child, Zach's always been this larger-than-life character. He's the one who leaves tears in his wake, he's never the broken one, barely holding on to his own emotions. His dad steps up and wraps his arms around the two of them.

Unable to look away from the three of them, I jump when Danni steps up behind me and wraps her arm around my shoulders. "I think you might be the best thing that ever happens to him," she whispers in my ear, and my tears finally drop.

"Oh, I don't know about that," I sniffle.

"You know what I do know," she states with a wicked smile on her tear-stained face. I arch a brow as I wait for what she's got to say. "Your parents are going to fucking hate him. Please can I be there when you introduce him?"

"Oh god," I groan, not needing the reminder that we've still got another set of parents to deal with at some point.

The trio in front of us breaking apart thankfully pushes thoughts of my family from my mind. One lot of family drama at a time is more than enough.

Zach's mum kisses him on the cheek before stepping away. He immediately searches me out and lifts his arm towards me. I don't hesitate in sliding my fingers into his and accepting his embrace when he pulls me into his side.

"I know you already know her, but this is Tabitha, my girlfriend, if she'll have me." The lump that climbs up my throat is so huge that there's no way I can answer him with words. Instead, I look up at him, a huge smile on my face, and nod.

His mum, who'd just about got herself under control, sobs once more.

"I think that might be the most shocking thing about this whole morning. Zach's found a girl who'll put up with him," Harrison goads, earning himself a slug to the shoulder.

After a few minutes, everyone says their emotional goodbyes and Zach leads me back to the front door.

His car, a huge blacked out BMW, sits out the front of his parents'. He opens the door and waits for me to climb in before heading to the driver's side to join me.

The second he's in, he rests his head back against the headrest, closes his eyes and blows out the longest breath.

Reaching over, I place my palm on his thigh, just so he knows I'm here while he takes a moment to process his information overload.

"There are two things I really want to do right now," he admits. I turn toward him, eager to find out what they are. "I need to ink someone, and I need to fuck someone." His eyes open and find mine immediately. My breath catches, because his eyes are telling me that that someone is me. My skin tingles in anticipation of both. Having his hands on me in any sense is mind blowing. "But there's something else I need to do first."

"Oh?" I watch as he pulls his phone from his pocket, taps the screen and places it to his ear.

"It's me. We need to talk. Where are you?" He's silent for a few seconds as he listens. "Okay, we'll be there in ten."

He drops his phone into the centre console and puts the car into drive.

The question is right on the end of my tongue to ask where we're going, but the determination on his face stops me. I'm already pretty certain I know anyway. I sit back and allow him the thinking time that he must so desperately need.

Ten minutes later, he pulls into a side road, and I'm

not surprised when a feisty little brunette steps out from the shadows. She looks just like she did the first time I saw her. Terrified. Her blue eyes are wide as she takes in the over the top car and walks towards the driver.

"You hungry?"

"Starved."

"Good. Hop in, we're going for lunch." And just like that, a brother-sister bond is formed.

CHAPTER THIRTY-SIX

ZACH

I THINK of the girl I'm driving toward and wonder what her life's been like. I barely know her, but from seeing the darkness that haunted her eyes in the few hours we spent together, I already know that she didn't grow up in a huge house in Kensington and spend her younger years at a private school.

My fingers white-knuckle the steering wheel as Tabitha's hand squeezes my thigh in support. Something settles inside me knowing that she's there. That she's supporting me. I don't deserve to have her by my side through all of this after everything I did to her. Her being here means everything and makes my chest ache in a totally different way, a way I've never experienced before and a way I don't think I ever want to stop.

"Are you okay?" she asks softly from beside me as we sit in the London traffic.

"Yeah," I say, and although I didn't think I would be after what we've just experienced, I really think I am. "I've always known that I don't fit. In a weird way, it's almost a relief to know that I was right all these years."

"You fit in just fine, Zach. You always have. Just because you like different things, it doesn't mean you're not part of your family."

Silence falls around us once again as I mull her words over.

The atmosphere in the car changes the second Kas pulls the back door open and steps inside. She wasn't expecting my call today. We've not spoken since she ran from the shop on Wednesday, making me wonder why she so easily accepted this invitation for an impromptu lunch.

Hardly any words are spoken as I drive us to a restaurant. It's one my parents used to take us to as kids. It's nothing fancy, but if Kas has had the kind of life I expect she might then I want to take her somewhere normal that brings me happy memories.

"Zach?" she asks as we leave the car behind and walk toward the restaurant.

"I'll go and get us a table. You two take your time," Tabitha says, taking another step from me, but I don't allow her to go. Giving her arm a tug, I pull her back so I can drop a quick kiss to her lips.

"Thank you," I murmur before releasing her and looking to my newly acquired sister.

We both watch Tabitha as she disappears into the front doors, the silence heavy around us.

"I'm sorry that I—"

"I spoke to my parents this morning. They told me everything," I admit, cutting her off and turning towards her. She's so short I almost feel like I'm talking to a child and have to remind myself that she's an adult.

She nods in understanding. "How was that?"

"Painful. More so for my mum than anyone else, I think."

"She must be an incredible woman."

"Yeah." A wide smile curls at my lips as I think about her and how strong she really is. "Yeah she is. You'll love her."

"I can't wait to meet her... if she wants to, of course."

"I'm sure she does." I take a step toward the restaurant, but I suddenly stop. "Kas?"

"Yeah?"

"I'm sorry about your mum." She nods, accepting my words, but I don't miss her eyes getting a little wet at the mention of her. "That must have been tough."

"You don't know the half of it," she admits before sealing her lips like she's said too much.

"Will you tell me about it, about her?"

"I will. Just... maybe not yet. Most of it isn't pretty."

"I feared as much." She steps up to me, and I can't help but rest my arm over her shoulders. I barely know her but I already feel a connection between the two of us. I felt it that first day she was in my studio, and it's only growing now I know the truth. I love my family, more than I can describe, but with Kas here, I can't help feeling like a few of my missing puzzle pieces have suddenly fallen into place. What with Tabitha as well, I almost feel like a whole person for the first time in my life. "Come on, let's eat."

CHAPTER THIRTY-SEVEN

TABITHA

IT'S BEEN a month since that morning at the Abbots' house when the truth about Zach and how he really came into this world was spelled out for him.

I want to be able to say that things were smooth and easy from then on out, but although his parents came and visited the studio and the three of them spent some time together, with everything out in the open it was like there was still a gaping hole between them.

As the days have gone on, things have started to improve. It's been devastating to watch, Zach's mum especially, as she's had to fight to prove to her son that she has only ever seen him as one of her own. Every time I look at her, I just want to pull her in for a hug for being so incredibly supportive and selfless where her family is concerned.

Tonight is Zach's twenty-eighth birthday, and although he was adamant that he only wanted to spend it celebrating with me in bed, as tempting as that idea was, I was even more adamant that he was to spend time out with those who love him.

With the help of his mum, I've organised an evening that will bring his two families together for the first time. I'm nervous, I can't help but be after he's kept his life split in two for so long, but I have every confidence that it'll be a great night.

"Are you sure we can't just stay here?" Zach asks, poking his head around the doorframe to his bedroom where I'm getting ready.

"No, we can't. I can, however, promise you that whatever your imagination is conjuring up right now can be done when we get back."

He pulls me into him so my back presses against his front. "Hmmm..." he hums against my exposed neck. "Is that right?"

"Yep."

"I could get used to this living together thing." His hands roam over my towel-covered body before tugging at the bottom and watching in the mirror as it falls from me. Neither of us has brought up the fact that since the morning we visited his parents I've barely been home. Every night I've found myself here in his arms, but at some point we're going to need to address it. "That's better." His hands skim up my stomach to palm a breast, teasing and pinching my nipples as we both watch. "You sure I can't convince you to stay in?"

"Absolutely not." My voice is breathier than I intended, giving away my desire now his hands are on me.

"But the things I could do to you." He kisses down the column of my neck. Goosebumps erupt across my skin as he moves down to my shoulder. "I could kiss every inch of your body. Trace every line with my tongue. I could part you and feast on you until you're crying out my name, begging to have my cock stretching you open."

"Zach," I part warn, part beg as his words ignite a hunger in me I'm not sure I'm going to be able to ignore.

"You can feel it, can't you? Me moving slowly inside you, stoking those flames that are only getting stronger."

My head falls back against his shoulder as he walks his fingers down my stomach. He teases over my heated skin before—finally—his fingertips connect with the exact place I need them to.

"Oh god," I moan, my eyes closing as I absorb the sensation.

"It's a real shame we're going out, eh?" His hands leave me, and after ensuring I'm not going to fall flat on my back, he takes a step away from me.

His eyes hold mine in the mirror. They're alight with desire and filled with hunger. "Hadn't you better cover that body up? We're going to be late."

A growl of frustration climbs up my throat. "I hate you," I call as he disappears into the bathroom.

"Likewise, Kitten."

I laugh, turning toward the clothes I'd laid out on his bed earlier to the sound of him getting ready in the distance. I've refused to tell him what I've got planned for tonight. I can only assume that he's expecting it to be just the two of us.

I'm in the kitchen, transferring things from my usual

handbag into my clutch for the night when his footsteps head towards me. I drop my lip gloss inside my bag before looking up, and I'm glad I do because if it were still in my hand then I've no doubt it would be heading for the floor right now. Zach's wearing a plain pair of black dress trousers and a classic white shirt that's open at the neck with the sleeves rolled up to his elbows. My mouth waters as I take in the way the fabric clings to his lean body. I bite down on my bottom lip to stop me sighing with contentment that this incredible man before me is all mine. He might be an arrogant arse, but he's *my* arrogant arse.

I make my way up to his face, running my eyes over the scruff that covers his jaw. My thighs clench as the memory of how it felt between them only this morning hits me like a truck. His lips curl into a sexy smirk, knowing exactly where my mind has gone before I find his eyes. The happiness in them sparkles back at me, but I don't miss the heat that threatens to overtake the longer he stares.

"It's not too late to change your mind," he taunts, taking a step toward me so he's close enough to take over every one of my senses. His scent fills my nose and I almost throw caution to the wind and drag him back to the bedroom.

"Nope, we've got people waiting for us," I blurt as an excuse, more for myself than him at this point.

"People?"

"Yep, people. And they're expecting to see the birthday boy."

"They're not expecting us to stay long though, right?"

I laugh at him, and somehow I manage to break our

connection so I can grab my jacket and slip my phone into my bag.

"The car should be downstairs. We need to go." He groans behind me but follows my lead when I head to the door.

The weather might be starting to warm up as spring progresses, but with the clear sky above us, it's bitterly cold as we wait for our car on the pavement.

Noticing my shiver, Zach pulls me into his body and wraps his arms around me. He stares down into my eyes as his warmth seeps into me.

"I've most definitely fallen out of hate with you, Tabby Cat."

"Oh yeah," I tease.

"Yeah, because I've fallen in love with you instead."

My breath catches at his confession and tears immediately burn the backs of my eyes. I've felt it from him a million times, his little touches here and there, the way he looks at me when he thinks I'm not paying attention. Deep down, I knew how he felt, but hearing it... Hearing those words from his lips... They're everything I didn't know I needed.

He drops his head until his lips brush against mine and he gives me the sweetest, most emotional kiss of my life. When he pulls back and rests his forehead against mine, a single tear slips from my eye and runs down my cheek.

"What's this?" he whispers softly, reaching up to wipe it away.

"I—I," I stutter, struggling to pull myself together enough to express how much he means to me. "I love you too." The smile he graces me with melts my heart. I know he's still struggling after the bombshell that his mum's not his biological one, but he's opened his heart up, not only to me, but also to Kas, in a way I never could have imagined when I first stumbled back into his life.

The arrogant bad boy I thought I hated has totally stolen my heart, and I couldn't imagine it any other way.

"Car for Zach?" a voice shouts, dragging our eyes from each other. We both laugh when we find our Uber sitting at the curb with an impatient driver waiting for us to surface.

"Shit, yeah. Sorry, man."

Zach drops one more quick kiss to my lips before taking my hand and guiding me to the car to begin our evening.

I left the details of tonight down to Diane. When we spoke on the phone a few weeks ago it was obvious to me that she needed to do something for Zach after the bomb they'd dropped on him so I left her to it, although not before I mentioned that a Michelin star restaurant might not have been a good choice and to keep it simple. Thankfully, when she messaged me with where she'd booked I discovered that she'd listened to me. Her restaurant of choice was a bistro that had recently opened up not far from the studio, and one glance at the website and I knew Zach would feel totally at home.

I'd mentioned that we were meeting people, but I'd refrained from giving any names. As we walk inside I'm assuming that Zach's only expecting to find one of his families waiting for him—either his Rebel boys, or his real family— but much to his surprise when we're directed to our table he finds everyone, both his worlds sitting together around one huge table.

"H-holy shit," he mutters beside me, his eyes wide as he takes everyone in.

"Happy birthday," everyone sings as he stands motionless.

"How did you—"

"I had a little help."

Diane choose that moment to get up from her seat. "You like it?" Her eyes are a little glassy as she looks up at her youngest boy.

"It's perfect. Thank you." Turning away from her once he's pulled her into a hug, he looks over everyone once again. "I guess some introductions are in order."

Zach names both his parents, Harrison, Summer, and Danni—who is suspiciously sitting as far away from Titch as possible. With all the family drama and the real beginning of mine and Zach's relationship, I've not had a chance to properly ask her about what's going on there. She's been giving us space, too. She tells me it's because this time is precious, but I have a suspicion she's just avoiding me.

He moves on to introduce the guys, and to his delight everyone happily accepts each other and conversations spark up around the table. We take a seat, and it's only then I realise there's an empty one beside Spike. Kas didn't show. My heart drops that she felt like she couldn't be a part of this. I can't say I'm overly shocked, she's never dealt with this kind of family thing, so I would imagine it's a little out of her comfort zone.

The waiter just comes over to begin taking our orders when someone comes rushing over and a huge smile spreads across my lips.

"I'm so sorry. The tube just stopped in the middle of a tunnel and gah!" She waves her hands around frantically while her chest heaves. "I ran from the station trying not to be late."

"It's okay, you're here now," Zach says, standing and pulling her into his arms. "Everyone," he says, turning toward the table and totally ignoring the waiter with this notepad poised to take down orders. "This is my little sister, Kas." He points everyone out, his parents getting up to hug her before Zach gestures to the seat beside Spike. She walks over and drops down and almost instantly gets dragged into conversation as Spike points at the tattoos on her exposed arms.

I look around at everyone as they chat or look down at the menu before them to make their final choice and pride swells within me.

Leaning over, I whisper in the Zach's ear. "You're really fucking lucky, you know that right?" He does a sweep of the table much like I just did.

"Yeah, I'm starting to understand that. Fuck knows why, I don't deserve half of it."

"Zachary Abbot, don't be so modest. You deserve this and so much more."

We have the best night—so much so that I almost forget about the desire he left me with earlier. Almost.

Everything about the night is perfect. Everyone chats like they've known each other for years. Well, everyone aside from Danni and Titch. No matter where Titch is, Danni makes sure she's as far away from him as possible, making both of us more and more curious as to what was going on.

As the evening progresses, Zach's parents say their goodbyes and we head to a club to dance the rest of the night away. Titch suggests we hit up The Avenue, so we all grab our coats and follow his lead.

The guys buy everyone two shots of tequila before we

hit the dancefloor. Zach pulls me into his body and moves his hips with mine in time with the music.

"Hmmm," I moan into his neck. "Why haven't we done this before?" With my arms resting over his shoulders, I absently play with the hair at the nape of his neck.

"Because I'd rather dance with you when you're naked." As he moves, I feel the length of his growing erection against the softness of my stomach.

"Is someone getting ideas?" I ask with a quirked brow.

"Kitten, you're pressed up against me. I have ideas when you're merely in the room, let alone touching me."

I laugh before he captures my lips with his and our tongues join in with the dancing. I'm totally lost to what everyone else is doing around me as I focus on the incredible man in my arms. We dance together until the burning desire that crackles between us gets too much and Zach excuses us to an Uber he has waiting outside so we can go home and continue his birthday celebrations in the privacy of his bedroom.

EPILOGUE

TABITHA

"I'VE GOT A SURPRISE FOR YOU," Zach whispers in my ear.

"If it's what's poking me in the thigh then I've gotta tell you, that's not so much of a surprise as it is expected," I joke, seeing as our mornings always start with a roll in the sheets.

"Well that, obviously, but there's something else too."

"Oh?" I turn onto my side so I can focus on him. My head spins a little from the amount I drank last night, but it's not enough to distract me from what my surprise might be.

"I need you to get up, get dressed in something comfortable, and then pack a bag."

"A bag? What sort of things am I packing?"

"The essentials."

"You know you're talking to a woman, right? Almost everything I own is essential. You're going to need to give me a little more. Clothes for hot or cold weather? How many knickers? What kind of shoes?"

He rolls his eyes at me. "Fine, pack for two weeks. Hot weather, sexy shoes and zero knickers. Anything you forget we'll buy, no biggie."

"Two weeks? Where are we going?"

"It's a surprise," he says teasingly before sitting up and pushing up from the bed.

"But what about—" My eyes drop to his body, and I bite down on my bottom lip.

"No time. But, there's always the mile-high club."

"We're flying?"

"Just get ready, Kitten. And don't forget your passport."

While I get myself sorted, Zach runs down to the studio to sort a few things.

With my bag loaded with everything I could possibly need, I lug it down the stairs after locking up the flat.

"I'd have come and got that for you," he says when I pull it into reception.

"It's fine. You ready to go?"

"I am." He shuts down my computer and spins towards me.

"Don't you have clients?"

"Nope."

"But the calendar was full."

"All fake. I made them up so you wouldn't be suspicious."

I narrow my eyes at him. "Sneaky."

"I thought so."

He grabs both of our cases before turning off the lights and pulling the front door open for me. There's a car waiting outside. He immediately opens the boot and loads our bags inside.

Before I know it, we're walking through Gatwick Airport and towards the desk to check in our bags.

My eyes flick up to the board and excitement explodes in my belly. "We're going to LA?"

"We sure are. Thought it was time you met Corey and experienced how things are done in America." I turn my wide smile from the board displaying our destination and look at Zach. "You happy?" he asks with a chuckle.

"Like you wouldn't believe." Pushing up on my tiptoes, I crash my lips to his and show him just how excited I am. Maybe we'll have to see about that mile-high club thing...

I'M PRACTICALLY BOUNCING on the balls of my feet as we drag our bags out to arrivals. Now we've touched down I'm desperate to experience the delights LA has to offer. The second we walk through the arrival doors, I spot a beast of a man, covered in tattoos, waiting for us.

His eyes light up the second he sees the two of us, and he steps forward with a wide smile on his face.

"Zach, my man. It's so good to see you."

Zach walks straight into him and embraces him in a man hug which involves a lot of back slapping while I laugh at their overexuberant greeting.

"And you must be Biff." Corey's joy at having us there is infectious, and I squeal in delight when he sweeps me off my feet and spins me around.

"Hands off, man. Get your own," Zach sulks.

He laughs at Zach's pouting face as he lowers me to the ground. The world spins a little and I cling to Zach for support.

"Nah, you're all right. I'm not one for tying myself down, you know this." Something passes between them, making me curious about the man I've only spoken to on the phone. Some kind of understanding that only comes from a long-standing friendship. Zach talks about him often but nothing more than a few memories of times they've spent together or related to tattooing, but I don't know much more than that.

"So, when do I get to walk on the golden sands of an LA beach then?" I ask, breaking the tension that suddenly descended around us.

"Not long now. Come on, I've got a car outside." Corey takes our cases, allowing Zach to pull me into his side.

The heat hits us the second we exit the airport, and it's glorious. I tilt my head towards the stunning blue sky and allow it to warm my face.

"You're going to like it here a little too much, I can sense it," Zach laughs, opening the car door for me.

I'm expecting to go to a hotel, so I'm a little surprised when we pull up outside a studio with a very familiar sign hanging out the front.

"It's like home from home," I say, staring at the neon pink Rebel Ink sign.

"Just with a little more sun," Corey adds, jumping from the car and taking our bags from the boot.

We follow him through to the studio and I can't help feeling like I've been transported straight back to London.

"Okay, this place is incredible, but it's a little freaky. I'm still in LA, right?"

Corey and Zach both chuckle as I look around at the familiar reception to the one I man at home.

"You like it?" Zach asks, his arms wrapping around me from behind as his heat warms my back.

"I can't not. It looks like home."

"I might have wanted to run away, but I needed a little bit of my old life with me," Corey says sadly, following my gaze around the space. "Tour?" he asks, coming back to himself and pulling his mind back to the present.

"I'd love one. Do you have a coffee machine Zach could make use of?"

"And here I was thinking Zach was the boss. I didn't realise you'd handed over your business as well as your balls, man."

Zach flips him off as he moves toward a closed door. "Don't go anywhere near her skin with your gun or you won't have any fucking balls left."

"Loud and clear, big man. Loud and clear."

It makes me laugh that Corey calls Zach that when Corey well outweighs him and has at least two inches on his height. He's a beast of a man.

I follow him as he shows me each room. Just like London, each room is different, decorated as its artist desires. "And this is mine." He pushes the door open and my breath catches at the amount of artwork adorning the walls.

"Wow, Zach said you were talented but... wow."

He's silent as my eyes take in design after design before me. I stop when I find one of an intricate heart with flames wrapping around the outside. I lift my finger and trace the lines, lost in the vibrancy of the colour. When I glance back, he's got his arm up, his hand pulling down on the back of his neck looking a little unsure of himself.

He startles at my attention.

"He... uh... he's really fallen for you, you know?" A little colour appears on his cheeks as he says this, telling me he hadn't planned it.

"I like to hope so." I think back to his confession before our meal last night and my heart swells in my chest.

"The way he talks about you on the phone, it's—"

"It's what?" A booming voice comes from behind him.

"Err... shit. Caught red-handed," Corey says with a laugh, lightening the mood a little.

"Don't let me stop you. Anything you need to say to Tabitha you can say in front of me."

"I was just going to say that you've swept him away. Stolen his heart and taken control of his balls. It's quite a sight to see. If he hadn't brought you so I could see you with my own eyes, I wouldn't have believed it possible."

"Aw, Corey. Are you a bit of a romantic a heart?"

"No. Definitely not. But equally I didn't have him down as one either."

"Your time will come, man," Zach says knowingly.

"Abos-fucking-lutely not. I've way too much baggage for one woman to deal with."

"Is that your way of saying you don't want a woman or that you need multiple?" I ask, when things suddenly get serious.

Corey barks out a laugh. "I really like this one, Zach. Don't fuck it up." He turns to me and whispers, "When he does, you can always have a job here."

"Thanks, I appreciate that."

"Right, that's enough. I don't need her to think you're more charming than me." Zach's hand slips into mine. "You've seen the place. Now we need to eat. Surf shack?" he asks, turning back to Corey.

"You bet." Corey pulls his phone from his pocket and books us an Uber.

Minutes later we're on our way to a surf shack that Zach's not stopped talking about since he mentioned it. Best seafood in the state, apparently.

We have a lovely meal looking out over the sea as the sun sets. Zach and Corey catch each other up on their lives as we eat and make easy work of our drinks that the waitress helpfully keeps topped up.

"And how's the lovely Lana?" Corey asks.

"She's good. Busy as always."

"I can't believe it's been almost six years, man." The atmosphere gets heavy as Zach lifts his hand to the dog tag around his neck.

He never talks about Jon. Even now I only know the basics. Corey gets a similar far-off look on his face as he thinks back, and I realise for the first time that this is how they're connected.

"D- did..." I hesitate, because I know Zach won't want to talk about it, but I need more. "Did you know Jon?"

"Yeah. We served together. Our military service ended on the same day."

Our eyes hold as what he's saying registers into my jet-lagged brain.

"Oh. But you're—"

"Surviving."

"Can I get you guys any desserts?" the waitress sings, distracting us from the heaviness of the conversation.

Thankfully, once we place our orders we manage to turn the conversation to lighter topics. Corey tells us about the new places he's discovered here, and ensures that Zach agrees to taking me to a few of them.

We have a great night. It's clear to see why Zach trusted Corey over here with this part of the business. He's so easy to get on with, despite his obvious issues that keep his eyes a little clouded most of the time.

"You ready to head to the hotel?" Zach asks, finishing off his pint.

Thoughts of a swanky LA hotel room fill my mind and all the things we could do in one have my temperature spiking.

"I think she is, if that look is anything to go by," Corey laughs. Perceptive fucker. "I'll get the bill, you two head off."

"Nah, man. My treat. You deserve a bonus for all you've done out here."

"Don't I fucking know it."

In only minutes we're saying goodbye to Corey, agreeing to meet him at the studio in the morning so the guys can go over some stuff. Excitement tingles in my belly of what's to come for our trip here.

The car drives along the coast, allowing us to take in the last of the evening sun before it dives into the sea, and before long we're pulling up in front of an incredible hotel right on the beachfront in Malibu.

The place is mind-blowing, but the reception is nothing compared to our room, which looks out over the stunning golden sand and perfectly clear night sky.

"Wow," I breathe, stepping out onto the balcony. Zach follows me out and wraps his arms around my waist. I really am in heaven.

HATE YOU

OUR FIRST WEEK FLIES BY. We spend time each morning at the studio and I get to meet the other artists whose names I know but mostly have never spoken to. We then head off and experience LA in the afternoons. Zach's yet to tell me when we're actually going home, but I can sense that our little bit of paradise is coming to an end.

"You think Corey would swap back? We could stay here instead," I suggest, resting my head back on Zach's shoulder as we enjoy the sunset over the sea one evening after our dinner in the hotel restaurant.

"I like your thinking, but I don't think it will get you anywhere. Corey belongs here. England was never where he was meant to be, not after everyth—" Zach stops abruptly when he realises he's said too much. "I'm sorry," he says softly, spinning me to face him. "He's not really one to talk about his life, I just—"

"It's fine. I get it. You're a good friend, Zach. He's lucky to have you." He shrugs off my comment as if it's nothing. "Fancy a walk on the beach?"

"Is that a trick question?"

We grab our shoes, and I pull a light jacket from the back of the chair. It feels like only seconds later, I'm slipping off my shoes and stepping onto the soft sand. The beach is almost empty, just a few late night surfing attempts going on and a couple of young families building sand castles, but other than that, it's just the sound of the crashing waves and a few birds overhead as we walk.

"Where do you see your future?" Zach suddenly asks.

"Um... To be honest, I've never really put that much thought into it. My biggest concern has always been what

I wanted to do. I seem to spend my life disappointing my parents or following their orders and disappointing myself. Starting work with you was the first time I properly did something for me and really felt like myself."

I wince as I think about my parents. I'm still yet to introduce Zach to them, but that's all going to come to an end at the beginning of next month, as I've agreed to attend their next event with a plus one. As scared as I am for them to meet Zach, I'm equally as excited to see the looks on their faces when they take him in.

"Okay, so now what? Do you want to stay at the studio? Do you want a room of your own?"

"What?" I ask, coming to a stop. "I can't have a room. I have no idea how to—"

"I know a few people who could teach you the ropes." His hand lifts to my cheek. "I've seen that sketchbook you think you hide in the bottom drawer of your desk, and I've now seen your own studio. You are more than capable of being one of my artists should you so wish."

I roll the idea around in my head before an idea sparks. "Would you let me ink you?" I wiggle my eyebrows in curiosity.

"Without a doubt. Which bit of me do you want, Kitten?" He takes a step back and holds his hands out to offer himself up to me, and I laugh.

"All of you."

His face suddenly turns serious and I panic that I've said the wrong thing.

He closes the space between us as he stares into my eyes, but he doesn't reach out for me. Instead he does something that I didn't see coming in a million years. He drops to one knee.

I gawp at him, thinking that he's going to burst out

laughing any second at his joke, but he never does. Instead, he takes my hand in his and brings it to his lips.

"You've got all of me, Kitten. But the question is, can I have all of you? Will you marry me?"

An unattractive snort falls from me as I wait for him to regret what he's just said, but he doesn't. He just stays down on one knee, in the Los Angeles sand with the sea as our backdrop and patiently waits for my answer.

"Yes," I blurt as the realisation starts to hit that he really means this. Zach Abbot is serious enough about me that he really wants to do this.

"Yes?"

"Yes." He launches himself at me and tackles me to the sand. He cradles the back of my head as he lowers me before dropping his weight onto my body and finding my lips.

He kisses me until we're both breathless and our lungs are screaming for air. He brushes his lips along my jaw until he gets to my ear.

"You know I've got a studio in Vegas, right?" His hand skims up over my hip and squeezes my waist.

"Of course. W-what are you suggesting?"

He pulls back and looks at me, something wicked twinkling in his eyes.

"Fancy a diversion before heading home?"

"Is that a trick question?" I ask, repeating my words from earlier.

He pulls back, cups my jaw in his hand and rubs his thumb over my bottom lip. "You want to invite anyone?"

Holy shit, he's serious.

FIVE DAYS LATER, the two of us are standing in a wedding chapel in Las Vegas with the biggest grins on our faces. I glance over my shoulder and take in our two and only guests, Danni and Titch. Corey was desperate to follow us, but he was booked solid at the studio. They both smile back at me, but I'm not convinced by Danni's delight. She might be happy that we're doing this, but she's anything but happy about being forced to spend time with Titch.

I'm dragged back to the here and now when the officiant before me speaks once again. "Tabitha, your vows," he prompts.

Opening my bag, I pull out the napkin I wrote them on the other night when we made the crazy decision to write our own.

"I, Tabitha Anderson, take you, Zachary Abbot, to be my husband. I promise to be there for you in good times and bad, in sickness and in health. I promise to be everything you want as well as things you don't even know you need. I promise to support you and be your partner in crime as well as your sounding board when you're growing your empire. I promise to love you, honour you, and hate you all the days of my life." He barks a laugh at my final words.

"Zachary," the officiant prompts. But unlike me, he doesn't pull out some scribbled notes, he just stares into my eyes and either makes it up as he goes along or he's been secretly memorising them.

"I, Zachary Abbot, take you, Tabitha Anderson, to be my wife. I had no idea I was missing something, but I now realise I didn't stop for long enough to notice as I ran from a part of my life I didn't think I wanted. But you came crashing in and forced yourself on me," Danni snorts behind us, but he's undeterred, "and showed me what I was missing. I've equally loved and hated our time together, and I know that I'm only going to love and hate it more with every day that passes. You're that final stroke of paint, the last drop of ink, that completes me. You make me whole, Tabby Cat, and I promise to show you how much I love you every day."

I wipe the tears from my eyes as he reaches out to take my hand.

I pretty much sob through the rings part of the ceremony, and before I know what's happening our very small congregation is clapping as we start to make our way back down the aisle.

Zach's hot fingers squeeze mine tightly, and the reality of what we've just done hits me. I look up at him and find the widest smile I think I've ever seen on his face.

"You okay, wife?" he asks when he notices me watching him.

"I can't believe we just did that."

"Believe it, Kitten." He lifts my hand and kisses my new rings. When we eventually dragged ourselves off the beach the night he spontaneously proposed we got an Uber to the closest jewellery shop and he bought me the most stunning platinum, princess cut engagement ring that now sits proudly next to the simple wedding band we chose to go with it.

Excitement shoots through me. I've never done anything so crazy in my entire life, but equally, I've never done anything that feels so right.

The second we're in the chapel's reception he pushes me up against the wall and crashes his lips to mine.

"Jesus, you might be man and wife now, but I still

don't need to see that," Danni complains when she and Titch appear behind us.

Zach releases me and accepts congratulations from our two best friends before the four of us walk out of the chapel.

It's dark out now, and the lights from the strip illuminate the sky.

"Mum and Dad are going to fucking kill you, you know that right?" Danni says, trailing behind us. "You remember what Mum was like when she found out Harrison did this with Summer without them? She forced that big wedding on them."

"I'm pretty sure they're in no position to criticise me ever again, Dan. And we're not having one of *those* weddings."

"Maybe, but they'll be gutted they didn't get to see that."

"You took pictures, right?"

"Of course, but I'm not sure they'll be happy with that. And your parents are going to go nuclear," she says, turning to me.

"Meh, it's a bit late now." Finally, I feel strong enough with who I am and what I want with my life that my parents' opinions no longer matter. The only person's opinion I care about is the one who's holding my hand right now and looking down at me like I'm the most amazing person in the world.

"I'm starving," Titch complains, much to Danni's disgust. "Where are we celebrating this epic union?"

"Burger place?" Zach suggests, and in that moment I couldn't think of anything better.

We fill up on burgers and chips before hitting the casino in our hotel, all delighting in watching Zach lose a bit of his well-earned money before we descend to the night club in the basement to drink and dance the night away.

I've no idea what the time is when we crash through the door to our hotel suite, but the sun's starting to come up and I'm more drunk than I've been in a long time. I think most of my buzz is due to the man who's currently pushing me up against the nearest wall than it is the drinks I've consumed.

"I didn't think I was ever going to get you alone."

His lips find mine, and his tongue plunges between my lips. His hands skim down my waist, bunching up the full skirt of my tea length wedding dress until he finds the soft skin of my thighs.

He works his way up until he finds the lace of my stockings and garter belt. "Umm... what are you doing to me?" he groans against my lips, his fingertips tracing the lines of my lingerie.

I gasp when he rubs at me over the lace of my knickers, my head falling back against the wall as he grazes his teeth over the sensitive skin below my ear.

"Zach," I beg, needing more than he's giving me.

He kisses down my chest and over the swell of my breasts that sit above the neckline.

"Have I told you how beautiful you look today? How lucky I am to be able to officially call you mine? How badly I want to show you just how I treat things that belong to me?" His fingers slip beneath the lace and I cry out when he connects with my clit.

"Fuck, I want to taste you right now."

"Go on then." My voice is no more than a breathy whisper. He glances up at me, a salacious smile playing on his lips before he disappears under the mass of fabric that hangs from my waist.

His fingers find the sides of my knickers and he slowly pulls them down my legs until he taps my ankles one at a time so he can remove them completely. He rubs his nose against my smooth skin before parting me and pressing his tongue where I need him most.

Lifting one of my legs, he drops it over his shoulder, leaving me balancing on one unsteady leg as he eats me until I'm crying out his name and clenching around his finger seated deep inside me.

When he emerges from my dress, his face glistens with my arousal and his hair's a mess from the lace it was brushing against.

He wipes his mouth before starting to undo his shirt buttons. He drops the fabric to the floor and my eyes feast on his inked skin. My mouth waters like always as I take in his sculpted torso and his deep v lines that disappear into his boxers. I bite down on the inside of my cheek as my need to run my tongue down the ridges gets too much to bear.

"I need you naked. Right. Now."

Taking my hand, Zach pulls me from the wall and spins me so he can find the zip at my back. Painfully slowly, he pulls it down and then pushes the fabric from my shoulders. The dress pools at my feet, leaving me in only my lingerie.

"As sexy as this is, I want you in nothing but my ring."

Heat floods my core, his hand brushing against my back as he finds the clasp of my bra and releases it. The lace joins my dress, and my shoes, garter belt and stockings join them only seconds later.

Once I'm naked, I reach for him and help him remove

his final items of clothing. The second he's bare, he pulls me into his body, his lips find mine, and he lifts me so I've no choice but to wrap my legs around his waist. The head of his cock teases my entrance. I grind my hips, trying to get more of him. He chuckles almost painfully as he walks us to the bed.

"So impatient," he murmurs.

"I want to feel my husband moving inside me."

He groans, his eyes darkening before me as he lowers me to the bed and settles himself between my thighs.

"I promise to love you now." Thrust. "Forever." Thrust. "And always." Thrust. "I fucking love you, Tabby Cat."

"I love you too, almost as much as I hate you." He laughs, but it's cut off when his lips find mine and he sets about spending what's left of the night showing me just how much he loves me.

I CAN BARELY MOVE when we wake the next morning. Every single one of my muscles pulls deliciously, reminding me of our wedding night.

"Morning, wife," he whispers, his rough, sleepy voice sparking a desire within me that really should be sated.

"Morning, husband."

"Hmmm... I love the sound of that."

"I don't want to ever leave this bed," I admit, snuggling into his side.

"Shall we order room service? I really need to eat."

I groan. "We promised Danni and Titch we'd meet them for lunch."

"My sister is such a cock block," Zach complains,

rolling on top of me, proving that I'm not the only one who's ready for our next round.

"Come on, hot shot. We've got the rest of our lives for that. I need a shower before gracing other human beings with my presence."

"Shower, that sounds perfect."

As expected, Zach gets his way in the shower and it takes much longer than I was anticipating to eventually get out of the suite to meet our two guests for a very late lunch.

Amazingly, they're not sitting at a table waiting for us when we get down to the restaurant we agreed on last night. We order ourselves coffees and are busy reading the menu when Danni and Titch join us at exactly the same time, looking much the worse for wear.

"Well, aren't you two a sight for sore eyes," I say, laughing at their slightly green faces as they keep the sunshine streaming through the windows to their backs. "Have a good night after we left you, then?"

"Can we not talk about it?" Danni asks, reaching across the table to steal my coffee.

"Sure but don't think—wait, what's this?" I ask when something on her finger catches me eye. "Is that a fucking wedding ring?"

All four of us stare down at her ring finger in shock, but none more so than Danni and Titch.

"Oh fuck," she groans, releasing her grip on the mug and holding her hand out in front of her. Reaching down, she lifts Titch's hand from his lap and her eyes almost pop out of her head. Titch, on the other hand, doesn't look so shocked. If anything, he looks smug as fuck.

Oh, this is going to be interesting.

TRICK YOU is NOW LIVE!
ONE-CLICK NOW to discover what's happened between Danni and Titch.

~~~~~~~~~~~~

Intrigued by Corey?
His story is INKED, my K Bromberg, Driven World book.
ONE-CLICK NOW!

ACKNOWLEDGMENTS

This story has been such a long time coming. When I wrote His Manhattan back in 2018, I fell in love with Zach and he's been begging me ever since to write this story—so much so I had to name drop him in the Forbidden books!

I'm so in love with Biff and Zach. Discovering their story has been so much fun, as well as finally getting to find out more about them and what makes them tick along with all my new guys.

I'm so excited to dive back into this series and learn more about Danni and Titch, along with a few others that I hope you're curious about as well.

As always, I've got a ton of people to thank. Michelle, who alpha read this for me as I was writing and kicked my arse when I wasn't going fast enough. Deanna, Lindsay, Susanne, Nicole and Tracy, thank you for dropping everything to beta read for me.

Sam, for everything! Seriously, I wouldn't be able to do this without you.

Evelyn, thank you for putting up with my repetitive typos that I seem to miss no matter what.

Paige, for polishing this up and making Biff and Zach as pretty as possible.

This book is a first for me in the fact that both the e-book and audiobook should be released at the same time.

So a massive thank you to Kim Loraine, Kylie Stewart and Shane East for making it happen at such short notice.

And last but never least, my husband and daughter for supporting me and the hours I spend with my laptop.

Until next time,

Tracy xo

ABOUT THE AUTHOR

Tracy Lorraine is a *USA Today* and *Wall Street Journal* bestselling new adult and contemporary romance author. Tracy has recently turned thirty and lives in a cute Cotswold village in England with her husband, baby girl and lovable but slightly crazy dog. Having always been a bookaholic with her head stuck in her Kindle, Tracy decided to try her hand at a story idea she dreamt up and hasn't looked back since.

Be the first to find out about new releases and offers. Sign up to my newsletter here.

If you want to know what I'm up to and see teasers and snippets of what I'm working on, then you need to be in my Facebook group. Join Tracy's Angels here.

Keep up to date with Tracy's books at
www.tracylorraine.com

ALSO BY TRACY LORRAINE

Falling Series
Falling for Ryan: Part One #1
Falling for Ryan: Part Two #2
Falling for Jax #3
Falling for Daniel (A Falling Series Novella)
Falling for Ruben #4
Falling for Fin #5
Falling for Lucas #6
Falling for Caleb #7
Falling for Declan #8
Falling For Liam #9

Forbidden Series
Falling for the Forbidden #1
Losing the Forbidden #2
Fighting for the Forbidden #3
Craving Redemption #4
Demanding Redemption #5
Avoiding Temptation #6
Chasing Temptation #7

Rebel Ink Series
Hate You #1

Trick You #2

Defy You #3

Play You #4

Inked (A Rebel Ink/Driven Crossover)

Rosewood High Series

Thorn #1

Paine #2

Savage #3

Fierce #4

Hunter #5

Faze (#6 Prequel)

Fury #6

Legend #7

Maddison Kings University Series

TMYM: Prequel

TRYS #1

TDYW #2

TBYS #3

TVYC #4

TDYD #5

TDYR #6

TRYD #7

Knight's Ridge Empire Series

Wicked Summer Knight: Prequel (Stella & Seb)

Wicked Knight #1 (Stella & Seb)
Wicked Princess #2 (Stella & Seb)
Wicked Empire #3 (Stella & Seb)

Deviant Knight #4 (Emmie & Theo)
Deviant Princess #5 (Emmie & Theo
Deviant Reign #6 (Emmie & Theo)

One Reckless Knight (Jodie & Toby)
Reckless Knight #7 (Jodie & Toby)
Reckless Princess #8 (Jodie & Toby)
Reckless Dynasty #9 (Jodie & Toby)

Dark Knight #10 (Calli & Batman)
Dark Princess #11 (Calli & Batman)
Dark Legacy #12 (Calli & Batman)
Corrupt Valentine Knight

Ruined Series

Ruined Plans #1
Ruined by Lies #2
Ruined Promises #3

Never Forget Series

Never Forget Him #1
Never Forget Us #2
Everywhere & Nowhere #3

Chasing Series

Chasing Logan

The Cocktail Girls

His Manhattan

Her Kensington

FALLING FOR THE FORBIDDEN SNEAK PEEK
CHAPTER ONE

Falling down on my bed, I blow out a long breath and tell myself that everything will be okay.

I had plans for this summer—a few weeks of fun before uni starts. The girls and I had been looking at last-minute holiday deals, and we had tickets for a music festival…but then my dad swooped in, in that way that he does, and ruined everything.

I knew it was coming.

I just wasn't expecting it quite yet.

I'd hoped agreeing to study what he wanted me to and working for him was enough—apparently not.

I decided a few years ago that I wasn't going to move away to study. I mostly love my life in London, and I loved living with Mum. I'm not ashamed to admit that she's one of my best friends. It was only as I started looking at universities that my dad piped up and told me that I would be studying accountancy and finance at The London School of Economics. He'd done his research and decided it was the best place for me to learn my trade so I could enter the family business.

I just about managed to contain my laughter when he emphasised the word *family*.

I've no idea how long I lie on my bed trying to convince myself that moving into his house with his new wife and her son isn't the worst thing to ever happen to me, but eventually my stomach rumbling has me moving. I sit on the edge of the bed and take in all my half-unpacked boxes. A large sigh falls from my lips. If I don't find everything a home, maybe I won't have to stay. I know it's wishful thinking. This is it for me now.

Disappointment floods me as I make my way through the silent house. It's not that I was expecting a welcome party or anything, but someone being here would have been nice. Someone to help me carry everything up to my room would have been even nicer. Since Dad moved in with Jenny a few years ago, I've been told to treat this place like my home.

It will never be.

It's just a house, a show home, a shell in which I'm scared to touch anything for fear of making a mess. Home is a place with character, with mess from day-to-day living, with people who love and care for you.

My dad isn't a bad man, per se, but he's not exactly what you'd describe as a doting father. Everything he does is for his own gain—if it happens to help others in the process, that's just a bonus.

My step mum, Jenny, is lovely. She really is, but I can't help feeling like she's just a little bit...broken. She makes all the right comments and does all the right things. She's a great mum. But there's such sadness in her eyes.

The fridge is full, as usual. It's strange, because I've never witnessed anyone eating more than a slice of toast or an apple in this kitchen.

I fix myself a salad with the unopened packets of fruit and vegetables, but it doesn't really have the effect I needed it to have. Being here makes me feel kind of empty, and no amount of lettuce leaves is going to fill the void after moving out of the flat Mum and I shared for the past few years.

Rummaging through the cupboards, I can't help smiling when I find a stash of naughty stuff hiding at the back.

Pulling my hair back into a messy bun, I put my thoughts to the side and set about making something that will make me feel just a little bit better.

The sun's just about to set, casting an orange glow throughout the kitchen. It almost makes it feel warm and inviting—almost. My mouth waters as I pour melted chocolate over the crushed biscuits and marshmallows I've managed not to eat already. Standing in only a vest and a small pair of hot pants, I decide to make myself a hot chocolate, grab a blanket, and enjoy my bowl of goodness out on the deck with a magazine. Chocolate makes everything that little bit better. If I eat enough, it might make me forget what this summer's actually going to be like for me.

I'm just waiting for the kettle to boil when a shiver runs down my spine. I'm sure it's just the size of the house that freaks me out. I've seen enough horror films to know there are plenty of hiding places in a place this big.

I'm still for a second, but when I don't hear anything, I continue with what I was doing. That is, until a deep rumbling voice has every nerve in my body on alert.

"Wow, step daddy sure is attracting the young ones these days." His voice is slurred, his anger palpable. It makes goosebumps prick my skin and a giant lump form in my throat. "You look too pure. Too innocent to be with that prick," he spits.

There's no love lost between my dad and my stepbrother, that's not news to me, but the viciousness of his voice right now makes me wonder what their relationship is really like. My dad might be many things, but he wouldn't cheat on Jenny—he loves her too much.

I can't remember the last time I saw him, but there's no way he can't know it's me. Who the hell else would be cooking in his kitchen? Deciding he's just trying to rile me up, I go to collect my stuff and get out of his way. Unfortunately, he seems to have other ideas.

His breath tickles up my neck moments before the heat of his body warms my back.

"You came here for the wrong man. I can put that right, though." The alcohol on his breath surrounds me. It's a reminder that there's a good chance he has no idea what he's doing right now.

The softness of his nose running up the length of my neck has tingles racing through my traitorous body. I don't realise he's smelling me until he blows out a long breath and the scent of alcohol hits me once again. I turn to leave, but his hands slam on the counter behind me and cage me in.

"Look at me," he demands.

"Let me go, Ben."

If he's surprised to discover it's me, he doesn't show it. If anything, his eyes shine with delight as he takes in every inch of my face before focusing on my lips. My stomach flips, knowing where his thoughts are.

Something passes over his face but it's gone too quickly to be able to identify. He pushes himself from the counter and away from me. No more words are said, but when he gets to the door, he looks back over his shoulder and runs his eyes over my body. They hold a warning I don't really understand.

Once he's disappeared from sight, I sag back against the counter. What the hell was that?

After putting half of the rocky road on a tray in the fridge, I forgo sitting outside and instead take my spoils to my room to hide. There's stuff everywhere in my room and, unlike the rest of this house, it makes me feel a little more relaxed.

Since the day Ben and I were introduced by our parents, we've not really had any kind of relationship. He's pretty much stayed out of my way and, in turn, I've done the same. It's not all that much of a task. When I'm here, he spends almost every minute somewhere else. When he's home, he's moody, arrogant, and generally a prick, so I'm more than happy to stay out of his way.

It's just a shame he's so damn pretty to look at. As the years have passed, he's only become more attractive, too. I've no idea if it's just his job or if he works out as well because every inch of him seems to be toned to perfection.

Jenny spends most of her time apologising for his attitude and trying to explain that he's got a lot going on. I'm yet to discover what that is. As far as I can tell, he seems to be your average twenty-year-old guy who'd rather be off his arse drunk or with a woman than spending time at home with his parents.

By the time I've dug my way to the bottom of the bowl, I feel pretty sick. There's still no sign of my dad or Jenny, but the music pounding from Ben's room across the hallway leaves no doubt as to what kind of mood he's in.

DOWNLOAD NOW to continue Lauren and Ben's story.

Printed in Great Britain
by Amazon